GROWTH AND REGIONAL PATTERN OF INDUSTRIAL COMPLEXES

GROWTH AND REGIONAL PATTERN OF INDUSTRIAL COMPLEXES

A Case Study of Bihar

RANA PRATAP

CONCEPT PUBLISHING COMPANY, NEW DELHI

First Published 1985

Rana Pratap (*b*. 1946-)

Published by

Naurang Rai
Concept Publishing Company
H-13 Bali Nagar
NEW DELHI-110 015 (India)

Printed in India by

Kiran Mudran Kendra
Mayapuri, Phase I,
NEW DELHI-110 064

PREFACE

THE clustered development of industries at a limited space has been a significant feature of modern industrial landscape. Such concentration gives rise to economies of production, encourages efficiency and augurs betterment at the regional level. When concentration of industrial units is interlinked to each other they form industrial complex. Industrial linkage constitutes the vital element of an industrial system and becomes the controlling factor for the growth, pattern and functional characteristics of an industrial complex. Industrial complex is a new concept in industrial geography and has become an interesting aspect of study. A scientific, analytical and systematic study of the geography of industrial complex may ultimately lead to the formulation of much needed industrial location models and theories particularly in the context of developing countries like India. But only in a few of the published research papers and books attempts have been made to present systematically the growth, regional pattern and functional characteristics of industrial complexes of India. The present study is a modest attempt to contribute in this direction. The State of Bihar, which is characterized as rich land and poor people, provides a suitable region for such type of exploratory studies. The purpose of this research work is to describe and analyze the growth, regional pattern and functional characteristics of industrial complexes of Bihar.

The present study is organised into eight chapters. The first chapter deals with the introduction of the study including the relevant review of the literature. The emphasis is given to nature and objectives of industrial complex as an aspect of industrial geography. In the second chapter an attempt has been made to focus the study area and its physico-socio-economic setting emphasizing the conditions responsible for the present industrial set up in the state. The third chapter deals with the delimitation of the industrial complexes of the state on the basis of employed workers and industrial units clustered together. The fourth chapter presents an account of the regional pattern of industrial complexes and also attempts to demarcate the zones of influence of industrial complexes. The fifth chapter provides a detailed account of growth and evolution of industrial complexes on the basis of production, employment, areal extension and urban population. An attempt has also been made to identify the order of magnitude of industrial complexes based on labour employment. The sixth chapter deals with the internal structure, e.g., linkages, pattern and functional characteristics of the complexes. The social relevance, problems and planning are discussed and presented in the seventh chapter. The eighth and the last chapter presents the summary and conclusions of this work indicating possible directions for future research.

Industrial geography has been author's aptitude from the beginning while he was an M.A. student in the Department of Geography, Patna University. This aptitude was induced to him by Dr. P. Dayal, the eminent Professor of Geography. In fact, he aroused the author's interest in the field of industrial geography by allowing him to work on 'Industrial Geography of Dalmianagar' as a special paper for his M.A. degree.

The present work could not have been completed without the help and assistance from other quarters. The author expresses his deep sense of gratitude to Dr. P. Dayal, University Professor and Head of the Department of Geography, Patna University, for suggesting this topic for research, direction and providing the library facilities in the Department. The author is thankful to Dr. S.M. Karimi, Professor and Head of the Department of Geography, Patna College, Patna for his occasional suggestions. The author is equally thankful to Dr. L.N. Ram, Professor of Geography, Patna University, for his helpful comments on research methodology.

The author is ever obliged to Shri Ram Lakhan Singh Yadav, M.L.A., Bihar for taking keen interest in the building up of his academic career and constant encouragement.

The author is particularly indebted to his supervisor Dr. B. Thakur, Reader in Geography, Delhi School of Economics, University of Delhi for his guidance, encouragement and stimulation. In fact, he was always available to him with his suggestions and critical comments in spite of his heavy engagements.

It would be a remiss for the author if he fails to appreciate the help rendered by Dr. M. Pathak, Reader and Head of the Department of Geography, Magadh University, Bodh Gaya. The author is thankful to him for providing the Departmental facilities and occasional suggestions. The author is equally thankful to all the members of the Department of Geography, Magadh University for their encouragement, especially to Dr. Ram Pravesh Singh, Lecturer in Geography, for providing valuable literature pertaining to the topic.

During the field work considerable helps were obtained from the offices of P.R.D. of Tisco, H.E.C., Bokaro Steel Plant, Sindri, Barauni and Dalmianagar. Besides, the maximum helps were received from the various departments, e.g., Industries, Statistics and Town Planning of the Government of Bihar. These helps were much valuable and hence the author is obliged to them.

The author expresses his gratitude to various authorities and librarians of A.N. Sinha Institute of Social Studies, Ratan Tata Library, College of Commerce Library, Magadh University Library, Gauhati University Library and Patna University Library for providing necessary facilities.

The author would be failing in his duty if he does not express his sincere thanks to Shri Chandra Shekhar Prasad, Shri Jai Shankar Prasad Singh, Shri Ram Pravesh Yadav and Shri Satyendra Singh all M.A. students for their help in Mathematical calculations and cartographic assistance. The author is especially obliged to his wife Sita for her sacrifice, constant encouragement and keeping the home quiet during the work.

Last but not the least, author's thank goes to Shri Sibeshwar Prasad for having carefully typed the manuscript within a short period.

Department of Geography
Magadh University
BODH GAYA

RANA PRATAP

CONTENTS

LIST OF MAPS AND DIAGRAMS

LIST OF TABLES

1

INTRODUCTION

STUDY OBJECTIVES AND APPROACH

THE INDUSTRIAL complex, where a set of specific industries is closely related, is an important aspect of industrial geography. The growth and development of industrial complexes are the significant features of modern industrial landscape not only in the technologically developed countries but also in developing countries. Therefore, the study of industrial complexes has become a major research theme in industrial geography particularly after the 1950. Its importance is so vital in modern economy that it has become an interdisciplinary topic with different approaches. Geographers are basically concerned with the descriptive and analytical aspects of the complexes. They try to identify, delimit and analyse the growth pattern of complexes at regional level with special reference to the factors affecting them. Linkage assumes the most fundamental aspect of industrial complexes and, therefore, this is the active frontier of research in this field. Many modern industrial geographers have described the linkage phenomena of industrial complexes as the vital element of industrial system. However, a scientific and analytical study of linkage aspect is handicapped due to the lack of adequate data particularly in India.

The primary purpose of this research is to study the growth and regional pattern of industrial complexes in Bihar. An attempt is made to analyse them from the initial growth to present period and seeks to discriminate between older and newer industrial complexes on the basis of growth, pattern and functional characteristics. Thus the main objectives of this work are : (a) to delimit the industrial complex quantitatively on the basis of industrial workers employed Anchalwise and also industrial units clustered together, (b) to describe the regional characteristics of industrial complexes in relationship to physical, economic and cultural aspects, (c) to present a chronological study of the growth of industries and industrial complexes analyzing the production, employment and population trends, and areal expansion, (d) to analyze the factors affecting the growth of industrial complexes, (e) to highlight the internal conditions of complexes emphasing the linkage, pattern and functional characteristics, and finally (f) to present a critical evaluation of social relevance, problems and planning of industrial complexes.

For this analysis of industrial complexes, the State of Bihar is chosen as the study area. Bihar happens to be one of the most promising industrial states in India. Its mineral richness and other physical, economic and social aspects have acted as the base of industrial growth. Hence the selected study area is suitable for the exploratory study of industrial complexes. Data related to the purposes are basically secondary in nature and are obtained either from the published Census records or from the published report available with factory offices. These data are statistically and cartographically analyzed to arrive at meaningful and logical conclusions.

THEORETICAL FRAMEWORK

The present trend of study of the industrial location is not only to assess the 'optimum location point',[1] or to locate a point of 'least-cost',[2] or 'maximum profit',[3] or both,[4] but also to evaluate the dynamic aspects of the economic processes incorporating human element[5] for betterment and effiquity. Moreover, industrial development has now to be viewed not only from the production and employment perspective, but also from the larger perspective of social goals and spatial pattern of human activities in general.[6] Like most of the developing nations, India is also trying to reorient her socio-economic set up by adopting the modern innovations and technical breakthrough for the development of regions in her vast potential backgrounds.[7] The new Indian Industrial Policy[8] adopted for the 6th Five Year Plan envisages securing of such socio-economic objectives as optimum utilisation of the installed capacity. It has also been for maximising production and achieving higher productivity, higher employment generation, correction of regional imbalances through a preferential development of industrially backward areas, strengthening the agricultural base by developing agro-based industries and also promoting optimum inter-sectoral relationships. However, faster promotion of export-oriented and import substitution industries would be the vital aspect. While making all efforts towards integrated industrial development, it is proposed to promote the concept of economic federalism with the setting up of a few nucleus plants preferably in the backward regions to generate as many ancillaries and small units as possible. These nucleus plants concentrate their activities on assembling the products of the ancillary units falling within the orbits on producing the inputs required by those smaller units and create adequate marketing conditions. Moreover, the nucleus will also ensure a widely spread pattern of investment and employment and will distribute the benefits of industrialisation at the maximum possibilities. It will also work for upgrading the technology of small units. All these conditions bring a region to an economic maximisation point. In this context it becomes most apparent to give an empirical study of the nucleus plants or the growth generating centres. These centres are located with a process of development and create 'a zone of influence' on the most decentralised pattern on micro, meso and macro level. Such nucleus plants establish a linkage system based on, input-output model, labour connection and even on spatial interactions, and are known as the industrial complexes.

DEFINING AN INDUSTRIAL COMPLEX

The term industrial complex has been widely used by the economists like Isard,[9] Klaassen[10] and several others. But the concept of industrial complex was developed by Perroux[11] and Boudeville[12] when they tried to explain the Growth Pole or Growth Centre Policy. Boudeville defines development poles as industrial centres which create Wealth and markets for their satellite areas.[13] Further on he defines a regional growth pole as a set of expanding industries located in an urban area inducing further development of economic activity throughout its zone of influence.[14] Likewise, Perroux used poles and centres as synonymous terms and interlinked the concept of development Pole or growth centre with the concept of economic space as fields of forces. He, however, postulated two forces: Centrifugal and Centripetal. The former emanates from the centres or poles or focii while the latter is attracted to them. Therefore, every pole or centre or focii is a centre of attraction and repulsion and in this process the whole region is brought under the economic upliftment.[15]

But these ideas of Boudeville and Perroux were subjects of criticism. The most serious objection is the methodological basis of the theory—input-output model, on which the concept of a pole is developed. It is static and unsuitable for a conceptual framework. Moreover, it is the most complicated method which requires detailed discussion by econometrician.[16] Further the ideas of space has been completely ignored. Friedman has tried to explain a systematic interrelation between development and space through his 'general theory of polarised development'.[17] Hermansen[18] has also found absence of a propulsive industries in the concept of Perroux and Boudeville. He, however, advocated that, "not every centre of a nodel region qualifies to be called a development pole, only those which contain propulsive firms—i.e., large scale firms, technically advanced, innovating and dominating, and working within propulsive industries (industries with a marked capacity for inducing growth in linked industries) which exert a strong influence on their environment and are capable of generating sustained growth over a prolonged period of time—should be regarded as geographical poles of growth".[19] Similarly, Hansen[20] and Richardson[21] also differ as they do not consider Perroux's development pole equivalent to industrial complex. Richardson notes that an industrial complex will be heavily concentrated in or around the growth point itself and other supporting industries dispersed over the zone of influence are induced by that complex.[22] Hansen mentions three basic characteristics of a propulsive industry, that is, nucleus plant which a complex : (a) it must be relatively large in order to assume that it will engender sufficient direct and indirect effects to have a significant impact on the economy, (b) it must be relatively fast growing sector, and (c) the quality and intensity of its inter-relations with other sectors should be important so that a large number of induced effects will be transmitted.[23] This idea was also expressed by Myrdal,[24] Hirschman,[25] Friedmann[26] and Robinson and Salih.[27] They developed the idea through their centre-periphery model of economic development and correctly argued that "the growth pole model depicts the transmission of economic prosperity as the result of two sets of opposing forces. On the one hand, growth tends to concentrate in some centre and erodes the economy of surrounding areas; on the other hand, development spreads over surrounding area as the result of growth in the centre".[28] The forces of increasing concentration are termed "back wash" or polarisation and those of dispersal "spread or trickle down". Backwash relates specifically to the tendency for the factors of production to be drawn from periphery to centre, setting up a vicious and virtuous circles respectively. For example, capital, raw materials, labour and other daily consumer goods are drawn to the centre. In contrast, "spread" relates to the tendency for initial disparities in the surface of economic development to be evened out. The relevant processes may be predominantly economic, social or political in nature.[29] This spread may be direct, indirect and induced.[30] Employment, general economic mobilisation and the transformation of social attitudes are few instances which are brought through the spread effect. This mechanism has received considerable attention in the context of developing countries, as elaborated by Misra in the Indian context.[31]

Indstrial complex is, therefore, a growth centre which propels industrial relations, sustains, economic growth and transforms social attitudes on the regional level. The region may be as large as a country, medium as state or zone or small as a town. Bernard[32] identified two types of growth centre in France-industrial complexes, both large and small, and higher order urban centres. In America an industrial complex is related to a large industrial plants, where industrial activities occur through a system of production, marketing or other interrelationships. This system is being adopted there for better production. In India, industrial complex is an industrial centre where large scale capital intensive plant is located. This location is meant for resource mobilization, employment creation and to spread economic and social goodwills to eradicate the regional imbalance.

Thus, Balassa defines an industrial complex as "one or more activities occurring at a given location and belonging to a group of activities which are subject to important production, marketing or other interrelationships".[33] Supporting this definition of industrial complex Allen and Maclennan,[34] have given the concept that an industrial complex comprises industries which are interrelated in so far as they make demands on each other. It needs to be of such proportion that its principal units can be assured of their input requirements from the immediate vicinity and the intermediate (auxiliary or subsidiary or both) units supporting the principal units will have a market of sufficient size to ensure profitable operations. From this the complex will be perfectly close-knit to continue its development by the inter-play of the market forces, once the nucleus has been set up. It will be 'an auto-sufficient system' capable of inserting itself in the general development of the area in which it was situated.[35] If the region is backward and lacks supporting industries, it will deter the progress of the principal industries and the region as well.[36] Its spread effect will be very week and in such a condition the industrial complex will act as "cathedrals in the desert"[37] around which "a primitive economy spreads in all directions".[38] Here an economic retardness grows and poverty persists accordingly.

Our knowledge about the industrial complex, that is clustering of industries as Klaassen[39] says, is complicated and dynamic. However, the definition of an industrial complex provided by Isard[40] seems appropriate and logical. Industrial Complex defined by him is a set of activities occurring at a given location and belonging to a group of activities which are subject to important production, marketing or other interrelations. Because of appropriateness this definition is accepted as the base of this study.

NATURE OF INDUSTRIAL COMPLEX

The location of industrial activities at a favourable point gives rise to many advantageous economic consideration, e.g., economies of scale, localisation economies, urbanization economies and spatial-juxtaposition economies. All those are also termed as agglomeration economics.[41] Since long it has been recognized by industrial location theorists that the existence of agglomerative forces combined with other factors attract industrial concentration. When such concentration of industrial units is interlinked to each other they form industrial bundles or industrial complexes. Bundles of industries selected in this way show mutual interrelations of spatial juxtaposition in a given region or country which lead to substantial economies.

Thus, the industrial complex analysis deals with spatial schemes of incidence and development of grouped industrial units.[42] It is a useful instrument for implementing regional industrial development. It is, however, concerned with the economic feasibility and industrial activities at an economically favourable location which avails the maximum advantages of the local, regional, national and even sometimes on international levels.[43] Industrial Complex analysis, therefore, "is a functional technique within the framework of a planned regional growth, since it allows one to identify and to evaluate combinations of industrial activities".[44]

The concept of an industrial complex contains two basic elements : (a) interrelatedness of economic activities and (b) proximity of their location.[45] Industrial units are related to one another by (a) direct inter-firm transactions, (b) joint demand for the products or services of other industrial units or joint supply of one or more partners, and (c) joint use of common resources and facilities, like labour and other social infrastructure.

The second element of a complex is proximity. Many inter-firm transactions taking place within a relatively limited geographical area result into an industrial complex. The relationship between firm is commonly known as linkage.[46] Linkage is a term which means inter-actions between firm in the transmission of goods, people, money and information. In this way the plants involved gain advantages from being near to each other. Industrial products or wastes of one plant are drawn upon by another situated in its proximity. This phenomena is popularly known as input-output model which was pioneered by Leontief.[47]

The technical relations dealt within industrial complex analysis are associated with inter-industrial relations and with internal industrial processes. The former is taken in the framework of input-output analysis, while the latter are related to the concept of engineering functions. In short, the cohesive force of an industrial complex derives from the operational advantages which a close geographical group of inter-related activities confers on its constituent units. These advantages are to be seen not only in reduction of transport cost but in more efficient and better co-ordinated operations made possible. The result is a low degree of spatial dispersion of exchanges of intermediate goods and services.

Size of industrial complex

The size of an industrial complex is not a fix-item either in space or dimensions (production, employment, capital investment, etc.). It may be of any size, small, medium or large, fluctuating from a few hectares to miles in its areal extent, a few tenths to thousands and thousands in its employment folds, and also from a few investment to a huge amount of investment in its capital capacity. Moreover, when it is studied from the points of view of raw materials, labour and flows of finished products, its locational dynamism touches a greater magnitude embracing thousands of kilometres. Finally, the size becomes important if prosperity seeps down in a continuous flows from the complex to its periphery.

Composition of industrial complex

Industrial complex in the manufacturing processes presents the most complicated phenomena. It is a technical operation passing through a series of phases. Isard and Schooler have identified several types of complexes, mostly based on activity or activities in the manufacturing processes.[48] Therefore, on the basis of composition different types of complexes have been

FLOW DIAGRAM OF COMPLEX FORMATION

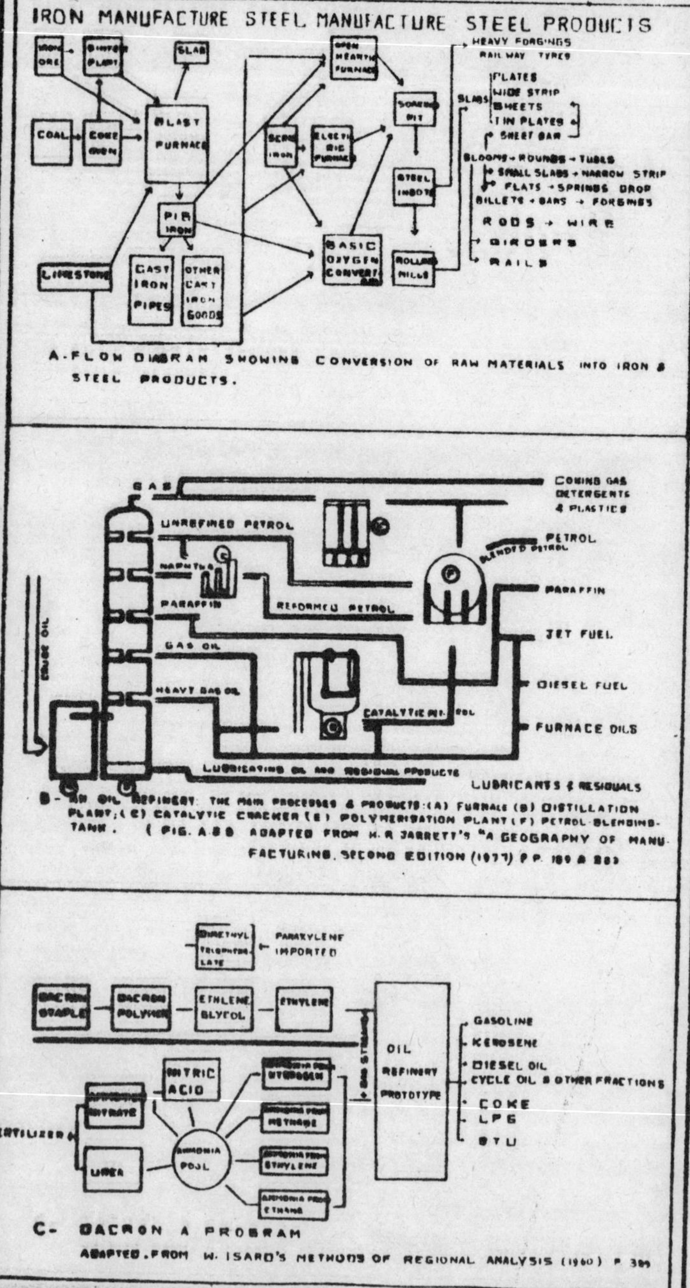

A-FLOW DIAGRAM SHOWING CONVERSION OF RAW MATERIALS INTO IRON & STEEL PRODUCTS.

B- AN OIL REFINERY: THE MAIN PROCESSES & PRODUCTS: (A) FURNACE (B) DISTILLATION PLANT; (C) CATALYTIC CRACKER (E) POLYMERISATION PLANT (F) PETROL-BLENDING-TANK. (FIG. A.B ADAPTED FROM H.R JARRETT'S "A GEOGRAPHY OF MANUFACTURING, SECOND EDITION (1977) P.P. 189 & 283

C- DACRON A PROGRAM
ADAPTED FROM W. ISARD'S METHODS OF REGIONAL ANALYSIS (1960) P. 389

FIG 1

recognised.

The first type comprises of the large establishments of basic industries. In such type numerous raw materials have to pass through several successive stages in the processing of an end product or group of end products. The initial raw materials are used and reused in a complex way by treating and processing them in a consequential manner. In this way, a cycle of production of an unlimited varieties by multi-stage transformations of mineral, animal and plant products, and even of water or air into industrial materials, is established.[49] Here advanced technology, large scale production and multiple stages, e.g. vertical, horizontal and diagonal structures are characterised. Mono or multi types of complexes are evolved. All the functions related to production or institutional organisations are set in motion on the corporated manner in integrated forms into one gamut. The examples are iron and steel, cement and engineering complexes. In the case of iron and steel; coal, iron-ore, limestone and other mineral pass through the processes of transformation into pig-iron, and again pig-iron to steel ingot, and finally into steel and other structurals. Here every stage depends upon the preceding stage for its basic inputs. Jarrett[50] provides a flow diagram showing conversion of raw materials into iron and steel products (Fig. 1. A.).

The second type of complex may derive from the joint production of two or more commodities from a single class of raw materials, such as, diverse food, fertilizer stock. The fertilizer is the final product of many bye-products. Therefore, the oil refinery centres become the centre of many units of varieties of products as explained by Jarrett[51] and Isard[52] as shown in Fig. 1. B and C respectively.

Such types are generally located at the centre of dense population either due to high transport cost or other distributional constraints or because of consumer service needs.

The introduction of chemicals and chemical methods in the utilization of resources has let to the development of a series of production cycles in the industrial sector. A wide variety or technological methods makes it possible to derive numerous chemical products from one and the same type of raw material. For example, plastics, synthetic rubber and synthetic fatty acids are all obtained from oil. The latest method from preparing synthetic paper out of oil has added the importance of petrochemical complexes. This methodological innovation has given rise to the great concentration of chemical industries around the location of petroleum, natural gas and non-ferrous, minerals like coal.

The modern industrial pattern tends to maximum utilisation of raw materials. Even the waste products are reused. This utilisation protects land and people from the danger of pollution hazards and unnecessary dumps of waste materials. For example, in smelting of copper ore or refining of crude oil, a host of bye-products are gained by arresting the escaping gases, liquids etc. Similarly, the slag, the waste product of iron and steel are being reused as a raw material for the production of cement. Bagasse and the molasses waste products of the Sugar factory are recycled in manufacturing of cardboard, synthetic rubber and power alchohol.

Lastly, a complex may be based on a single but fairly broad industrial process, such as a nucleonics complex oriented to either fission, fusion, or both.[53]

GROWTH OF INDUSTRIAL COMPLEX

The establishment and growth of an industrial complex at a particular location is the outcome of the interaction of varied physical, economic and social factors. When and where the causation factors exceed in favour of one major industrial activity industrial concentration takes place. Since these factors are not ubiquitous, the industrial concentration presents uneven trend having a distinct cultural landscape. They are known as industrial districts, regions and belts.

The modern industrial regions of the world have developed; firstly, where coal, petroleum and hydro-electric power are available in abundance; secondly, where exploitation of raw materials is done; thirdly, in or near large centres of population, where cheap labour and good markets of consumers are available; fourthly, at trading centres and port cities, in order to gain labour, materials, and wider markets of national and international extents and finally advanced technology, huge capital supply and also due to the welfare schemes of the socialistic governments. Therefore, "in no phase of geography is the inter-dependence of all regions—rural, mineral and urban—more clearly visible than in manufacturing".[54]

Industrial complex near coal fields

Coal has remained one of the major sources of power prior to the Industrial Revolution. Any type of industrial development was drawn upon by means of the steam engine, which was found in or near coal fields. Even though it was used as the raw materials in the smelting of iron-ore, its importance became most essential. At present, inspite of the great demand of petroleum and hydel power, the demand of coal has not dwindled. Since it is a bulky and the most weight losing material of relatively low value, it cannot be transported over longer distances except by water. Naturally heavy industries which are large consumers of coal, congregate near coal fields to minimise the high freight rates. The iron and steel industries are the best example of this. There are many other industries for which cheap fuel and power are essential and, therefore, they concentrate in the vicinity of coal fields. Examples are the glass industry, the pottery industry and those chemical industries which use coal tar as basic raw materials.

Contrary to this, petroleum, fuel oil, Jasoline and natural gas tend to flow out of their source-region. This is simply because of better distributional facilities and also due to the means of cheap pipelines or by tanker transportation. These materials are supplied to the larger urban agglomerations which become the most logical sites for many types of industry.

Industrial complex near raw materials

The food processing industries, the sugar industry, the cement industry, the copper smelting and lumbering and several other industries are located at the centres of their respective raw-materials. These are bulky and perishable raw materials and involve the heavy weight of waste material in proportion to the finished products. Hence, the production-economies are gained locating near raw material sites.

Industrial complexes in and near population agglomerations

Large urban centres provide a variety of sources for markets and labour. Therefore, different type of additional industries are attracted on account of infrastructures and other services available. Printing and publishing, electrical industries, instrument making industries such as telephone and telegraph equipment, X-ray apparatus, aircraft and aircraft engine industries, are some of the examples. Contrary to this, industries like, cane and beet sugar, cheese, saw mills and pulp-mills are seldom common in urbanised areas.

Industrial complex in port-cities

Usually port-cities are favoured centres of trade and commerce, capital, large population and other infrastructure facilities. Even if they have no local resources either of fuel or raw materials, they are excellently linked by sea, rail, road and frequently by inland waters. In all cases raw materials, finished or semi-finished goods, fuel and power are always available. All these attract the industries in folds and that is why industrial complexes are very common in large ports of the world.

Advanced technology and industrial complex

The technological innovation has influenced the industrial growth to a great extent. The use of large machineries on the basis of these developed technology has led to the establishment of numerous engineering complexes. These engineering complexes manufacture series of heavy or light machines, vehicles etc. for use in other industries. Even the raw materials are now being extracted from difficult terrain and localities and are consumed in various industries. Thus, growth of industrial complex seems to be highly associated with the technological innovation.

Governments' welfare schemes and industrial complex

The socialistic pattern of society invests the public money for the general welfare of people. All the development schemes are launched for the elimination of regional imbalances and also to provide employment opportunities to its millions. For this purpose public enterprises are established in the economically backward region just to raise the standard of living of people. Here location of enterprizes is not considered in the term of maximum profit as it is done in the capitalistic pattern of society. Sometimes, the location of enterprises is not least-cost or optimum location. Therefore, a group of industries are located to utilize the maximum advantages in close proximity resulting into large and small industrial complexes.

Advantages and disadvantages of industrial complex

In the preceding section it has been stated that industrial complex symbolises a number of advantageous points. These points include economies of agglomeration, economies of scale and several considerations. This provides a better economic point not only to the firm or related firms but to the whole region. People and materials are revolutionised. The centre becomes self-sustaining with economic and social aspects well marked. That is why, such type of industrial complexes are becoming the most strong measure especially in the developing societies, through which economic disparities are being eliminated. Industrial firms located in isolation increase the regional climaxes. Hence the study of industrial complex is of utmost importance in the developing economy.

When the growth of industrial complex touches its apex at a particular urban centre and peripheries are not fully benefitted, a lot of disadvantages grow. Traffic congestion, haphazard growth of colonies, environmental pollution, high cost of living, working inefficiency due to noise, unionism and other social drawbacks like, accident, prostitution, etc are the outcome of this larger concentration. But these problems are subject of improvement through several urban planning methods.

WHY THE TERM 'INDUSTRIAL COMPLEX'?

The 'industrial complex' is an Economic term usually related to industrial complications in production technology and economic growth of a region. Most of the economists like Perroux and

Boudeville have called 'growth pole' or 'growth centre' synonymous to industrial complex. It has been found that the French Economists call it by 'Developmental Pole', whereas American Economists, especially Isard, call it 'Industrial Complex'.[55]

In Industrial Geography, industrial centres, industrial concentrations and spatial agglomerations of industries are generally used. Industrial centres are centres of industrial location, whereas industrial concentration gives a sense of numerous individual industries located together in one urban or local system. And when several industrial centres are located in one spatial system then the complete system is called industrial agglomerations.

Similarly, Sociologists use the term 'Industrial Organisation' equivalent to industrial complex. Therefore, 'industrial complex' is the inter-disciplinary term and its nature of implication is always confusing when studied in one discipline. For this author has used the geographic terms like industrial concentration, or industrial agglomeration could have been a better substitute than industrial complex. But these terms give a view of spatial configuration of the industrial units and lack to provide a sense of technological complications in manufacturing processes. 'Industrial complex' gives a sense of integrated phenomena not only in spatial dimensions but also in technological processes in production, and other social systems. It also justifies the complexity of the problems related to industries and industrial phenomena in regional makings. The problems of this study are not entirely related to industrial landscape only but industrial study in regional perspective and hence the term industrial complex has been used.

DIFFERENCE BETWEEN AN INDUSTRIAL CENTRE AND AN INDUSTRIAL COMPLEX

Generally confusion persists between industrial complex and industrial centre. Industrial centre means a town or a city where one type or several types, large, medium or small industrial unit or units establish just to sell out the products in the markets available, or just to enjoy the benefits of the urban agglomerations. The establishments are generally unplanned and their growth is mushroom without any strong system or interdependence. Technologically, these enterprises are mostly isolated and are unable to enjoy agglomeration economies.

The industrial complex or production combination as called by Socialist writer[56] is a major progressive form of modern organisation in industry. Under this form a single major production enterprise covers a variety of lines of production. The waste or products of one type of enterprise serve as the raw materials for the intermediate products or auxiliary materials for others. The branches of production are organically, technologically and economically linked in a single production complex. Therefore, complex means not just one firm, one branch of industry in one factory, but a totality of economic relations, a totality of economic exchange, even if only in small locality.[57] It is an integrated approach to develop a region on micro, meso and macro basis.

APPROACHES TO INDUSTRIAL COMPLEX STUDIES

The Industrial Complex approach has its roots in antiquity. The concept of industrial complex was developed by Weber,[58] but the idea, however, was anticipated from the writings of such early economists as Smith,[59] Ricardo,[60] Mill[61] and Launhardt,[62] who assumed the existence of conditions of perfect or near perfect competition. The industrial complex as an hypothesis was given a serious consideration after the Second World War, especially by Isard and his co-writers.[63] Later on the idea of the industrial complex was adopted by several economists[64] and regional planners[65] in their industrial and regional studies. Geographers[66] have also contributed to this idea to a large extent. Economists have emphasised through analytical approach and have drawn conclusions about the least production cost and better production system. Geographers, like the regional planners, have contributed to the spatial configuration and its impact on the socio-economic aspect of the people as a whole. The concept of region or regionalism has also been explained through the idea of an industrial complex. The European and American Writers have realised the idea as a 'growth pole' or 'growth centre' or 'Development pole', as self sustaining centre throwing enormous lights of development in its zone of influence. It has been accepted as a policy which is considered as a process of decentralised concentration of development in order to accelerate regional growth. The Russain Writers, however, have tried to establish the interdependency. Criteria of several production systems into one production-combination of "Territorial Production Complex". Therefore, the literature related to industrial complexes has been reviewed under three headings: (a) economists approach, (b) Geographers or regional planners approach and (c) Socialistic approach.

Economists approach

Weber through his least cost location theory[67] has explained the term agglomeration economies. A number of industrial establishments diffused on a limited geographical space give rise to several economies, e.g. scale economics, localisation economies, urbanisation economies and special juxtaposition economies. These are known as agglomeration economies when combined together. This view of Weber, later on was adopted and explained by several economists like Palander,[68] Hoover,[69] Losch,[70] Greenhut[71] and also by Isard.[72] They all agree with Weber that agglomeration economies exert a positive influence on industrial clustering. Thus, the concept of industrial concentration came into existence. Isard became the only one who elaborated the terminology as a hypothesis. Therefore, his views are discussed at length in the following section.

Isard's comparative cost approach

Like Weber, Isard also used the term agglomeration economies in the establishment and growth of an industrial centre. This view is explained in his book on Location and Space Economy.[73] But his monumental work on industrial complex is discussed and elaborated in his another book on Industrial Complex Analysis and Regional Development : A Case Study of Refinery-Petro, chemical Synthetic-Fiber complexes and Puerto Rico.[74] Again he analysed the industrial complex as a parameter for the growth of a region through his another work

Methods of Regional Analysis.[75]

Besically Isard's approach rests on a modern Weberian doctrine, viz., a comparison of costs and revenues of a number of relevant industrial complexes in Puerto Rico with the corresponding complexes on the mainland of the U.S.A. He has forwarded a number of parameters to study the industrial complex in which, broad economic development approach, individual comparative cost analysis, location Quotients, labour coefficients, coefficients of localization, the study of commodity flows, the interregional input-output approach, a linear programing approach and gravity model techniques are important to mention. All of these are exhaustive and conclusive, though most of them are valid in certain respects.

While presenting the case study of Puerto Rico and its Petrochemical and other complexes, Isard has gone through several stages. The first stage is related to site. The economic proximity of Venezuela's oil fields and availability of cheap labour led to the production processes of oil refineries and natural gas giving rise to Petro-Chemical and other synthetic Fiber complexes. The second stage is a technological association of all individual and inter-industrial production activities. Activity-matrix and engineering functions have been evaluated. Moreover, for each separate programme, detailed feasible combinations and chain of activities have been constructed. The third and final stage discusses the total input-output production programme and their associated costs and revenues differential in comparison to the mainland location (U.S.A.).

Isard's approach, although original, has failed in the selection criterion of comparative costs interpreted as a social indicator in a planned regional context of industrial location. Klaassen, has pointed out several disadvantages of a comparative cost approach.[76] He points out that comparative cost analysis does not deal with the problems of inter-temporal schemes of industrial complexes.

Klaassen's attraction-theory approach

Klaassen has contributed his well known attraction theory, a theory of inter-industry relations, in which demand and supply effects are treated equally. This specific kind of input-output analysis enables one to divide industries into three main groups: market-oriented industries, supply oriented industries and foot-loose industries.

Klaassen's contribution to the selection of bundles of industries presents guidelines to be followed by policy makers for industrial location in depressed areas. The first step is the attraction of the industry fitting best into the existing industrial pattern of the area. On taking account of the indirect effect of this location, the procedure is repeated in order to select the industry with the next-best possibilities of settlement in that area, supposing that the first industry selected is actually a part of the industrial structure of that area. Continuing in this way a combination or complex of mutually linked industries is created. The method proposed by Klaassen can be considered as an important contribution to regional development.

Besides Isard and Klaassen several other economists have contributed to the formulation of complex-idea. Florance[77] in a notable study on the relationships among size of plant investment and location has given the idea of the localization of industry-index. He developed "location quotient"—a device for comparing a region's percentage share of a particular activity with its percentage share of some basic aggregate such as employment or income as a measure of regional industrial concentration. Through this method he has correlated size of plant with degree of localization and capital intensity of the production process. Since then location quotient method has been used frequently in regional economics. The main disadvantage of this measure is the use of national average as a norm implying something inherently correct about one area having a similar industrial structure to the nation as a whole.[78]

Among the modern contributors Peter[79] is the most notable. He has studied the industrial complex by means of geometric programming and has realised the fact that the development of industrial complexes and their growth effects is a dynamic process, which should, in general, be accomplished within a planning horizon of 5 to 15 years. This time horizon is, in general, considered to be long enough to attract new industries and to plan for the associated changes in the regional infrastructure, population, employment, social and institutional conditions, etc. In this way planning of complexes in under-developed countries as well in stagnating regions of economically advanced countries falls within the scope of this study.[80]

But the method adopted by Peter is primarily based on the engineering functions and involves a lot of mathematical approaches. Again he is less conscious about the spatial interaction which is most vital aspect to be dealt within the study of regional planning.

Geographers and regional planner's approach

Geographers have devoted considerable attention towards the development of industrial location theory. In this direction most of the works done by industrial geographers are on the choice of the best location. Other studies are empirical in nature emphasizing locational factors such as labour, materials, markets and transport. These factors have also been extensively analysed in the regional context. The modern view has shifted from these classic considerations to the humanistic approach.

Among the industrial geographers, Smith[81] is the pioneer, who has tested the economists' location theories in the geographic context. His masterwork, industrial location : An Economic Geographical Analysis is an example to cite.[82] Another pioneering attempt has been made by Harris,[83] Alexander,[84] Estall,[85] Alexandersson,[86] Alonso,[87] Hamilton[88] and Casetti.[89] Among the recent geographers who are critical to the idea of optimum location have emphasized human element in location decisions, as 'behavioural approach'. They are Rawstron,[90] Pred,[91] McNee[92] and Gilbert.[93]

The literature on industrial complex in geographical field is very few. In the knowledge of this author probably a few remarkable works have been done by geographers in this direction. Geographers like Richter,[94] Steed,[95] Britton,[96] Karaska,[97] Logan[98] and Townroe[99] attempted to identify the structure and functions of Complexes. They have stressed the role of linkage in the development of industrial complex. Linkage is one aspect of industrial complex and hence these studies are partial in their approach. The idea given by Luttrell[100] on the industrial complex is the only contribution in the real sense. He has formulated the conceptual framework and has established industrial complex as a factor of measurement for the growth of an economic region. Chaudhuri[101] has also presented the important characteristics and associated problems of an industrial complex. But the formulation of theoretical bases and functional linkages essential for a complex are less emphasized. The atomistic economy of the nineteenth and early twentieth centuries is raidly giving way to the economy of giant industrial combines. And hence, the study of those combines in their regional context has become essential for geographers. But lack of requisite data is a hindrance to this type of study.

The industrial geographers are aware of the significance of structural changes in the economy and are able to interpret them. A geographer also studies the characteristics of new economy and its corporations. In the modern corporation, owner ship and control are now separated. The growth of corporate regional planning is recognised. The value of a particular location depends not so much on its own inherent advantages and disadvantages of site and position, but on its corporate position also. These are good grounds to agree with McNee that "in the large scale corporate regional systems of our time, the geography of price has fused with the geography of administration."[102] Therefore, the study of specific corporate regional systems would seem to be one of the most fruitful avenues of investigation for the industrial geography.[103]

Socialistic approach

The Swedish and Russian schools have developed several fundamental concepts. The Swedish school is dominated by Hagerstrand.[104], Tornqvist[105] and Warneryd.[106] Tornqvist, for example, has argued that face to face contacts are the most effective means of exchanging information and believed that personal contacts occupy a large part of the working time of high administrative personnel. As result of this development time has become the major constraint. The spatial solution to this time constraint has been for managers to locate their offices in close proximity to the offices of other 'contact intensive' personnel. The work of Pred,[107] particularly on the question of business behaviour and its links with information flows, has attracted a great deal of discussions. His basic behavioural matrix interprets locational action as dependent upon two factors, the first being the quantity and quality of information available to each decision-maker, the second the ability of each manager to use this information correctly in the selection of sites for the Company's location. Another behavioural concept about industrial location has been advanced by Taylor.[108] According to his seed-bed growth theory the majority of small companies tends to locate in the vicinity of existing industrial concentrations. The reason for this tendency is that all industrial companies possess a quality of potential entrepreneurs. These entrepreneurs try to locate companies in the area which they know best; a tendency supported by the availability of second hand machinery, potential customers, suppliers and labour forces in that area. The consequence of this process, therefore, is that a large number of small companies are likely to emerge in the vicinity of existing industrial concentrations.[109]

Contrary to this view, the Russian School is becoming more and more familiar with the mechanism of concentration of economic activity. The spatial aspects of development have been the focus of attention since the very first year of existence of the Soviet State. The early work on regionalization of the U.S.S.R. made the point that "regionalization is not a technique for achieving decentralization, but, on the contrary, a key method for concentrating forces, attention, purpose, management and organization in Soviet development".[110]

Since the inception of the Five Years Plan in the Soviet economy, the new concept of territorial production complex has been accepted. The spatial division of labour and the expansion of power production or other resource based production cycles give rise to the formation of territorial production complexes. These complexes prepare the ways for determining the economic type of region. The idea of territorial production complex was formulated by a Russian Planner Kolosovskiy.[111] By this term he means all branches of social production in a certain area which are interconnected by the principle of interdependence. Here one economic region depends upon other and vice-versa. In such a way the whole region becomes economically more viable. The industrial units along with its associaries become the part of a sub-system, and numerous old and new sub-systems are thread together into one system or production complex. Each industrial unit acts independently and also interdependently. A production complex is, in other words, the total economic landscape of a territory or a region.[112]

INDIAN APPROACH

The different aspects of Indian Industrial Geography have been highlighted in good length by various contributors. These contributions are related to individual industry, growth of industries in regional context and also on the aspect of Industrial complex. These studies are categorised into three sections : (a) foreigners approach to Indian industrial aspect; (b) Indian's approach to industrial aspect and (c) Geographers of Bihar on industrial aspect.

Among the foreign writers, Thomas,[113] Brush,[114] Kay,[115] Kirk,[116] Baldwin,[117] Johnson,[118] Baranson[119] and Shirokov[120] are the most important. They have studied the locational characteristics problems and development of various industries. For example, Thomas has emphasized the importance of basic industries in the growth of Indian economy. Baranson and Baldwin have analysed the problems related to the manufacturing activities. Brush and Johnson have discussed the location aspects of the iron and steel industry in India. Kay and Kirk have highlighted the problems of Cotton and Jute Industries. Shirokov has described the industrialisation trends, especially in the Pre and Post-independence periods of India. These studies are considered to be the basic and have given directions to many Indian geographers.

Among the Indian Contributors on the industrial aspect both economists and geographers are included. Sharma,[121] Ghose,[122] Mehta,[123] Kuchhal,[124] Kuriyan,[125] Dayal,[126] Karan,[127] Chaudhuri[128] and Sinha[129] are the significant contributors. Sharma has described in detail the growth and location of six major industries; cotton, jute, iron and steel, cement, sugar and fertilizers in india. Ghose, Mehta and Kuchhal have followed the same pattern. Kuriyan has stressed the industrial development since independence and also has mentioned the spatial distribution of Indian industries.[130] Dayal has emphasized over the recent trends in the locational aspect of industries like aluminium,[131] iron and steel and cement[132] and sugar.[133] He has also indicated the characteristics of the major industrial belts of India.[134] Karan has highlighted the distributional aspect of manufacturing in India and has indicated the changes in the industrial location.[135] Chaudhuri has carried out research on various aspects of Indian industries. He has analysed the locational aspect of iron and steel[36] and other industries. His emphasis on the growth of small scale industry and decentralisation aspect is very much interesting.[137] Further on his attempt on the Industrial Landscape of West Bengal is a landmark in the industrial field of India.[138] Likewise, Sinha's contribution is also valuable in fulfilling the long required geographer's view on industrial aspect of the country. Besides these contributions, hundred other works have been attempted to analyse the different aspects of industrial economy of India. To assimilate all of these would be a herculian task. Although, few names are important to be mentioned. They are Ganguli,[139] Dixit,[140] Indrapal,[141] Ghosh,[142] Thapan[143] and Patni.[144]

Studies on industrial geography in Bihar have remained a shy field. Although Bihar happens to be one of the potential states in its industrial economy, no any exhaustive industrial account in the form of book has been published. Six Ph.D. works have been completed on various industrial aspects of Bihar. Several research papers have been published on the industrial aspects of Bihar since independence. Majid is to be credited being the pioneer industrial geographer of Bihar, who completed his Ph.D. work on Industrial Geography.[145] Later on he published several papers on different aspects of Bihar in which copper,[146] silk,[147] lac and shellac[148] and sugar[149] industries are important. Other geographers have contributed to the importance of geographical factors on the growth of industries in Bihar. For example, Azam has highlighted the industrial potentialities of the Lower Son Valley.[150] He has also analysed the Cement industry of Bihar.[151] Sinha is the next industrial geographer who has studied the growth and industrial landscape of Bihar particularly with reference to the Chhotanagpur Highlands.[152] Thakur studied sugar industry of Bihar[153] and Pandey on Mica processing industry of Giridih.[154] The Chhotanagpur Plateau Region has been the main attraction for many researchers, among them Karan,[155] Ram,[156] Singh,[157] Mukherjee,[158] Pandey[159] and Prasad[160] are important to mention. Likewise the munufacturing regions of North Bihar have been delimited by Mandal.[161] Among the individual industrial centres, Dalmianagar Ranchi, Bokaro have been greatly considered. The industrial phenomena of Dalmianagar has been studied by Azam,[162] Sinha[163] and Singh.[164] Similarly, industrial aspect of Ranchi has been described by Pandey,[165] Sinha[166] and Singh.[167] The small scale industry of Bihar has been studied by Singh[168] especially its role in the economic development of Bihar Plain.

Indian Geographers have relatively paid scant attention to the identification and analysis of industrial complexes of India. Chaudhuri has taken a distinct lead in this field. He has already published four and five research papers on the various industrial complexes of West Bengal. Kulti-Burnpur Complex[169] and Durgapur Complex[170] have developed around the nucleus of respective iron and steel industries. The formation of Greater-Calcutta industrial Complexes[171] is due to the urban agglomerations and various industries like jute and engineering. He has also highlighted the future potentialities of Haldia, which is in the process of development as a major industrial complex in India.[172] Ghose and Chakravorty have contributed jointly a paper on the aspect of location of an industrial complex.[173] They have emphasized the essential condition like creation of a nucleus plant for the establishment of an industrial complex. Singh in his paper, on Industrial complex of Dalmianagar[174] has highlighted the interdependability of industrial units as the major factor for the growth of an industrial complex. His second paper deals with the factors affecting the growth of industrial complex.[175] In his further research he has identified six industrial complexes of Bihar.[176] This identification is based on the clustering of various industrial units at a limited geographical space and thus has availed the advantages of agglomeration economies.

NEEDED RESEARCH AND STATEMENT OF PROBLEMS

The above reviews on industrial complex reveal that most of the works are basically theoretical and descriptive. Only in a few of the published research papers and books attempts have been made to present systematically the growth, regional pattern and functional characteristics of industrial complexes. Other problems which invite research attention are : (a) role of Industrial Complexes in the Regional Development, (b) growth of industrial complexes for the socio-economic betterment, (c) industrialisation through industrial complexes, (d) industrial complexes and industrial planning, and (e) industrial linkage as a factor of Industrial Complex growth. All these problems may be analysed and discussed with case studies.

The role of industrial complexes in the regional development is a pertinent question. Regional development is the main aspect of our Five Year Plans. Industrial complexes provide better conditions through the mobilization of the resources, erecting employment opportunities and achieving at the better productions. All these are meant for better social needs. And this way a regional development is achieved.

Industrial complexes develop around a nucleus plant. Such plants act as a mother plant and nurishes several other large, medium and small industries. These industries are related to various other industries on the regional plane and thus an industrialisation is achieved.

The industrial planning is always sought to decentralise the industrial activities to several new centres. These centres when functionally interlinked to one another become more operative. But when these centres become nodes, they accumulate huge wealth and survive at the cost of peripheries and accentuate regional disparities. Industrial Complexes are, however, inherently opposite to the industrial nodes. And, therefore, industrial planning is truely conditioned to industrial complexes.

Industrial linkage is the main factor for the growth of an industrial complex. An empirical study will show, how much growth of linkage affects the growth of an industrial complex.

A need, therefore, remains for understanding the growth, regional pattern and functional characteristics of industrial complexes. Such studies would lead ultimately to the formulation of much needed industrial location models particularly in the context of developing countries like India. Karaska, Steed, Walker and Choudhary have strongly advocated the systematic study to the geography of industrial complexes and it is in this direction that the subject is most likely to advance. The present study attempts to contribute to that need.

REFERENCES

1. Smith, A. (1776), Inquiry into the Nature and Causes of the Wealth of Nations, Ricardo, D. (1817), The Principles of Political Economy and Taxation and Mill, J.S. (1848), *Principles of Political Economy*.

2. Weber, A. (1909), Theory of the Location of Industries. Translated into English by C.J. Freiderich in 1929, University of Chicago Press, Chicago, p. 11.

3. Losch, A. (1940), *The Economics of Location*, Yale University Press, New Haven, p. 17.

4. Isard, W. (1956), Location and Space Economy, MIT Press, Cambridge, Mass; and Smith, D.M. (1971), *Industrial Location An Economic Geographical Analysis*, John Wiley and Sons, New York, London.

5. McNee, R.B. (1960), "Towards a More Humanistic Economic Geography : the Geography of Enterprise", *Tijdschrift Voor Economische Sociale Geographfie*, 51, pp. 201-6.

6. Misra, R.P. (1971), *Growth Poles and Growth Centres in Urban and Regional Planning in India*, University of Mysore, Mysore, p. 11.

7. Mountjoy, A B. (1966), *Industrialization and Under-developed Countries*, Hutchinson University Library, London, p. 165.

8. "*The New Industrial Policy of the Government of India*", The Searchlight, Patna, 24th July, 1980, p. 3.

9. Isard, W., and Schooler, E.W. and Vietorioz, T. (1959), *Industrial Complex Analysis and Regional Development*, M.I.T. Press, Cambridge, Mass.

10. Klaassen, L.H. (1967), Methods of Selecting Industries For Depressed Areas, OECD, Paris.

11. Perroux, F. (1950), "Economic Space, Theory and Applications", *Quarterly Journal of Economics*, Vol. 64, pp. 89-104.

12. Boudeville, J.R. (1961), "A Survey of Recent Techniques for Regional Economic Analysis", in W. Isard and J.M. Cumberland (eds.), *Regional Economic Planning, Techniques of Analysis for less Developed Areas*, Organisation for European Economic Co-operation, Paris, pp. 383-84.

13. Boudeville, J.R. (1961), op. cit., p. 383.

14. Bondeville, J.R. (1966), *Problems of Regional Economic Planning*,

Edinburgh University Press, Edinburgh, p. 11.

15. Perroux, F. (1950), op. cit., p. 366.

16. Lasuen, J.R. (1969), "On Growth Poles", *Urban Studies*, vol. 4, pp. 137-61.

17. Friedmann, J. (1972), "General Theory of Polarised Development", in N.M. Hansen (ed.) *Growth Centres in Regional Economic Development* The Free Press, New York, pp. 87-107.

18. Hermansen, T. (1972), "Development Poles and Development Centres in National and Regional Development; Elements of a Theoretical Framework", in A.R. Kuklinski, (ed.), *Growth Poles and Growth Centres in Regional Planning*, Monton, Paris and the Hague, pp. 29-30.

19. Hermanson, T. (1972), op. cit., p. 29.

20. Hansen, N.M. (1972), *Growth Centres in Regional Economic Development*, The Free Press, New York.

21. Richardson, H.W. (1969), *Regional Economics*, Weidenfeld and Nicolson, London.

22. *Ibid.*, p. 425.

23. Hansen (1972), op. cit., p. 97.

24. Myrdal, G.M. (1957) *Economic Theory and Underdeveloped Regions*, Gerald Duckworth, London.

25. Hirschman, A.O. (1958), *The Strategy of Economic Development*, Yale University Press, New Haven and London.

26. Friedmann, J.R. (1966), *Regional Development Policy : A Case Study of Venezuela*, MIT Press, Cambridge, Mass.

27. Robinson, G. and Salih, K.B. (1971), "The Spread of Development Around Kuala Lumpur : A Methodology for an Exploratory Test of Some Assumptions of the Growth Pole Model", *Regional Studies*, vol. 5, pp. 303-14.

28. *Ibid.*, p. 303.

29. Moseley, M.J. (1974), *Growth Centres in Spatial Planning*, Pergamen Press, New York, p. 116.

30. Hansen, W.L. and Tiebout, C.M. (1963), "An Inter-Sectoral Flows Analysis of the Californian Economy", *Review of Economics and Statistics*, 45, pp. 409-18.

31. Misra, R.P. (1972), "Growth Poles and Growth Centres in the Context of India's Urban and Regional Development Problems", in A.R. Kuklinski (ed.), *Growth Poles and Growth Centres in Regional Planning*, Mouton. Paris and the Hague.

32. Bernard, P. (1970), "*Growth Pales and Growth Centres in Regional Development* : vol. III, Report no. 74.14, UNRISD, Geneva, p. 64.

33. Balassa, B. (1969), *The Theory of Economic Integration*, Pitman & Sons, London, p. 197.

34. Allen, K. and Maclennan, M.C. (1970), *Region, Problems and Policies in Italy and France*, Allen & Unwin, London.

35. Allen, K. and Maclennan, M.C. (1970), op. cit., p. 257.

36. Prasad, K.N. (1980), *Problems of Economic Development in the*

Third World with Special Reference to India, Sterling Publishing Co., New Delhi, p. 377.

37. Moseley, M.J. (1974), op. cit., p. 5.

38. Prasad, K.N. (1973), "*Economic Development of Chotanagpur*", *Commerce* (Bombay), vol. 17, p. 55.

39. Klaassen, L.H. (1967), op. cit., p. 22.

40. Isard, W. (ed.) (1960), [*Methods of Regional Analysis: An Introduction to Regional Science*, M.I.T. Press, Cambridge, Mass, p. 377.

41. Isard, W. (1956), Location and Space-Economy, M.I.T. Press, Cambridge, pp. 172-79.

42. Peter, N. (1972), Planning of Industrial Complexes by Means of Geometric Programming, University Press, Rotterdam, p. 8.

43. Tinbergen, J. (1961), "The Spatial Dispersion of Production: A Hypothesis", *Schweiz Zeitschrift fur Volkswirt and Statistie*, vol. 97, No. 4, pp. 1-15.

44. Peter, N. (1972), op. cit., p. 8.

45. Luttrell, W.F. (1972), "Industrial Complexes and Regional Economic Development in Canada", in A.R. Kuklinski (ed.), *Growth Poles and Growth Centres in Regional Planning*, Mouton, Paris, p. 245.

46. Richter, C.E. (1969), "The Impact of Industrial Linkages on Geographical Association", *Journal of Regional Science*, vol. 9, p. 19.

47. Leontief, W.W. (1951), "Input-output Economics", *Scientific American*, vol. 185, p. 6.

48. Isard, W. and Schooler, E.W. (1959), "Industrial Complex Analysis, Agglomeration Economics and Regional Development", *Journal of Regional Science*, vol. 1, pp. 19-33.

49. Joshi, K.L. (1978), *Geography of India: Resources and Regional Development*, NCERT, New Delhi, p. 113.

50. Jarrett, H.R. (1977), *A Geography of Manufacturing*, Macdonald and Evans, Norwich, p. 189.

51. Jarrett, H.R. (1977), op. cit., p. 283.

52. Isard, W. (eds.) (1960), op. cit., p. 389.

53. Isard, W. (ed.) (1960), op. cit., p. 377.

54. Royen, W.V. and Bengtson, N.A. (1971), *Fundamentals of Economic Geography*, Prentice Hall of India Private Ltd., New Delhi, p. 548.

55. Prasad, K.N. (1980), op. cit., p. 367.

56. Kolosovskiy, N.N. (1961), "The Territorial Production Combination in Soviet Economic Geography", *Journal of Regional Science*. vol. 3, pp. 1-25.

57. Nekrasov, N. (1974), *Territorial Organisation of Soviet Economy*, Progress Publishers, Moscow, p. 24.

58. Weber, A. (1909), op. cit.

59. Smith, A. (1776), op. cit.

60. Ricardo, D. (1817), op. cit.

61. Mill, J.S. (1848), op. cit.

62. Launhardt, W. (1885), *Mathematisole Begrundung der Volkwirtscha-*

flsleure. Leipzig.

63. Isard, W. and Schooler, E.W. and Victoris, T. (1959), op. cit.

64. Klaassen, L.H. (1967), op. cit., Balassa, B. (1969), op. cit., Peter, N. (1972), op. cit.

65. Hansen, N.M. (1968), French Regional Planning, University Press, Edinburgh. Kuklinski, A.R. (ed.) (1972), *Growth Poles and Growth Centres in Regional Planning*, Mouton, Paris and the Hagut, and, Moseley, M.J. (1974), Growth Centres in Spatial Planning, Pergamon Press, New York.

66. Karaska, G.J. (1969), "Manufacturing Linkages in the Philadelphia Economy. Some Evidence of External Agglomeration Forces", *Geographical Analysis*, pp. 354-69, Britton, J.N.H. (1961). "A Geographical Approach to the Study of Industrial Linkages", *Canadian Geographer*, vol. 13, pp. 135-36 Luttrell, W.F. (1972), op. cit.

67. Weber, A. (1929), op. cit., p. 139.

68. Palander, T. (1935), Beitrage Zur Standortstheorie, Almquist and Wiksells Boktryckeri, Uppsala.

69. Hoover, E.M. (1948), The Location of Economic Activity, McGraw Hill, New York.

70. Losch, A. (1954), op. cit.

71. Greenhat, M.L. (1956), *Plant Location in Theory and Practice*, University of North Carolina Press, Chepel Hill.

72. Isard, W. (1956), op. cit.

73. *Ibid.*

74. Isard, W. and Schooler, E.W. and Victorisz, T. (1959), op. cit.

75. Isard, W. (ed.) (1960), op. cit.

76. Klaassen, L.H. (1967), op. cit., p. 51.

77. Florence, S.P. (1948), *Investment Location and Size of Plant*, Cambridge University Press, Cambridge.

78. Salt, J. (1969), "Progress in Industrial Geography", in R.U. Cooke and J.H. Johnson (eds.), *Trends in Geography : An Introductory Survey*, Pergamon Press, London.

79. Peter, N. (1972), op. cit.

80. *Ibid.*, p. 13.

81. Smith, D.M. (1966), "A Theoretical Framework for Geographical Studies of Industrial Location", *Economic Geography*, vol. 43 (2), pp. 95-113.

82. Smith D.M. (1971), *Industrial Location : An Economic Geographical Analysis*, John Wiley and Sons, New York, London.

83. Harris, C.D. (1954), "The Market as a Factor in the localization of Industry in the United States", *Annals of the Association of American Geographers*, 44, pp. 315-48.

84. Alexander, J.W. (1958), "Location of Manufacturing : Methods of Measurement", *Annals of the Association of American Geographers*, 48, pp. 20-26.

85. Estall, R.C. (1966), *New England : A Study in Industrial Adjustment*, Pitman and Sons, London.

86. Alexandersson, G. (1967), *Geography of Manufacturing*, Prentice Hall, Englewood Cliffs, New Jersey.

87. Alonso, W. (1967), "A Reformulation of Classical Location Theory and Its Relation to Rent Theory", *Papers and Proceedings of the Regional Science Association*, 19, pp. 23-44.

88. Hamilton, F.E.I. (1967), "Models of Industrial Location", in R.J. Chorley and P. Haggett (eds.) *Models in Geography*, Methuen, London, pp. 361-485.

89. Casetti, E. (1966), "Optional Location of Steel Mills serving the Quebec and Southern Ontario Steel Market", *Canadian Geographer* 10, pp. 27-34.

90. Rawstron, E.M. (1958), "Three Principles of Industrial Location", *Transactions and Papers*, Institute of British Geographers, 25, pp. 132-142.

91. Pred, A. (1967), Behaviour and Location, Foundations for a Geographic and Dynamic Location Theory, Part I, Lund Studies in Geography, Series B, 27.

92. McNee, R.B. (1960), "Towards a more Huamanistic Economic Geography : The Geography of Enterprise", *Tisdscrift Economische Voor Sociale Geographie*, 51, pp. 201-6.

93. Gilbert, A. (1974), "Industrial Location Theory : Its Relevance to an Industrialising Nation", in B.S. Hoyle (ed.), *Spatial Aspects of Development*, John Wiley, London, pp. 271-289.

94. Richter, C.E. (1970), "Systematic Relationship between Industrial Linkages and the Agglomeration of Manufacturing Industries", *Review of Regional Studies*, 1, pp. 37-48.

95. Steed, G.P.F. (1970), "Changing Linkages and Internal Multiplier of an Industrial Complex", *Canadian Geographer*, vol. 19, pp. 229-243.

96. Britton, J.N.H. (1969), op. cit.

97. Karaska, G.J. (1969), op. cit.

98. Logan, M.I. (1966), "Location Behaviour of Manufacturing Firms in Urban Areas", *Annals of the Association of American Geogaphers*, vol. 56, pp. 451-60.

99. Townroe, P.M. (1970), "Industrial Linkage, Agglomeration and External Economies", *Journal of Town Planning Institute*, vol. 56, pp, 18-20.

100. Luttrell, W.F. (1972), op. cit. pp. 242-262.

101. Chaudhuri, M.R. (1967), "Kulti-Burnpur : Case Study of the Growth and Problems of An Industrial Complex", *Geographical Review of India*, vol. 29, no. 1, pp. 18-35.

102. McNee, R.B. (1960), op. cit., pp. 201-206.

103. Salt, J. (1969), op. cit., p. 181.

104. Hagerstrand, T. (1967), Innovation Diffusion as a Spatial Process, Translated by A. Pred, Chicago University Press, Chicago.

105. Tornqvist, G. (1970), Contact Systems and Regional Development, Lund, *Lund Studies in Geography*, Series B. No. 35.

106. Warneryd, O. (1968), Interdependence in Urban Systems,

Goteberg.

107. Pred, A. (1967), op. cit.

108. Taylor, M.J. (1969), "Industrial Linkages, Seedbed Growth and the Location of Firms", *Occasional Paper* no. 3, University College, London.

109. Gilbert, A. (1974), op. cit., pp. 271-289.

110. Gokhman, V.M. (1981), "The Significance of Growth Poles in Regional Development", *Soviet Geography*, vol. 22, pp. 255-271.

111. Kolosovskiy, N.N. (1961), op. cit , pp. 1-25,

112. Joshi, K.L. (1978), op. cit., p. 115.

113. Thomas, P.J. (1948), *Basic Industries of India*, Orient Longmans Ltd., Bombay.

114. Brush, J.E. (1952), "The Iron and Steel Industry of India", *Geographical Review*, vol. 42, pp. 37-56.

115. Kay, S.J. (1952), "India's Cotton Textile Industry", *Journal of the Royal Society* of Arts, vol. 100, pp. 848-59.

116. Kirk, W. (1956), "The Cotton and Jute Industries of India; A Study in Concentration and Dispersal", *Scottish Geographical Magazine*, vol. 72, pp. 38-52.

117. Baldwin, G.B. (1959), *Industrial Growth in South India*, Glencoe Free Press, Glencoe.

118. Johnson, W.A. (1966), *The Steel Industry of India*, Cambridge.

119. Baranson, J. (1967), Manufacturing Problems in India, Syracuse University Press, Syracuse.

120. Shirokov, G.K. (1973), *of Industrialisation of India*, Progress Publishers, Moscow.

121. Sharma, T.R. (1946), Location of Industries in India, Hindkitab, Bombay.

122. Ghose, B.C. (1949), *Indian Location*, Oxford University Press, Delhi.

123. Mehta, M.M. (1952) *Location of Indian Industries*, Allahabad.

124. Kuchhal, S.C. (1969), *Industrial Economy in India*, Allahabad.

125. Kuriyan, G, (1956), "Industrial Development in India since Independence", *Indian Geographical Journal*, vol. 33, pp. 71-78.

126. Dayal, P. (1958), "Location and Development of Aluminium Industry in India", *National Geographical Journal of India*, vol. 4, pp. 67-78.

127. Karan, P.P. (1958), "The Areal Distribution of Manufacturing in India", *Journal of Geography*, vol. 57, pp. 294-300.

128. Chaudhuri, M.R. (1962), Indian Industries : Development and Location, Oxford and IBH Publishing Co., Calcutta.

129. Sinha, B.N. (1972), *Industrial Geography of India*, The World Press, Calcutta.

130. Kuriyan, G. (1962), "An analysis of the Spatial distribution of Industry in India", *Indian Geographical Journal*, vol. 37, pp. 1-7.

131. Dayal, P. (1958), op. cit.

132. Dayal, P. (1964), "Aspects of Industrial Location in India", *Transactions of Indian Council of Geographers*, vol. 1, pp. 1-9.

133. Dayal, P. (1968), "Sugar Industry in India', *Abstracts of Papers of 21st International Geographical Union Congress*, New Delhi, p. 187.

134. Dayal, P. (1975), "Characteristics of the Major Industrial Belts of India", in A.K Dutt and A.G. Noble (eds.), Rural Urban Change in India, Patna University Regional Council for International Education, Pittsburgh, pp. 166-169.

135. Karan, P.P. (1964), "Changes in Indian Industrial Location" *Annals of the Association of American Geographers*, vol. 54, pp. 336-54.

136. Chaudhuri, M.R. (1964), Iron and Steel Industry in India, Oxford Book Co., Calcutta.

137. Chaudhuri, M.R. (1965), "Industrial Estates in West Bengal", *Geographical Review of India*, 27 (1).

138. Chaudhuri, M.R. (1971), *The Industrial Landscape of West Bengal*, Oxford and IBH Publishing Co., Calcutta.

139. Ganguli, B.N. (1949), Iron and Steel Industry in Bengal-Bihar Industrial Belt", *Calcutta Geographical Review*, 11 (3 & 4).

140. Dixit, K.R. (1963), "Growth and Distribution of Indian Paper Industry", *National Geographical Journal of India* vol. 9 (3 & 4), pp. 218-35.

141. Indrapal (1963), "Prospective Site for a Fertilizer Factory in Uttar Pradesh", *Indian Geographical Journal*, 8 (1, 2).

142. Ghosh, A. (1965), *Efficiency in Location and Inter-Regional Flows : The Indian Cement Industry During the Five Year Plans* 1950-1959, North-Holland Publishing Co., Amsterdam.

143. Thapan, D. (1966), "The Iron and Steel Belt of India", in R.L. Singh (ed.), *Applied Geography, Varanasi*, National Geographical Society of India, pp. 173-180.

144. Patni, R.L. (1968), "A New Method for Measuring Locational Changes in a Manufacturing Industry", *Economic Geography*, vol. 44, no. 5, pp. 210-217.

145. Majid, S.A. (1949), The Industrial Geography of Bihar, Unpublished Ph.D. Thesis, London University, London.

146. Majid, S.A. (1956), "Copper Industry of Bihar", *Geographical Outlook*, 1 (1).

147. Majid, S.A. (1959), "Silk Production and Weaving in Bihar", *National Geographical Journal of India*, 5 (2).

148. Majid, S.A. (1960), "A Geographical Study of Lac and Shellac Industries of Bihar", *The National Geographer*, vol. 3, pp. 1-10.

149. Majid, S.A. (1968), "Sugar Industry in Bihar", Abstracts of papers of *21st International Geographical Union Congress*, New Delhi, p. 193.

150. Azam, S.S. (1968), "Industrial Landscape of the Lower Son Valley in Bihar", unpublished Ph.D. Thesis, Ranchi University, Ranchi.

151. Azam, S.S. (1975), "Cement Industry in Bihar", *Geographical Outlook*, vol. 10, pp. 59-70.

152. Sinha, R.P. (1970), *Industrial Landscape of the Highlands of Chhotanagpur*, Unpublished Ph.D. Thesis, Bhagalpur University, Bhagalpur, and Sinha, R.P. (1972), "*Growth of Industries in Bihar*", The Geographical Progress, (R.B.I.), pp. 19-69.

153. Thakur J.N. (1975), *Sugar Industry of Bihar*, Unpublished Ph.D. Thesis, Patna University, Patna.

154. Pandey, S.C. (1979), *Mica, Processing Industry of Giridih (Bihar)*, Unpublished Ph.D. Thesis, Patna University, Patna.

155. Karan, P.P. (1953), "Economic Regions of Chotanagpur", *Economic Geography*, vol. 29, pp. 216-250.

156. Ram, L.N. (1968), "Industrial Belts in South East Chotanagpur", *Transactions of the Indian Council of Geographers*, vol. 5. pp. 79-90.

157. Singh, U.P. (1975), Industrial Landscape of Upper Damodar Valley, Unpublished Ph.D. Thesis, Bhagalpur University.

158. Mukherjee, M.M. (1970), "Aspects of Recent Industrialisation in Chhotanagpur", *National Geographical Journal of India*, vol. 16, pp. I01-109.

159. Pandey, P. (1970), *Impact of Industrialisation on Urban Growth (A Case Study of Chhotanagpur)* Central Book Depot, Allahabad.

160. Prasad, A. (1970-71), "Industries of Chhotanagpur : A Study in Regional Pattern of Distribution, Growth and Amplitudes", *Geographical Outlook*, vol. 7, pp. 71-83.

161. Mandal, B. (1971), "Manufacturing Regions of North Bihar", *The National Geographical Journal of India*, vol. 17, pp. 58-62.

162. Azam, S.S. (1970), "Pattern of Industrial Development at Dalmianagar", *Geographical Outlook*, vol. 7, pp. 148-54.

163. Sinha, R.P. (1974), "Growth of Industries at Dalmianagar", *The Bihar Information*, vol. 18, pp. 26-37.

164. Singh, R.P. (1968), Industrial Geography of Dalmianagar, Unpublished Master Thesis, Patna University, Patna.

165. Pandey, P. (1969), "Industrial Landscape of Greater Ranchi", *Geographical Outlook*, vol. 6, pp. 41-47.

166. Sinha, V.N.P. (1968), "Industrialisation in Ranchi" *Transactions of the Indian Council of Geographers*, vol. 5, pp. 91-97.

167. Singh, R.P. (1961), "Bokaro : The Future Steel Town", *Natianal Geographical Journal of India*, vol. 7.

168. Singh, R.P. (1980), "Growth of Small Scale Industry and its Impact on the Economy of the Bihar Plain", Indian Geographical Studies, *Research Bulletin* no. 14, pp. 29-35.

169. Chaudhuri, M.R. (1967), op. cit.

170. Chaudhuri, M.R. (1969), "Growth Pattern and Problems of Durgapur Industrial Complex", *Proceedings of the Indian Science Congress, Session* 56, Part III.

171. Chaudhuri, M.R. (1972), "Industrial Activities in the Greater Calcutta Industrial Complex", *Industrial Situation in India*, vol. I, no. 1, pp. 21-26.

172. Chaudhuri, M.R. (1973), "Haldia—A Major Port Industrial Com-

plex and City in Making", *Industrial Situation in India*, no. 2, pp. 48-53.

173. Ghose, A. and Chakravorty, A. (1971), "Location of An Industrial Complex", *Indian Journal of Regional Science*, vol. 3, no. 2, pp. 1-13.

174. Singh, R.P. (1974), "Dalmianagar : A Study of the Industrial Complex", *Indian Geographical Studies, Research Bulletin*, no. 2, pp. 36-43.

175. Singh, R.P. (1976), "Factors Affecting Growth of Industrial Complexes in Bihar", *Indian Geagraphical Studies, Research Bulletin* no. 7, pp. 66-72.

176. Singh, R.P. (1980), "The Industrial Complexes of Bihar" *Geographical Review of India*, vol. 42, pp. 229-237.

2

THE STUDY AREA

THE ESTABLISHMENT and growth of an industrial complex in any region is the outcome of the commulative effects of its physical, economic and social set of factors. Even the structure, shape, size and spatial diffusion of industries are to a great extent guided by those basic determinants. Hence, the discussion of these factors, prior to the discussion of main problem, becomes imperative. The State of Bihar is selected as a case study. Bihar one of the most populous Indian States is often known as "a rich country inhabited by poor people".[1] This paradox of 'poverty amidst plenty' has been repeated so often as regards the state that it almost sounds platitudinous.[2] This state is an exceptionally endowed with the natural resources like vast rolling plains with rich fertile lands extremely suitable for agriculture, inexhaustible resources of water, ample rainfall with amicable climatic conditions, considerable forest resources, wide range of mineral, fuels and metallic ores which provide a strong base for varied industrial growth and evergrowing vast human resources 'enriched by a cultural heritage of millenia of years'.[3] Besides, under planned development scheme several heavy industrial giants, e.g., Tisco, Telco, H.E.C., Bokaro Steel Plant, Sindri Fertilizers, Barauni Oil Refineries and others have developed, yet it is a deficit state in food grains and industrially most backward. Thus, both the vital sectors—agriculture and industry remain less rewarding.[4] The grim faces of her teeming millions reeling under the acute poverty justify the byword of destitute under the shadow of development.[5] The causes of this contrast of economy exist in the promise and potentiality and its relative non-fulfilment.[6] Vast resources are still awaiting exploration, and utilization

TABLE 2.1 : **Plan allocation (per capita plan expenditure) for different states**

(*in Rupees*)

Selected states	First plan	Second plan	Third plan	Fourth plan
Andhra Pradesh	34.71	52.16	98.82	104.04
Gujarat	46.41	77.51	115.19	182.34
Maharastra	46.41	57.85	109.62	191.71
Karnataka	48.45	56.75	106.29	126.95
Orissa	58.04	52.80	127.68	109.79
Punjab	101.02	88.20	135.76	214.11
Tamil Nadu	28.22	52.34	101.62	140.98
Uttar Pradesh	26.26	33.14	75.97	151.70
West Bengal	58.56	47.36	86.02	73.64
Bihar	18.89	41.76	70.73	99.01
India	89.44	50.87	97.02	127.64

Source : The Economic Times, Wednesday, September 22, 1976, p. II.

TABLE 2.2 : **Selected socio-economic indicators for Bihar and India.**

Economic indicator	Ref. year	Unit	Bihar	India
General				
Population	1971	Million	56.35	547.95
Density of population	1971	Per sq. km.	324	171
Percentage of Urban Population to total	1971	Per cent	10.0	19.9
Percentage of scheduled castes, tribes to total	1971	Per cent	22.9	21.5
Percentage of agricultural workers to total workers	1971	Per cent	82.3	69.7
Percentage of working force to total population	1971	Per cent	31.0	32.9
Agriculture				
Net cultivated area as per cent of total area	1969-70	Per cent	48.6	45.5

TABLE 2—(*Contd.*)

Economic Indicator	Ref. year	Unit	Bihar	India
Net irrigated area as per cent of net cultivated area	1969-70	Per cent	27.1	21.8
Net sown area per cultivator	1970-71	Hectares	1.1	1.8
Consumption of fertilizers per hectare of cropped area	1969-70	Kg.	8.9	16.9
Per capita average food grains production	1969-70	Kg.	147	188
Yield per hectare of principal crops :				
(a) Food grains		Kg.	879	830
(b) Pulses		Kg.	489	464
(c) Sugarcane		Kg.	33805	49434
Industry				
Working factories	1970	Number	515	976
Average daily employment of factory worker per lakh population	1972	Rs.	134	253
Per capita gross output in industry	1970	Rs.	31	59
Miscellaneous				
Per Capita Power consumption	1972-73	Kwh.	66	96
Total road length per 100 sq. km. of area	1973	Km.	63.79	36.10
Bank offices per lakh of population	1974	Number	1.3	3.1
Per Capita Income	1972-73	Rs.	489	698

Source : The Economic Times, Wednesday, September 22, 1976, p. II.

due to less developed infra-structural facilities.[7] Floods and droughts—two natural calamities to which the State is frequently exposed stand for the economic hazards. Heavy agricultural dependency has caused lack of capital and entrepreneurship. Poor people have no savings to put into banks and therefore, no investment is done for producing more.[8] The huge Plan expenditures on major projects have proved overtly optimistic without any significant spread effect.[9] The plan allocation for Bihar has remained comparatively lower in comparison to other Indian States (Table 2.1). The complex socioeconomic phenomena have operated through decades to accentuate the poverty and are responsible for the absence of a healthy middle class.[10] "The absence of a healthy middle class in the State has arrested the economic development, affected the savings potential and has almost polarised the society into high-income and low income groups, the latter left with little wage to raise material standard of life".[11] And finally inefficiency, corruption and immorality in politics, administration, business, education, legal and other fields have become the public life in which Bihar has no equal in the country.[12] In the context of the limited opportunities and the growing demand by different groups, group rivalaries have evolved giving an adverse impact on the economic stability. Moreover, the recent political instability has caused low production, high prices and economic stagnation and has compelled the state to remain at the lowest economic ebb on the national vertex (Table 2.2).

LOCATION AND EXTENT

Bihar is named after the Viharas,[3] Buddhist monasteries which were in larger numbers during yore. It extends between 21°58′10″ to 27°31′15″ N. latitudes and 83°19′50″ to 88°17′40″E. longitudes and covers an area of 1,73,876 sq. miles with 69,822,154 population (1981).[14] Thus the state accounts for 5.3 per cent of the total Indian territory and 10.5 per cent of the country's population. Bihar is a compact unit with a roughly quadrilateral shape.[15] It is a landlocked state bounded by the Himalayan Kingdom of Nepal on the north, Orissa on the south, West Bengal on the east and the Uttar Pradesh and Madhya Pradesh on the west. From the administrative point of view, the state has been divided into 8 divisions, 31 districts, 72 sub-divisions, 587 Blocks and 67,566 villages (Fig. 2.2 & 2.3). The figure 2.2 and 2.3 give a comparative values of Bihar in the years, 1971 and 1981.

TABLE 3 : **Two Major divisions of Bihar**

Regions	Area in thousand sq. km.	Percentage of the total states land	Pop. (crores) 1971	Percentage of the total state's pop.	Density (per sq. km.)	Percentage of rural population
Northern bihar plains	94.3	*54.20*	*4.21*	*74.75*	*446*	*92*
(i) North Bihar	54.2	30.96	2.61	46.68	484	95
(ii) South Bihar	40.1	23.24	1.60	28.07	399	87
Southern Plateau	79.6	*45.80*	*1.42*	*25.25*	*179*	*84*
Bihar	173.9	100.00	5.63	100.00	324	90

Source : Approach to the Fifth Five Year Plan, Planning Department, Government of Bihar, Patna, September, 1972.

PHYSICAL SETTING

Topography

The topography of Bihar is easily divisible into two distinct physical units, e.g., Northern Plains and Southern Plateaus. These two units present regional contrasts in their physical economic and social character. They are also known as the Bihar Plains and the Chhotanagpur Plateau region. The former is further sub-divided into two unequal blocks, the North Bihar Plain and the South Bihar Plain (Table 2.3). The Ganga river occupies almost the middle portion of the vast monotonous aggradational surface of the Ganga Plain.[16] The Plain is flat and rolls towards the southeast direction. Most of the portion is below 150 metres from the sea level, except the extreme North-west portion in West Champaran district, where Siwalik rises to 450 metres. Sumeshwar and Dun Hills are separated by the Dun or Harsha valley. Below the foothills of these hills a marshy lowland area is found which is known as Tarai region. The whole Northern plain is almost a dead level alluvial Plain liable to floods. However, a series of raised riverside lands, called 'levees' are intermittently noticed and are characterised by coarser materials. The South Bihar Plain with a roughly triangular shape is separated from the abrupt rise of the Plateau region of the south and extends upto Raj Mahal hills in the east where it is again separated from the Bengal Plain.[17] Like the North Plain, this plain is also a flat alluvial tract but presents more diversified surface. The monotony of the plain is interrupted by a number of isolated granite hills of Barabar, Rajgir, Kharagpur, etc. which are better known as the outliers of the Chhotanagpur Plateau.

The Southern Plateaus or the Chhotanagpur Plateau region is characterised by the undulating, criss-crossed river valleys, rugged spurs, tilted, faulted and warped terrain. It is a region of great inequalities having Plateaux of varying elevations, hills and hillocks of differing altitudes and intermontane valleys of varying width and size.[18] The plateau abruptly rises from the South Bihar plain in the form of escarpments and gradually increases its height mainly towards south and west. It consists of a series of plateaus of different altitudes ranging between 300 to 1000 metres. The two large plateaux namely Hazaribagh and Ranchi separated by the Damodar trough occupy the heart of the region. Ranchi Plateau, especially the western part, known as 'Pat' region is the highest surface with an average height of 1000 metres from the sea level. From there the plateau rolls down towards north, south and east giving a panormic view by streams which pass through waterfalls into erosional plains of Ranchi and Singhbhum districts. The remarkable features of the Plateaus are the huge isolated, rounded or conical protuberances of rocks which rise suddenly from the general level.[19] The Parasnath hill of this type is the highest territorial vertex of 1500 metres and occupies the eastern margin of the Hazaribagh Plateau. Similarly, the hills of the Kaimur Plateau, structurally a distinct unit in the western marginal portion, are worth mentioning and the average height rounds about 400 metres from the sea level. Hills of Barabar (300 ms.), Rajgir (445 ms.), Kharagpur (300 ms.) and Rajmahal (600 ms.) are the remnants of the ancient crystalline rocks (Fig. 4).

Geology

The geology of Bihar is very interesting. It is characterised by several special features. First of all, Bihar consists of rocks of the oldest and the youngest of the geological eras ranging from the ancient Archaean at the base to the recent cainozoic on the top, subsequently passing through the Dharwar, Cuddapah, Vindhyan, Gondwana systems of rocks followed by the Siwalik and the Gangetic alluvium deposits (Fig. 5). Secondly, almost the ninety percent of the Chotanagpur Plateau is composed of the Archaeon gneisses and granite which are supposed to represent an originally solidified crust acted as the basement on which later deposits occurred.[20] The Dharwars are the first deposited sedimentary soil which became metamorphic by igneous intrusions. These rocks are confined in two parts: one in Hazaribagh, Giridih, Gaya and Monghyr districts mainly consisting of pegamatites deposits of quartz schist, mica-schists and phyllites etc. and the other is located in Singhbhum and south-eastern margin of Ranchi district. Here this deposit is known as the Iron-ore Series containing all grades of unmetamorphosed to highly metamorphosed rocks, like hacmatite-quartzites, manganese, copper, kyanite, chromite, etc. Then follows the Cuddapah system which is almost absent here. But the Kolhan series of the Southern Singhbhum is very similar to this system with unmetamorphosed shales, limestones and conglomeretes.

In the next succession of deposit comes the Vindhyan system of rocks which is horizontally bedded deposit of limestones, sandstones and shales. These rocks are found in the limited areas of Rohtas and Palamau districts, either side of the river Son. These deposits had remained above the marine transgression except the Vindhyan system and hence had gone through the acute denudational operation, exposing the ancient granite to the surface in the Southern Singhbhum and also in the northern portion of the Plateau. Even the iron-ore series of the Dharwar system is outcropped into Iron-ore hills and consequently ores are not mixed but are simply extracted here,

The Palaeozoic era opens with the advent of the Permo-Carboniferous earth movement which caused a chain of basin shaped depressions or rift valleys in the east-west directions.[21] The Damodar river flows through it. These depressions were subjected to the sedimentation from Carboniferous to Jurrasic period of the Mesozoic era. These deposits are known as Gondwana rock system, which contain the largest deposits of coal, fireclay, iron-stones, sandstones, etc. Due to the depressional occurrences, these precious rocks remained untouched by the agents of denudation. Then followed the Jurrasic lava eruption of the Rajmahal Hills which over-topped the Gondwana rocks especially in the eastern part of Santhal Parganas. The Western Ranchi Plateau was overlaid by the eastern extension of the Deccan lava flows of Cretaceous period. These rocks are new weathered to laterites.[22]

With the start of Cainozoic era, especially in the Tertiary period, the making up of the Himalayas has affected the topography of the Chotanagpur Plateau region which were tilled, faulted and uplifted. They have gone through several fluvial cycles of erosions.

The north-western marginal portion of the state is covered by the Siwalik of Tertiary period. Finally, the alluvium deposits of the gangetic plains are the most recent of the Cainozoic era. The deposits are divided into older or 'Bhanger' and newer or 'Khadar' alluvium. The former occupies comparatively higher places and also along the foothills, while the latter concentrate the flood plain areas of the main streams. The deposits consist of kanker, silt, clay, sand and finesand. The whole tract is devoid of minerals. Only salt petres and sodium salts are found in the north-western and middle western portions of the State (Fig. 16).

Drainage

Bihar is fortunate for having numerous rivers of perennial and seasonal character. The Ganga river traverses the State from west to east in full length and develops a river system of its own known as the Ganga River system. In this system the affluents of two different watersheds, the Himalayan from the north and Chotanagpur plateau from the south, arise and gravitate towards the mono-mighty water-way of the Ganga, the Ghaghra, the Gandak, the Burhi Gandak, the Baghmati, the Kosi and the Karamnasa, the Son, the Punpun, the Phalgu, the Sakri, the Kiul and other wet-weathered streams from the south merge with the Ganga (Fig. 4).

The rivers of the Chotanagpur region are the Damodar, the Subernarekha, the South Koel and their tributaries. These rivers descend down from the Hazaribagh and the Ranchi Plateau watersheds, mostly towards east and southeast directions and flow through the rugged topography. The Damodar river rises in Palamau and flows eastward through the structural valley of the Damodar Basin. The Bokaro, the Barakar and the Konar river are the main tributaries. The Subernarekha originates from the Ranchi Plateau, passes through the Hundru waterfall and flows in south eastern direction. The Kharkai meets the Subarnarekha in the Singhbhum district and at their confluence, the famous Steel city of Jamshedpur is located. The River South Koel also rises in Ranchi Plateau and passes through the circuitous course tending towards south and meets to the Sankh, another southerly flowing river.

These rivers are of much economic importance, since their water is used in irrigation, drinking purposes to the urban centres, in production of electricity and they support the localization of major industrial establishment.

Climate

Since the Tropics of Cancer passes through this State, climatically Bihar occupies a tropical and sub-tropical location. Naturally, high temperature with higher percentage of humidity is the main feature of the climate. Moreover, Bihar presents transitional climatic phenomena, between the West Bengal Delta to the east and the drier U.P. to the west.[23] In Bihar itself the condition is not uniform throughout. The plain region seasonally differ from the Chotanagpur Plateau region in temperature and percipitation.

A year is divided into three main seasons on the basis of the variations of temperature and humidity. They are, the winter season, from November to February; the Summer season from March to June, and the rain season from July to October.

During winter the temperature falls to 15°C in the northern plain and it gradually increases towards south. Patna experiences nearly 16.5°C of temperature. Further south near Ranchi it goes upto 17.3°C at Chaibassa to 18°C. This increase of temperature is only due to the decrease of latitudes towards the south. The season is almost dry without any rain except in the month of December and January when temperate cyclones bring rains, known as "wheat rain or rabi rain". Thus Motihari (14.5°C) and Netarhat (14°C) are the coldest places in Bihar during winter. The former suffers from the continentality effect while the latter is due to its higher altitudes (Fig. 6).

After February the temperature starts increasing. Temperature increases day by day and so pressure and humidity fall accordingly. In April the mean temperature remains upto 29°C. But during May it abruptly rises to 42°C and sometimes it goes upto 46°C and thus May becomes the hottest and driest month of the year. 'Loo' the hot, dusty and drier forceful local winds, which frequently blow in the afternoon is the chief feature of the plains. The Plateau region of the south is not affected by this scorching hot wind due to the higher altitudes. All these conditions led to the formation of intense low pressure which attracts S.W. Monsoon.

The rainy season starts with the breakthrough of the S.W. Monsoon at the end of June or in the beginning of July, As the rain occurs the temperature falls down to a very pleasant point. Rain increases from July to August. High humidity results in dullness in the weather. Heavy rain causes water stagnation in the plains leading to marshy prevalence. But the Plateau region is better as no water stagnation takes place here.

After September rain decreases gradually. Humidity falls rapidily during nights in the form of heavy dew. The retreating monsoon with high rains during 'Hathyia Nachhatra' covers the whole Bihar in the form of the last rain of the season.

The distribution of rainfall is uneven in the State (Fig. 7). The extreme north-east and the extreme north-west portions get the highest rain more than 2000 mms. The rain decreases gradually towards south-west. The average rainfall is 1200 mm. The Plateau region experiences more rain than plains.

ECONOMIC SETTING

Economic structure

The economic setting of Bihar is governed by its physical characteristics as well as human efforts. The presence of both plains and plateaus has influenced the economy. A brief discussion presented here to assess the economic conditions of the State.

The economic structure of state is primarily rural and agrarian. The 1971 Census reveals that almost 90 per cent of population lives in villages and its main economic pursuit is agriculture. The occupational structure as shown in Table 2.4 clearly indicates that nearly 83.0 per cent of the state working force is engaged in agriculture. Out of this 39 per cent is agricultural labourers. They are landless, poor and without any economic incentives. The mining, industries, trade and commerce and other services

TABLE 2.4 : **Bihar's occupational structure of working Force : 1971**

Class of Workers	Bihar Percentage of total force	India Percentage of total force
Primary Sector	*83.2*	*72.0*
Cultivators	43.3	43.3
Agricultural labourers	38.9	26.3
Other activities	1.0	2.4
Secondary sector	*7.1*	*11.2*
Mining	1.5	0.5
Manufacturing :		
(i) Household	2.5	3.5
(ii) Other than household	2.6	6.0
Construction	0.5	1.2
Tertiary sector	*9.7*	*16.8*
Trade and commerce	3.3	5.6
Transport & communication	1.5	2.4
Other services	4.9	8.8
Total Workers	100.0	100.0

Source : (i) Bihar, Primary Census Abstract, March, 1973.
(ii) Director of Census Operations, Bihar, of Census India, 1971.

are very poorly shared and this also justifies the poor economy of the State. Fortunately, in recent years, this lop-sided economy and its advance impact on the general economic growth has been realised and the State Government is trying her level best to divert its working force from agriculture to small industries and another infrastructure activities.

Land use

The total land of the state is 17,330,000 hectares. Out of which nearly 49 per cent is under cultivation, 19 per cent under culturable waste, 16.5 per cent under forest, a little over 9 per cent under non-agricultural uses and 6 per cent barren (Table 2.5) (Fig. 10).

TABLE 2.5 : **Land use pattern in Bihar, 1975-'76**

Land use	Area in '000 hectares	Percentage of total land
Net sown area	8,465	49.0
Culturable waste land	3,351	19.1
Forest	2,821	16.5
Non-agricultural uses	1,649	9.4
Barren land	1,044	6.0
Total	17,330	100.0

Source : Bihar Statistical Hand-Book, 1979, p 34.

This shows an unbalanced leaning of economy on agriculture. The most striking feature is apparent from Table 2.6 that the percentage of land under forest and culturable waste is gradually decreasing while the land under plough and non-agricultural use are increasing. This indicates a heavy pressure of increasing population on agriculture to meet the growing demand of the food products. Moreover, the increase of land under non-agricultural uses justifies the population growth and also gradual development of railroad etc.

TABLE 2.6 : **Variations in land use pattern in Bihar**

Different heads	Percentage of total land 1958-59	Percentage of total land 1969-70	Percentage of total land 1975-76
Net Sown Area	46.0	48.4	49.0
Culturable waste land	19.3	19.1	19.1
Forest	21.8	17.9	16.5
Non-agricultural uses	7.9	8.8	9.4
Barren land	5.0	5.8	6.0
Total	100.0	100.0	100.0

Source : Computed from Bihar Through Figures, 1965, 1973, 1977.

Agriculture

Agriculture is the mainstay of Bihar's economy which supports more than eighty per cent of State's population. Nearly half of the State's income is obtained from it (Table 2.7). This is simply on account of fertile soils, (Fig. 8), mostly alluviam type, abundant water and agriculture dominated economy. But unfortunately, it has proved to be the weakest link of the State's economy as it is highly crowded by the poor people in the traditional manner and is most unstable due to frequent floods and droughts.

TABLE 2.7 : **State income by industrial origin, 1960'61 to 1974'75**

(*crores of rupees*)

Sector	1960-61	1970-71	1974-75
Agriculture and allied activities	531.89	1214.38	2515.53
Mining, manufacturing and small enterprises	149.32	439.53	743.48
Commerce, transport & communication	154.74	371.60	603.39
Other services	157.07	354.42	473.75

Source : Bihar Through Figures. 1977, p. 45.

Bihar produces a variety of crops. Production of cereals dominates the cropping pattern. Nearly 94 per cent of the total cropped area is under food grains, most under rice, wheat and maize. Rice, however, is the most dominant crop in acreage and production. Nearly half of the net sown area is under rice (Table 2.8) (Fig. 12). It is a staple food and is grown throughout the state. But Bhojpur, Patna, Nalanda, Gaya, West and East Champaran and Purnea districts are important producers. Wheat follows rice in production. The western portion of the state is the main wheat growing region (Fig. 13). Maize occupies Saran, Patna, Monghyr and Bhagalpur districts. Similarly pulses and cash crops are also significant here. Only 4 per cent of the total land is under cash crops mostly shared by sugarcane, jute, tobacco, etc. (Fig. 14 and 15).

TABLE 8 : **Trends of crop production in Bihar (in '000 m. tonnes)**

Crops	1970-71	1971-72	1972-73	1973-74	1974-75	1975-76	% variation from 1970-71 to 1975-76
Food Crops							
1. Rice	4154	5273	4465	4158	4550	4768	+ 14.7
2. Wheat	1259	2494	3136	1649	2000	2297	+ 82.4
3. Maize	1113	139	812	1000	684	687	– 38.0
4. Barley	163	141	119	107	124	108	– 34.0
Cash Crops							
5. Jute	788	673	559	542	550	612	– 22.0
6. Sugarcane	6209	5281	4331	5157	5568	4907	– 16.0
7. Pulses	987	887	656	685	870	750	– 11.0

Source : Bihar Statistical Hand Book, 1978.

The above table shows an unhealthy trend in the production of crops. Except rice and wheat, decline trend in other crops is quite obvious (Fig. 11). When it is compared with production of all India level this also gives a discouraging result as shown in Table 2.9. Agricultural production data for Bihar of two decades indicate an average annual growth rate of less than one per cent compared to 3 per cent per annum for the country. This growth rate of agricultural production is very slow in comparison to the growing demands of grains—2 per cent per annum, due to States population growth. Consequently deficit in food grains continues despite the slight improvement in the production of cereals like wheat and rice.

Bihar produces only 8 per cent of total food grains of India ranking third after the Uttar Pradesh and Madhya Pradesh.

TABLE 2.9 : **Trends in agricultural production in Bihar**

Period	Percent per annum	
	Bihar	All india
1952-53 to 1964-65	+ 1.8	+ 3.7
1964-65 to 1969-70	— 2.1	+ 1.4
1952-53 to 1969-70	+ 0.7	+ 3.0

Source : (1) Growth rates in agriculture, 1949-50 to 1964-65, Ministry of Food and Agriculture, Directorate of Eco. & Statistics, 1966.
(2) For the years 1965-66 to 1969-70, Bihar through figures, 1971.

The growing pressure of population and the shortage of food grains have changed the cropping pattern. During the Plan periods the emphasis were laid on the production of food grains through the intensive measures just to meet the growing demands of food. Naturally land under cereals especially wheat has increased by several folds giving the worst effect to other cereals and non-cereal crops like, barley, gram, jute, maize, sugarcane; etc. The net sown area under these crops is gradually decreasing as the Table 2.10 indicates. Shortage of cereals is caused by high prices of grains in the consumer's markets. Farmers not getting ready cash or getting very poor rate from the factories for their raw jute or sugarcane were compelled to shift from cash-crops to cereals. The irregular supply of irrigational facilities, shortages of fertilizers, poor incentives provided by banks, and the corrupt developmental schemes, inordinate delay in the completion of irrigational and power projects and several other social parameters have remained the main constraints which have gagged the agricultural growth.

TABLE 2.10 : **Changing cropping pattern in Bihar**

(Area in '000 hectares)

Crops	1960-61	1971-72	Variation in percentage 1960-61 to 1971-72	1976-77	Variation of percentage, 1971-72 to 1976-77	Variation of percentage 1960-61 to 76-77
Food Crops						
(a) Rice	5240	5206	— 1	5326	+ 1	+ 1.7
(b) Wheat	652	1397	+ 114	1945	+ 139	+ 293
(c) Maize	805	823	+ 2	934	+ 13	+ 15
(d) Barley	393	235	— 40	149	— 36.6	— 76.6
Cash Crops						
(e) Jute	147	131	— 11	125	— 4.7	— 15.7
(f) Mesta	38	32	— 16	N.A.	—	—
(g) Sugarcane	186	142	– 24	128	— 9.8	— 338

Source : Bihar Through Figures, 1968, 1972, 1977 and Bihar Statistical Handbook, 1978.

Other pursuits associated with agriculture are fishing, animal husbandry, poultry farming and hunting. In all these pursuits only 2.6 per cent of the working persons is engaged. These provide supplementary food for the population. Some raw materials are also obtained for the industries like tanning, blanket making; etc. Rivers are the natural sources for fishing. Bihar produces about 1.20 lakhs tonnes of fish annually which is only one third of the total requirement. Cattle like cows, buffaloes, sheep, goats, etc. provide milk, hides and skins. Bihar accounts for about 28.7 million livestock. Poultry farming is becoming a household industry now.

Forest

The state's economy is to great extent contributed to by the forest products. These products are woods, bamboos, timbers, kendu-leaves, sabai grasses, lac etc. Bihar is the largest producer of lac and it produces nearly 60 per cent of the total national production. In 1972-73 about 48 lakh people were engaged in the forest and its related industries. Rupees 11 crores and 16 lakhs were realised from these products in 1974-75. Bamboo and sabai grasses are the main raw materials for the states Paper factories (Table 2.11).

About 16.5 per cent of the total area of the state is under forest. Unfortunately, despite the Government's policy of reserving the forest, deforestation is going on and the percentage of land under forest is gradually decreasing from 1951 onwards. Table 2.6 clearly points out that during 1958-59 the total land under forest was about 23 per cent which has gradually been reduced to 21 per cent in 1964-65, 18 per cent in 1970-71 and 16.5 per cent in 1975-76. Now, deforestation has reached a point which requires a special attention to protect and preserve it from further deterioration.

TABLE 2.11 : **Outturn of the forest products in Bihar**

Periods	Stick lac (Quintal)	Timber (cubic metres)	Firewood (cubic mtr.)	Bamboo (Tonnes)	Sabai grass (tonnes)	Kendu-leaves (tonnes)
1950-51	N.A.	139136	225286	N.A.	1640	3510
1964-65	119995	411560	289483	89000	6068	N.A.
1966-67	150975	335594	305247	120483	3964	26236
1970-71	162083	407136	350505	111004	67251	N.A.
1972-73	73884	423843	569061	145664	33271	N.A.
1975-76	138537	N.A.	N.A.	N.A.	N.A.	N.A.

Source : Bihar Through Figures, 1968, 1971, 1977.

The Chotanagpur Plateau is the main land of forest where nearly 95 per cent of the State forest is concentracted. Ranchi, Palamau, Singhbhum, Hazaribagh, Giridih, Santhal Parganas, Gaya and Nawadah are the districts for forest-occupations in order of importance. The Gangetic plains are almost cleared off from forest. The north-western portion of West Champaran district is also under forest of considerable economic importance (Fig. 9).

Minerals

Bihar is very rich in metallic and non-metallic minerals. The vast reserves of minerals like coal, iron-ore, copper, mica, bauxite, kyanite, limestone, fire clay, china clay, uranium and several others are concentrated here. This state has been leading all the Indian States in reserves and production of minerals since long. From 1951 to 1965 she has produced 100 per cent copper, mica and kyanite, 80 per cent of bauxite, nearly 50 per cent coal, 25 per cent of iron-ore, 20 per cent of limestone and 10 per cent of manganese of the country (Fig. 18). During 1950-51 the state produced half of the total value of minerals' output of the country. But, after 1965 its relative national importance in production is gradually getting down. In 1974, Bihar produced only 42.3 per cent of coal, 14 per cent of iron ore, 58 per cent of copper ore, 52 per cent of apatites, 78 per cent of kyanite, 43 per cent of mica, 26 per cent of bauxite and 13 per cent of limestone (Table 2.12). Likewise the value of the output of minerals of Bihar in comparison to Indian output has gone down gradually from 1965 to 1974 (Table 2.13). This is simply due to increased production of minerals in other parts of the country while the production of minerals in Bihar has remained more or less the same. The value of output has increased in several folds due to increase in prices of the commodities.

Almost, the entire mineral of the state is concentrated in the Chotanagpur region and hence this region is often called the "Ruhr of India". The northern Gangetic alluvium tract is almost devoid of any minerals except, salt petre, and sodium salts (Fig. 16).

In 1971 about 1.4 per cent of the total population was engaged in mining and quarrying activities. Coal mining employs about 85 per cent of total workers employed in the mining followed by 6 per cent in stone, 4 in mica, 1.6 in iron-ore, and 2 per cent in other non-metallic minerals. The exploitation of these minerals has yet to increase at the maximum. The less developed railroads, poor supply of electricity and unscientific methods of quarrying have been the

TABLE 2.12 : **Bihar's share in the production of principal minerals in India**

Minerals	1965 India (a)	1965 Bihar (b)	(b) as % of (a)	1969 India (c)	1969 Bihar (d)	(d) as % of (c)	1970 India (e)	1970 Bihar (f)	(e) as % of (f)	1974-75 India (g)	1974-75 Bihar (h)	(g) as % of (h)
Apatite (Tonnes)	7,076	6,104	85.0	9,316	2,245	23.0	15,987	11,186	66.0	17,325	9,301	52.0
Bauxite (Tonnes)	1,05,649	3,22,329	45.6	10,84,899	4,53,721	45.0	13,69,522	4,93,496	36.0	11,03,000	2,84,000	26.0
China Clay (Tonnes)	3,07,341	1,30,965	42.0	3,74,418	1,41,925	39.8	3,42,537	1,12,724	32.6	Not Available		
Coal ('000 Tonnes)	67,162	31,007	46.0	75,411	35,000	46.6	73,696	34,737	46.0	83,312	35,496	42.0
Copper-Ore ('000 Ts.)	468	468	100.0	511	509	99.9	518	506	98.0	1,500	818	58.0
Fire-Clay ('000 Ts.)	473	165	34.0	598	188	31.0	576	199	29.0	Not Available		
Iron-Ore ('000 Ts)	22,833	4,272	18.0	29,564	5,349	18.0	31,366	5,135	16.0	35,944	5,184	14.0
Kyanite (Tonnes)	37,481	37,369	100.0	84,172	73,431	88.0	1,19,043	1,02,231	86.0	45,000	30,000	78.0
Limestone ('000 Ts.)	19,957	2,247	12.0	22,512	2,228	9.0	23,800	2,181	9.0	2,60,139	3,387	13.0
Mica (Tonnes)	23,840	13,323	48.0	18,508	8,887	44.0	16,485	9,000	60.0	14,325	6,000	43.0

Sources : (i) Mines and Geology Dept., Patna, 1971. (ii) Bihar Through Figures, 1977, pp. 116-117.

TABLE 2.13 : **Value of output of minerals in Indian level**

(in Thousand of rupees)

Year	Bihar (a)	India (b)	(a) as % of (b)
1	2	3	4
1965	9,48,336	29,05,250	35.0
1966	10,00,390	32,79,220	35.2
1967	10,48,114	36,98,731	33 3
1968	12,59,307	41,65,587	31.8
1969	14,14,582	46,62,736	30.5
1970	14,30,147	48,77,092	27.8
1971	13,62,334	49,51,257	27.3
1972	13,31,103	47,11,364	29.6
1973	16,46,557	57,35,000	28.0
1974	21,04,500	74,84,000	28.0

Source : Bihar Through Figures, 1970 and 1977.

least hurdles in the development of minerals. However, the exploitation of various types of minerals, like coal, iron ore, manganese, lime stone, copper ores, mica, bauxite, etc. have given the impetus for the localization of heavy industries like Iron and Steel, Cement and other engineering works. Therefore, the value of minerals is immense.

Power

Power is most important infra-structure to assess the economic standard of a region. Despite enormous resources like inexhaustible perennial water, ample coal deposits and atomic minerals, the state is trailing behind several other Indian states in the power production and consumption. Power development in Bihar had a very late start. Practically there was insignificant development of power till 1960 and the state was purchasing power from the D.V.C. Bihar started its first generating station of 45 M.W. (3×15). Capacity at Barauni and another 50 M.W. unit at Patratu during the Third Plan Period after the creation of Bihar State Electricity Board on April, 1958.[24] Most of the works related to power generation, transmission and distribution have been done in the last decades only.

The installed generating capacity including both Public and captive units has developed from 244 M.W. in 1950-51 to over 1400 M.W. in 1971. Again the generation of power improved from 14.33 M.W. in 1971-72 to 20.70 M.W. in 1974-75[25] similarly, the per capita consumption of electricity has increased since 1951 from 15 Kwh to 62 Kwh in 1970, and 67 Kwh in 1974-75. This consumption figure is very poor in comparison to those of other states like Maharastra, Punjab, and Gujarat with 171, 168 and 143 Kwh respectively.[26]

Within the State itself, the per capita consumption of electricity is highly unequal. In North Bihar the per capita consumption of electricity is only 8 Kwh. The Southern Plateau region is better in per capita consumption of power with 110 kwh. The number of electrified towns and villages rose from 10 and 52 in 1950-51 to 161 and 11,000 in 1971-72 and again it rose to 200 and 17,000 in 1975-76. As Fig. 17 shows that Bihar produces both hydel as well as thermal power. There are several hydel and thermal plant schemes which are generating or about to generate power in Bihar (Table 2.14).

The state requires 2400 M.W but the supply is only about 1460 M.W. Naturally this shortage has become the major constraint in the economic development of the state especially in its industrial and agricultural fields. Several small scale and ancillary industries have been compelled to close down their firms due to the erratic and low shedding of power. Even the large-scale public undertakings are suffering and they are bearing a loss of crores.

Transport network

Transport networks are the physical expressions of integration within and between economies but they are both cause and effect of the movement demands induced by this integration.[27] Like power, rail-roads are also an essential infra structure which act as arteries in the economic development of a region.

The state of Bihar has suffered a great deal in her economic and social growth due to insufficient development of rail-road communications. The Ganga river flows through the centre of state and acts as a natural barrier between the north and south. These two regions are connected by rail-roads at

TABLE 2.14 : **Major power projects in Bihar**

Projects	Location	Year of Start	Year of completion or to be completed	Capacity of power generation (M.W.)
Barauni				
Stage I	Barauni	1960	1966	45
Stage II	do	1960	1971	100
Stage III	do	Under construction	1981-82 (expected)	220
Patratu				
Stage I	Hazaribagh	1963	1972-73	400
Stage II	do	Started	1982-83 (expected)	220
Subarnarekha Hydel	Getathul (Ranchi)	1965-66	1980	110
Muzaffarpur Thermal	Muzaffarpur	1971	1983-84 (expected)	220
Tenughat Tharmal			1985-86	420
Koel Karo hydel	Proposed	—	—	6×115 mm

Source : Commerce, November 17, 1973, p. 15, and The Eco. Times, June 9, 1980.

Mokama Bridge. To avoid this traffic congestion, construction of another road bridges at Patna has been completed recently which has provided easy movement of traffic.

The northern plain is comparatively poor in rail-road development in comparison to the south plain and south plateau regions. The reasons are physical as well as economic. North Bihar is frequently marred by floods and unreliable shifting courses of rivers. This has adversely affected the smooth construction of rail-roads. The poor agricultural economy and high density of population have caused economic constraints. In contrast the southern region is minerally and industrially more developed and this has helped in the development of rail-roads. However, dissected scarps, high plateaus and inaccessible tracts have restricted the development of rail-roads. Roads in comparison to rails are more expandable since they runover rough

FIG. 2

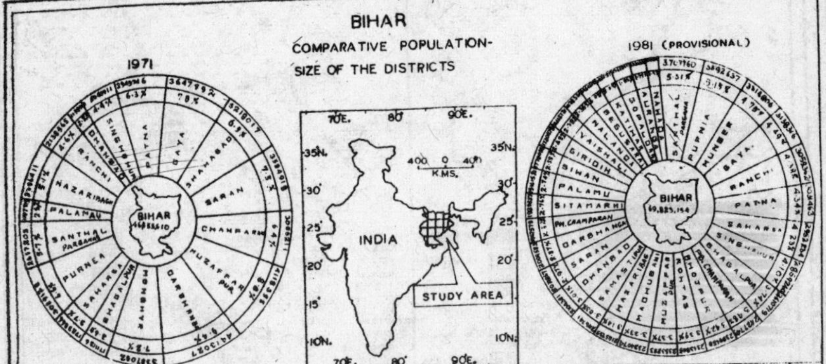

BIHAR
COMPARATIVE POPULATION-
SIZE OF THE DISTRICTS
1971
1981 (PROVISIONAL)
BIHAR
BIHAR
INDIA
STUDY AREA
KMS.

BIHAR
DIVISIONS & DISTRICTS
0 100
KMS.
1971
1981
N E P A L
CHAMPARAN
SARAN
MUZAFFAR PUR
DARBHANGA
SAHARSA
PURNEA
PATNA
SHAHABAD
GAYA
MONGHYR
BHAGAL PUR
SANTHAL PARGANAS
HAZARIBAGH
PALAMAU
DHANBAD
RANCHI
SINGHBHUM
I PATNA DIVISION
II TIRHUT
III BHAGALPUR
IV CHOTANAGPUR
PASCHIM
CHAMPARAN
PURBI
GOPALGANJ
SITAMARHI
MADHUBANI
SIWAN
MUZAFFAR PUR
DARBHANGA
SAHARSA
PURNIA
SAMASTIPUR
VAISHALI
BEGUSARAI
KATIHAR
BHOJPUR
PATNA
NALANDA
MUNGER
BHAGALPUR
ROHTAS
GAYA
NAWADA
AURANGA BAD
SANTHAL PARGANA
PALAMU
HAZARIBAG
GIRIDIH
DHANBAD
RANCHI
SINGHBHUM
I PATNA DIVISION
II TIRHUT
III DARBHANGA
IV KOSI
V BHAGALPUR
VI NORTH CHOTANAGPUR
VII SOUTH CHOTANAGPUR
VIII MAGADH
INDEX
INTERNATIONAL BOUNDARY
STATE
DIVISION
DISTRICT
O R I S S A

FIG. 3

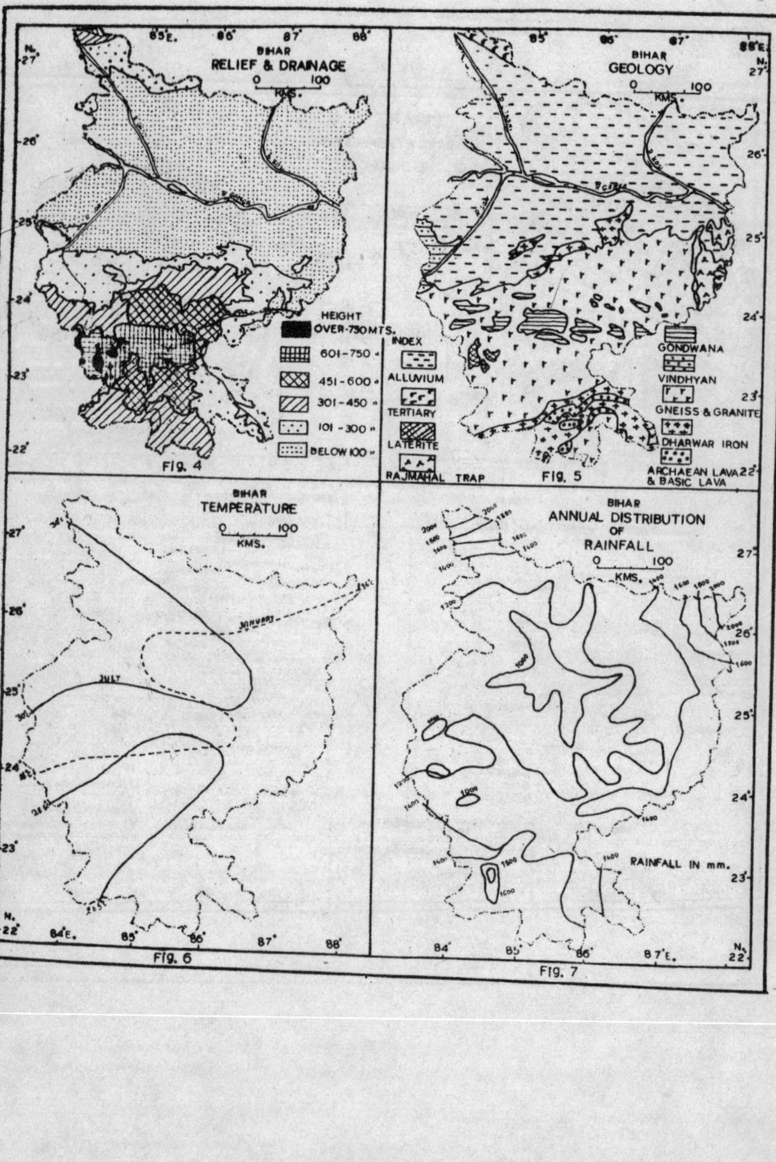

Fig. 4 Fig. 5

Fig. 6 Fig. 7

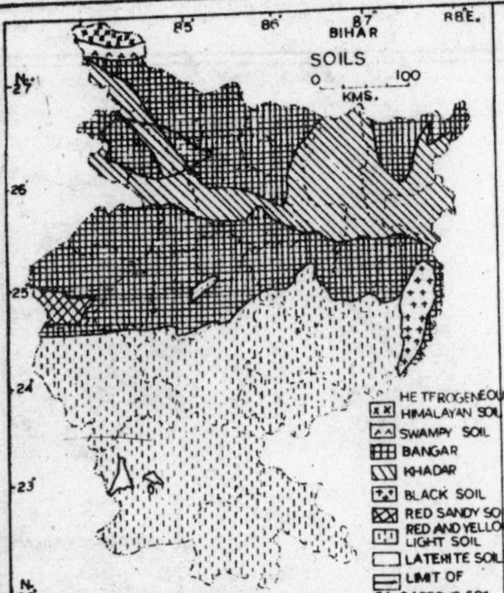

Fig. 8

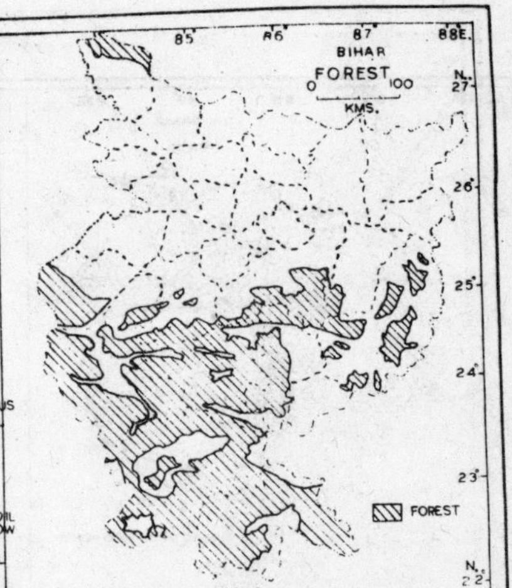

Fig. 9

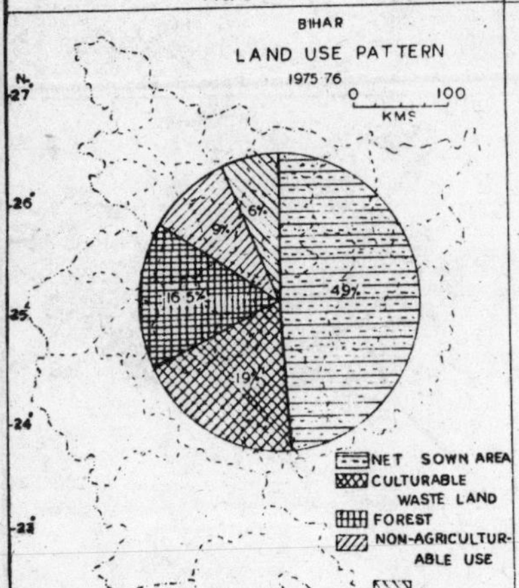

Fig. 10

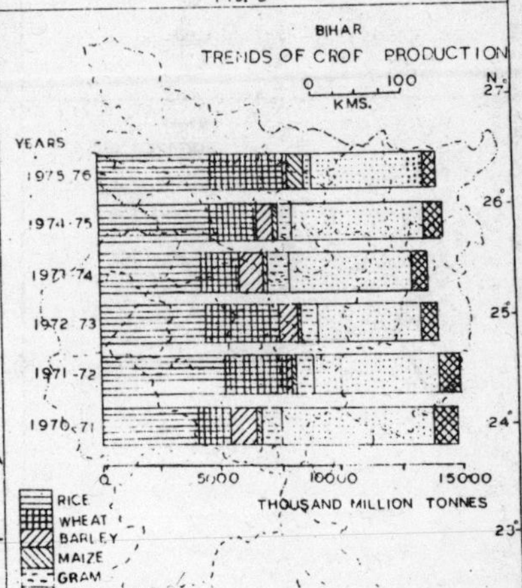

Fig. 11

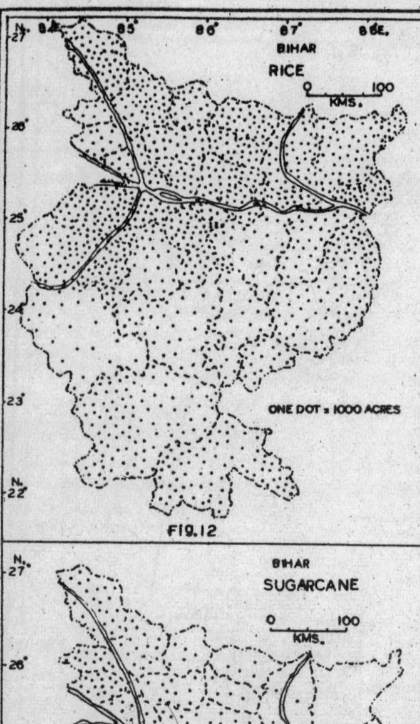

FIG. 12

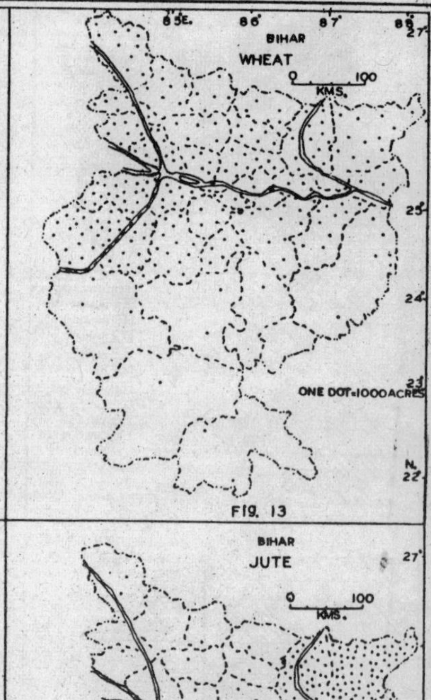

FIG. 13

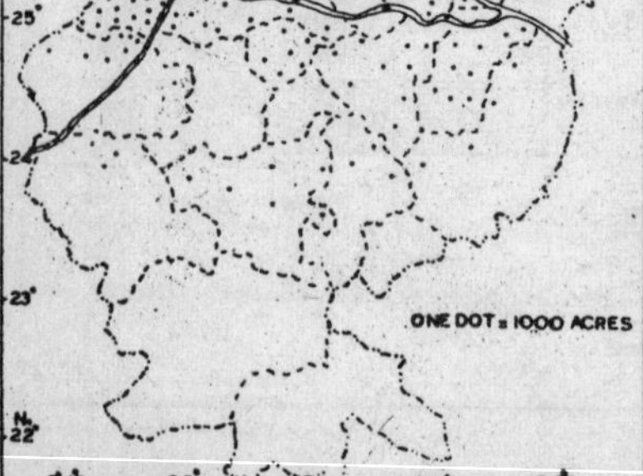

FIG. 14

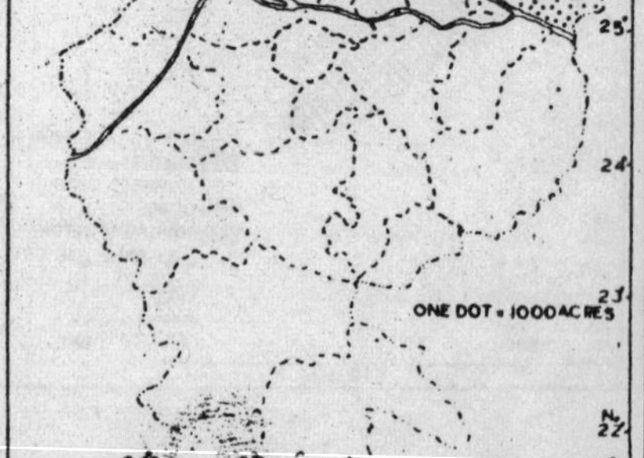

FIG. 15

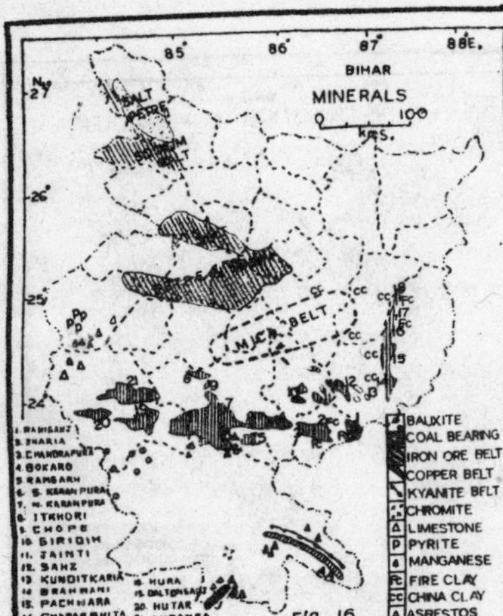

Fig. 16

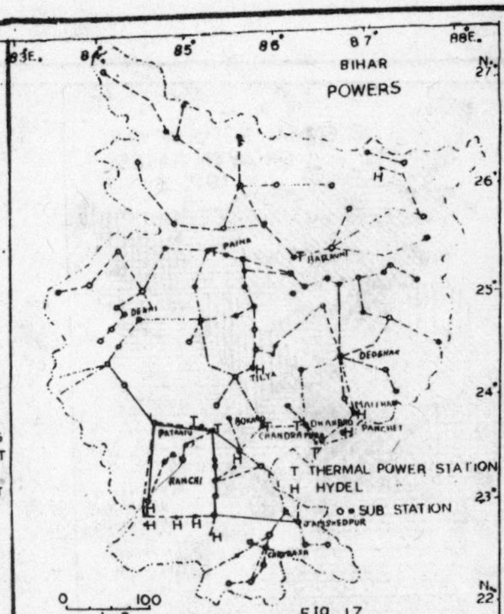

Fig. 17

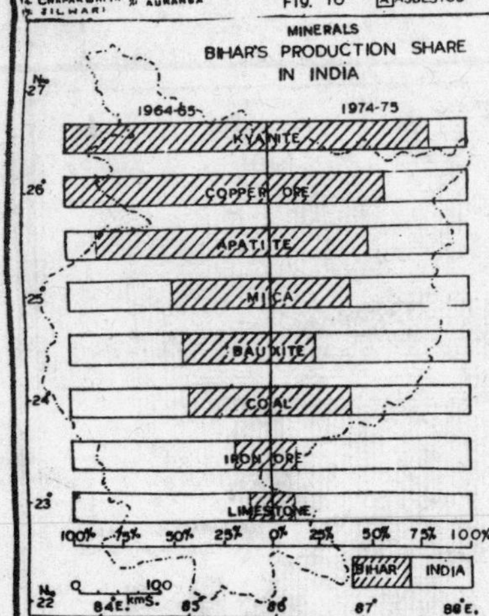

Fig. 18

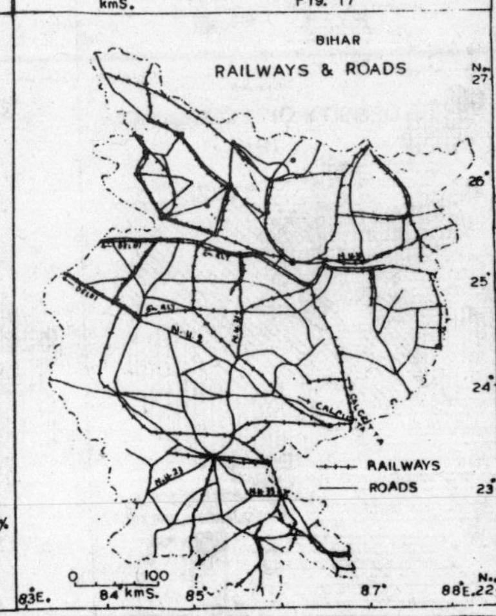

Fig. 19

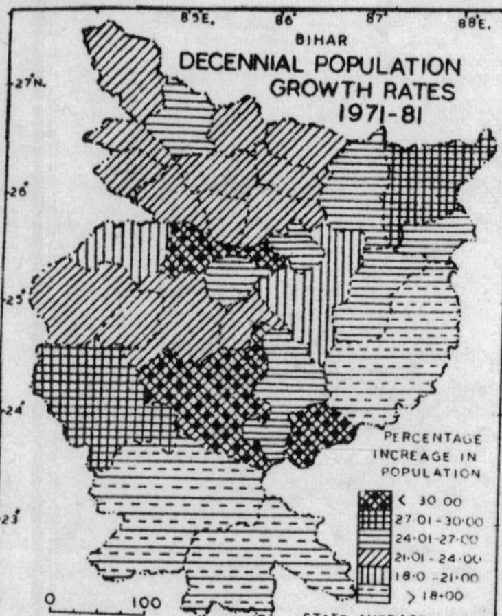

FIG. 20

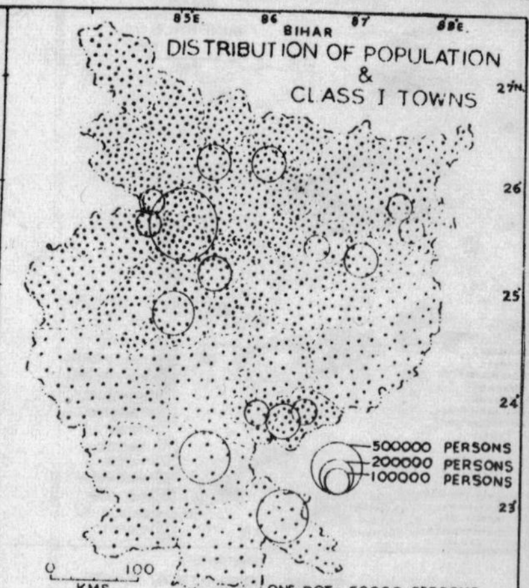

FIG. 21

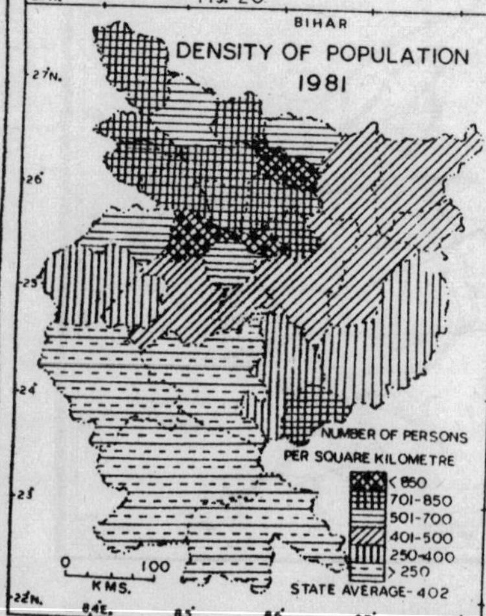

FIG. 22

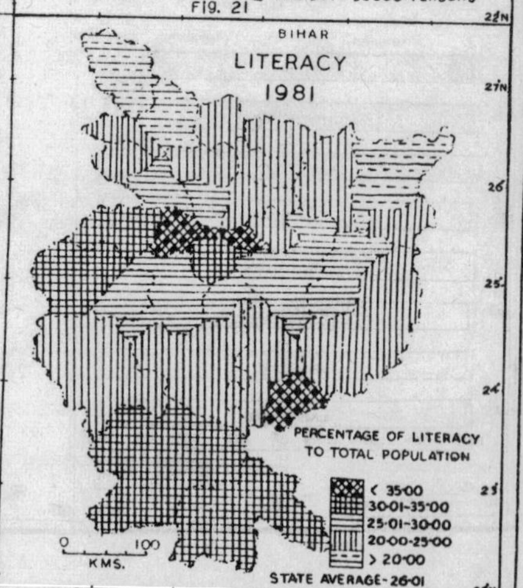

FIG. 23

and difficult terrain whereas rails require workable gradient and, therefore, follow easier relief lines and valleys.[28]

The Damodar River Valley is the most developed region. Coal transportation has given an impetus for this development. The Singhbhum district is the second densest region. The industrial establishment at Jamshedpur, Chaibasa and several mining centres, e.g., Gua, Noamundi, Ghatsila has caused the growth of rail-roads. The third region is around Ranchi where industrial centres and bauxite mining have influenced. Hazaribagh, Kodarma and Giridih come next where mica processing industries and other forest products have influenced the transport development. Palamau, Rohtas, Gaya, Aurangabad and Nawadah are comparatively poor in railroad development. Likewise Champaran, Katihar and Purnea are the most backward districts in rail-road development as Fig. 19 depicts.

The present length of railways in the state is about 5200 kms. with 3100 kms. of broad gauge, 2000 kms. metre gauge and less than 100 kms. of narrow gauge. Almost entire North Bihar has metre gauge lines except Barauni-Muzaffarpur-Chapra line whereas South Bihar including Plateau region has broad gauge line. The Grand Chord line, Mughalsarai-Patna-Asansol rail-line, Gorakhpur-Gauhati via Barauni rail-line, Hajipur-Muzaffarpur, Patna-Ranchi via Gaya and Ranchi-Ghatsila via Tatanagar are the important rail-routes of great economic significance.

The length of surfaced roads increased from 4800 kms. in 1951 to 12206 kms. in 1968-69. In 1973-74 the length increased to 14840 kms. Several National Highways run through the state. N.H. 2 (old G.T. Road) passes through the main industrial and mineral belt from east to west. It is the main artery of economic life in the state. N.H. 6 (Chirkunda to Mohania), N.H. 28 (Dalsingsarai-Samastipur to Jalalpur), N.H 28 A (Pipra to Raxaul), N.H. 30 (Bakhtiarpur, Patna-Arrah-sasaram), N.H. 31 (Barhi, Kodarma-Bihar-Bakhtiarpur, Mokama, Khagaria Purnia), N.H. 32 (Gobindpur, Dhanbad, Chas Road), N H. 33 (Barhi-Hazaribagh, Ranchi and Chandil) are the roads of economic singnificance (Fig. 19).

Industry

Industry is the third important economic aspect of the state after agriculture and minerals. The resource potentiality of the industry is very high as it is directly or indirectly dependent upon agriculture, minerals, foresty and other economic persuits. The state has remained industrially backward. Hardly 2.6 per cent of the total population of the state is engaged in industries. The per capita income of Rs. 489 in 1972-73 was lower by 30 per cent than the per capita national income of Rs. 698 and was the lowest of all the Indian states. The per capita gross output in industry for the state in 1970-71 was consequently considerably lower at Rs. 134 compared to Rs. 253 for the country as a whole. Similarly, the per capita value added for Bihar at Rs. 31 was only about half of the national average of Rs. 59. The industrial backwardness of the state has also reflected in the low average daily employment of factory workers, which at 515 persons per lakh population in 1970 was lower by 47 per cent compared to the country's average of 976 persons per lakh population[29] (Table II). This industrial backwardness is caused by several factors. These are poor agrarian economy, dearth of local entrepreneurs, inadequate infra-structural facilities, lack of technical consultancy service, small investments by banks and other agencies and social complex phenomena. The recent study has concluded that the agricultural and allied activities, transport, communications and storage, banking and insurance and power sectors have shown virtual stagnation or ever slight decline in their contribution to the net domestic product over the 15-year period beginning from 1960-61.[30] Between 1970 and 78 the industrial growth rate had been as low as half per cent per annum. Moreover, there has been marked instability in the level of output from year to year.[31]

The structure of industries in Bihar during 1970 (Census sector) revealed the predominance of the engineering and mineral-based industries (Table 2.15). These two groups accounted for more than half of the total number of factories and nearly 75 per cent of the factory employment and 65 per cent of value added by manufacturing.[32] These industries are highly concentrated at a few industrial centres like Jamshedpur, Ranchi, Bokaro, Sindri, Dhanbad, Dalmianagar, Barauni, etc. These are

TABLE 2.15 : **Industrial structure of Bihar, 1970**

Industry group	Factories reporting		Productive capital		Employment		Output		Value added	
	No.	Per-cent to total	Rs. crores	Per-cent to total	No. ('000)	Per-cent to total	Rs. crores	Per-cent to total	Rs. crores	Per-cent to total
Food	69	14.9	24.33	2.8	18	7.8	60.01	8.7	7.49	4.5
Spinning, weaving etc.	10	2.2	1.77	0.2	6	2.6	6.52	0.9	1.59	1.0
Printing, publishing etc.	13	2.8	1.62	0.2	3	1.3	3.67	0.5	1.37	0.8
Chemicals	17	3.7	31.83	3.6	10	4.3	33.23	4.8	9.11	5.5
minerals & products	13	2.8	80.35	9.2	7	3.0	62.67	9.1	8.92	5.3
Structural clay products	20	4.3	5.88	0.7	7	3.0	7.35	1.1	2.42	1.5
Glass & glass product	12	2.6	2.74	0.3	3	1.3	3.69	0.5	1.31	0.8
Cement	7	1.5	15.56	1.8	5	2.2	15.42	2.2	1.16	0.7
Non-metallic minerals	70	15.1	2.69	0.3	7	3.0	9.09	1.3	1.47	0.9
Engineering	149	32.1	471.02	53.8	118	50.9	421.16	60.9	111.65	66.9
Elect. light & power	41	8.7	225.56	25.8	34	14.7	33.44	4.8	11.22	6.7
Miscellaneous	43	9.3	11.94	1.3	14	5.9	35.60	5.2	9.11	5.4
Total	464	100.0	875.29	100.0	232	100.0	691.85	100.0	166.82	100.0

Source : Annual Survey of Industries, 1970 (ASI Census Sector), Central Statistical Organization, Deptt. of Statistics, Govt. of India, New Delhi.

the main industrial centres accounting for more than 80 per cent of the total industrial output and employment. They act like "oases outside a few miles of which the desert of the primitive economy still stretches in a wide expanse".[33] Besides these, only a few sugar factories are scattered in the northern plains especially in the Tirhut division of the state. Agro-based industries of commercial value have developed at several urban centres.

But fortunately this gloomy phase of economy is now under perceptible changes. However, the current favourable agricultural trend has touched only the periphery of feudal Bihar. The 'big push' given by the public sector projects is having a slow but steady spread effect on its industrial economy.[34] For the first time to the traditional category of Bihar, entrepreneurs who consisted of the members of business houses and retired civil servants and their family-members are being added into a new class of Kulak entrepreneurs. Unemployed engineers, diploma holders and the other educated are also coming into this fold giving a breakthrough of the industrial revolution by adapting modern technology. Therefore, the increase in the number of small-scale industries is rapid (Table 2.16).

TABLE 16 : **Growth of small-scale industries in Bihar**

Year	Units	Year	Units
1967	1630	1971	12,477
1968	2100	1972	16,395
1969	3601	1973	19,412
1970	6301	1974	24,347

Source : Industrial Directory of Bihar, 1972 and Statistical Hand-Book, Bihar, 1978.

This industrial strides was due to several incentives granted by the State Government as a new strategy for industrial development. The incentives are applicable to large, medium and small-scale industries. Sick industries are also entitled to these incentives. This incentive includes the substantial electricity tariffs and sale tax ommissions. The price of land is subsidised to the extent of 50 per cent in backward districts and 25 per cent in other districts. Provisions of raw materials and consumption of finished products have also been assured.[35]

Another development is the creation of the Industrial Area Development Authority (IADA). Seven authorities have already been created, out of which six are around the larger industrial centres, e.g. Jamshedpur, Ranchi, Bokaro, Barauni, Dehri and Sindri and the seventh at Patna is to cover the industrial growth areas, and stimulate the development of ancillary industries around the giant industrial complexes.[36] Besides, several Industrial Estates and Industrial Areas have been established almost at the important industrial centres of the state in order to provide the industrial activities and generate new jobs for unemployed engineers and other educated persons.

Despite all these developmental measures, the structural constraints are the main hurdles which have been gegging the industrial growth.[37] These constraints are important to be mentioned. First of all, capital intensive large public sector undertakings and the investment of Rs. 1500 crores by the Central Government have little spread effect on the economy due to the lack of other socio-economic overheads. Secondly, inspite of a series of incentives announced by the state Government of entrepreneurs, these have been the least conceived and some of these are never implemented. Thirdly, the electricity tariff for the small sector remained the highest in the country.[38] Naturally, entrepreneurs outside the state were least attracted. Fourthly, the capitalists, and previous Zamindars had shown negative attitudes to invest on industries and they have kept capital under curtain, simply to evade the tax payment. Therefore, pecuniary genesis system was dead giving a fatal blow to the growth of industries. Fifthly, during the Plan periods, the industry-sector was neglected. It was not accounted for more than 2 to 3 per cent of the total outlay except in the 2nd Plan. Sixthly, institutional finance has remained shy. The investment by IDBI, IFCI and ICICI was only 5 to 6 per cent of the total investment during 1971-72, though deposits by Bihar was more than 300 crores and the banks invested only 10 per cent thereof. The investment even by the Central Agencies like DGS & D was also minimum. Seventhly, changing industrial policy by the State Industries Department, non-implementation of schemes and neglect of geographers and economists and the furnishing of poor industrial information have caused the adverse impact. Lastly the total neglect of the Khadi and Village industries, handloom and handicraft industries has made a very poor impact on the economy. Until and unless these constrains are wiped out, a healthy industrial environment is not possible for the state a contrasting economy.

SOCIAL SETTING

Like physical and economic setting, social setting has also its relevance. A region is primarily known by its people and hence to study the people and their characteristics becomes essential. In the succeeding pages a brief account of spatial pattern of population and other social characteristics is presented. This analysis is made on the basis of Census figure.

Population

According to 1981 Census (provisional) the population of Bihar is 69,823,154, out of which 35,865,467 is males and 33,957,687 females.[39] This population figure accounts for 10.21 per cent of the population of the country, which is only next to that of the Uttar Pradesh.

Growth of population

Since the beginning of the present century, the population of Bihar has been increasing except during the periods of 1911-21 and 1941-51 (Table 2.17). The population depression was

TABLE 2.17 : **Growth rates of population in Bihar 1901-'11 to 1971-'81**

Census year	India	Bihar
1901-11	+ 5.73	+ 3.67
1911-21	− 0.30	− 0.66
1921-31	+11.00	+11.45
1931-41	+14.23	+12.20
1941-51	+13.31	+10.27
1951-61	+21.64	+19.27
1961-71	+24.57	+21.33
1971-81	+24.75	+23.90

Source : 1971 Census of Bihar, B.L. Das, Commerce, Nov. 17, 1973, p. 4 and also from Census of India, 1981, Series-4, Bihar Paper I of 1981.

caused by famines and epidemics during 1911-21 and large scale migration between 1941-51 on account of the partition. After 1951, the growth rate is very rapid. But in comparison to national growth rate it is slightly lower (Fig. 20).

The district-wise population growth rate during 1971-81 varies from 16.32 per cent for Santhal Pargana district to 43.50 per cent for Dhanbad district. Thirteen districts namely Dhanbad, (43.50), Patna (34.68), Hazaribagh (33.41), Purnea (23.09), Palamu (27.37), Begusarai (26.94), Giridih (25.91), Saharsa (25.61), Katihar (25.52), Nalanda (25.44), Bhagalpur (24.85), East Champaran (24.11) and West Champaran (23.98) have recorded higher growth rates in comparison to the Bihar's (23.98) average. Again, growth rates of Darbhanga (23.53), Muzaffarpur (23.27), Gaya (23.19), Vaishali (23.17), Samastipur (23.13) are slightly lower than that of Bihar. The remaining districts recording growth rates below 20 per cent are Bhojpur (19.77), Singhbhum (17.29), Ranchi (17.15) and Santhal Pargana (16.32), (Fig. 21). The phenomenal growth of population in Dhanbad district is contributed by the fast pace of industrialisation, coming up of Bokaro Steel City and rise in mining activities. Similarly, Hazaribagh has recorded higher growth rate possibly because of its growing industrial and mining activities. Other districts probably having agricultural economy have experienced a marginal growth rate or have even shown a declining trend. Similarly, the industrial-cum-mining belt of Ranchi and Singhbhum have also shown a decline in growth rate. The tribal belt has also followed a declining trend due to migration. The growth rate of Patna is only due to its greater employment opportunities in the capital city.

Density of population

The average density of population of the state is 402 persons per sq. km. It ranks third among the Indian states only after Kerala and West Bengal. The population distribution in the state is very uneven. Table 2.3 clearly indicates that almost three-fourths of the population are concentrated in the Ganga Plains. The northern plain is by far the most populous having almost half of the States population. The Chotanagpur plateau region is sparsely populated except the Dhanbad district. The high density of Dhanbad is mainly because of rapid growth of urban areas, large number of mines and industrial activities (Fig. 22).

Sex ratio

The sex-ratio of Bihar is 947, that is, for every 1000 males there are 947 females. In 1971, it was 954. This sex-ratio of the state is higher than that of the country (935). The district of Siwan (1071), Saran (1023), Gopalganj (1006), and Nawada (1002) are the only districts of the state having more females than males. This is simply because males have migrated to different parts of the country in search of livelihood and hence the industrial regions of state shares very low sex-ratio. The district of Dhanbad has the lowest sex ratio, that is 815 in the state.

Urbanization

The degree of urbanization, which is presumably a concomitant of industrial growth, is 12.46 per cent of the total population. It accounts for only half of the all India's average (23.73). In 1971 the percentage of urbanization was only 10 per cent. North Bihar is the least urbanized region since its economy is based on agriculture, while the Chotanagpur region has the highest percentage due to mining and other industrial activities (Table 2.3). Among the districts Dhanbad records the highest percentage of urban population, that is, 50.70% of its total population. This is the result of rapid industrialisation and development in coal mining and associated activities. Patna is the second most urbanized district (36.87%) due to its larger employment in services. Singhbhum is another district having more than 32% of urbanization. Samastipur, Siwan, Gopalganj and Palamau are the districts of very low urbanization. According to 1981 Census Bihar contains 14 cities and 220 towns. These cities are Patna (8.1 lakhs), Ranchi (4.8 lakhs), Jamshedpur (4.6 lakhs), Gaya (2.5 lakhs), Bhagalpur (2.2 lakhs), Bokaro Steel City (2.2 lakhs), Muzaffarpur (1.9 lakhs), Darbhanga (1.8 lakhs), Biharsharif (1.5 lakhs), Munger (1.3 lakhs), Arrah (1.2 lakhs), Katihar (1.2 lakhs), Dhanbad (1.2 lakhs) and Chapra (1.1 lakhs) (Fig. 21).

Literacy

The Census of 1981 reveals that nearly 26 per cent of the total population is literate. This figure is much lower than that of literacy of the country (34.8%). The percentage of literacy was 20per cent according to the Census of 1971. It has displayed growth of 6 per cent in literacy percentage during 1971-81. Table 2.18 indicates the gradual growth in literacy percentage since 1901. Among the districts literacy rate is the highest in Patna (39.7%) followed by Dhanbad (39.3%), Singhbhum (33.6%), Nalanda (91.0%) and Ranchi (31.3%). The lowest literacy is found in the districts of West Champaran (13.8%), East Champaran (19.0%), Purnea (19.3%), Sitamarhi (19.4%) and Saharsa (20.2%), as is apparent from the Fig. 23.

TABLE 2.18 : **Variations in literacy : Bihar**

Year	1901	1911	1921	1931	1941	1951	1961	1971	1981
Literacy rate in percentage	3.42	3.83	4.35	4.15	9.18	12.13	18.13	19.94	26.0

Source : Arranged from different census records.

Scheduled castes and scheduled tribes

According to the Census of 1971, about 14.11 and 8.75 per cent of the total population constituted of scheduled castes and scheduled tribes respectively. The former is found throughout the state while scheduled tribes are concentracted in the Chota-nagpur region only Palamau and Gaya districts have the highest percentage of scheduled castes with 25.4 per cent and 24.6 per cent respectively. The tribal people known as the Adivasis with Munda, Oraon, Santhal, Ho etc. are dominating in the hilly and forested areas of Ranchi, Santhal Parganas, Southern Palamau and Hazaribagh districts.[40] They are economically very poor without any incentive in industry, trade and commerce. They thrive mostly on the primitive activities and are least benefited by the industrial revolution of the region.

Working classes

Table 1.4 states that nearly 82.2 per cent of the working force is engaged in agriculture, 2.6 in manufacturing, 2.5 in household industry, 3.2 in trade and commerce and the rest is engaged in services, etc. North Bihar has very high percentage in agricultural labour, while Dhanbad district has the lowest. Again, Dhanbad, Singhbhum and Ranchi districts have mostly non-agricultural workers primarily engaged in mining, manufacturing and other services.

One interesting feature of the society in Bihar is the absence of healthy middle class who can invest money in trade, commerce and other industrial organisations. The absence of this class has adversely affected the economic development of the State. Recently, the State Government has launched a number of measures to improve the conditions of the rural poor. They are abolition of bonded labour, fixation of minimum wages and stopping of eviction of Harijans from their lands. But, unfortunately, reports are pouring in that these reforms are facing rough weather from the hostile landlords, who are often in the league with their caste brothers in bureaucracy. In the true sense, these reforms have become political and a vote-catching device. Until and unless some dynamic steps are taken, the tendency of exploitation will not be rooted out. Bihar will continue as one of the most backward states—"an exporter of raw materials and importer of basic necessities".[41]

On the basis of above discussion, it may be concluded that Bihar in spite of her rich economy, is a poor state. This colossal poverty is due to her lower productivity of land and people combined with the vicious social system. Therefore, the only question, how to overcome that problem is burning and the most serious one. Thus, besides agriculture, stress on industrialisation may be a correct approach to this problem.

REFERENCES

1. Bose, B.R. (1977), *The Economy of Bihar*, K.L. Firma Publication, Calcutta, p. 1,

2. Kidwai, A.R. (1980), "Bihar : Constraints Gagging Growth", *The Economic Times*, Monday, June 9, 1980, Fourth Anniversary Supplement, Bombay, p. 1.

3. Singh, R.L. and Singh, K.N. (1971), "Middle Ganga Plain", in R.L. Singh (ed.), *India : A Regional Geography*, National Geographical Society of India, Varanasi, p. 208.

4. *Commerce* (1973), "The Economy of Bihar", Vol. 127, No. 3263, Nov. 17, 1963, p. 12.

5. Sengupta, N. (1979), *Destitutes and Development : A Study of Bauri Community in the Bakaro Region*, Concept Publishing Co., New Delhi.

6. Singh, K.S. (1973), "Industrial Development of Bihar", *Commerce*, Vol. 127, No. 3263, November 17, p. 41.

7. Sengupta, K.K. (1973), "Bihar : A Paradox of Plenty and Poverty", *Amrita Bazar Patrika*, Calcutta, March 28, p. 10.

8. Prasad, K.N. (1980), *Problems of Economic Development in the Third World with special reference to India*, New Delhi, Sterling Publications, p. v.

9. Myrdal, G. (1967), *Asian Drama*, Pelican Book, Vol. I, Chap. 7, p. 285.

10. Fifth Five-Year Plan, 1974-79, Industry Sector, Industries and Technical Education (Industries) Deptt. Government of Bihar, Patna, pp. 2-3.

11. *Techno-Economic Survey of Bihar* (1959), NCAER, New Delhi, p. vi.

12. Narayan, J.P. (1973), "The Problem of Self-Renewal in Bihar", *Commerce*, Vol. 127, No. 3263, Nov. 17, Bombay, pp. 3-5.

13. Dayal, P. (1968), "The Bihar Plain : A Regional Study", *Transactions of the Indian Council of Geographers*, Vol. 5, p. 1.

14. Lal, B.B. (1981), *Census of India*, Series 4, Bihar Paper I, Provisional Population Totals, Director of Census Operation Bihar.

15. Ahmad, E. (1965), "*Bihar*; A Physical, Economic and Regional *Geography*" Ranchi University, Ranchi, p. 11.

16. Spate, O.H.K. (1960), *India and Pakistan : A General and Regional Geography*, Methuen & Co. Ltd., London, p. 3.

17. Dayal, P. (1968), op. cit., p. 4.

18. Singh, R.P. and Kumar, A. (1970), *Monograph of Bihar*, Patna, p. 12.

19. Diwakar, R.R. (ed.) (1969), *Bihar Through the Ages*, Calcutta, p. 26.

20. Dayal, P. (1953), op. cit., p. 12.

21. *ibid.*, p. 16.

22. *ibid.*, p. 23.

23. *ibid.*, p. 14.

24. Ojha, B.N. (1976), "Power : Crux of the Problem", *The Economic Times*, Sept. 22, Special Volume I, p. VIII.

25. Ojha, B.N. (1976), "The Success Story of Electricity in Bihar", *Bihar Information*, Patna, March and April, Vol. 24, No. 5, pp. 31-32.

26. *Bihar Information*, Patna, August 15, 1973, Vol. 21, No. 13, p. 29.

27. Das, H.P. (1978), "Transport and Economy", unpublished paper.

28. Singh, R.P. and Kumar, A. (1970), op. cit., p. 138.

29. *The Economic Times* (1976), "Bihar : Economy Turns Buoyant"—A Special Feature : Part I, September 22, 1976, p. I.

30. Singh, K.S. (1973), op. cit., pp. 41 & 44.

31. Kidwai, A.R. (1980), op. cit., p. I.

32. *The Economic Times*, (1976), op. cit., p. II.

33. Prasad, K.N. (1973), "Economic Development of Chotanagpur", *Commerce*, Vol. 127, No. 3263, Bombay, Nov. 11, pp. 54-55.

34. *The Economic Times* (1976), op. cit., p. I.

35. Couto, A.F. (1973), "Opportunities for Industrial Growth of Bihar", *Commerce*, Nov. 17, Vol. 127, No. 3263, pp. 31-39.

36. Singh, K.S. (1973), op. cit., p. 44.

37. *ibid*., p. 42.

38. Punjab, Haryana and Tamil Nadu have been getting hydel power at an average cost of 3 to 5 paise per KWH over the last four and five plans, whereas Bihar has been purchasing power from DVC at an average cost of 9 paise per KWH and its own generation cost has been 11 to 13 paise per unit which also has recently increased very much. (Ojha, B.N. (1976), "Power : Crux of the Problem", *The Economic Times*, September 22, p. VIII).

39. Lal, B.B. (1981), *Census of India* 1981, Series-4, Bihar Provisional Population Totals, Paper I and Supplement of 1981, Director of Census Operation, Bihar.

40. Sinha, V.N.P.; (1976), *Chotanagpur Plateau : A Study in Settlement Geography*, New Delhi, Rajesh Publications, p. 41.

41. Dhar, H. (1976), "Bihar lags behind despite resources", *The Economic Times*, Sept. 22, p. 14.

3

DELIMITATION OF INDUSTRIAL COMPLEX

IN THE preceding chapters a general overview of theoretical framework stating problems and purpose was presented. The geographical description of the study area has also been discussed and analysed. In this chapter, however, a general industrial framework is provided in the beginning to enable to delimit industrial complexes quantitatively. The study is entirely based on different demographic literature related to industry and industrial concerns, which are obtained from different agencies under different captions by the State or the Central Governments. The 1971 Census Report is considered as the base of all discussions and results.

INDUSTRIAL SET-UP

Bihar happens to be one of the most promising industrial States in India. Its mineral richness and other physical, economic and social aspects have acted as the base of industrial growth. The industrial growth started from the very inception of the 20th Century and since then it has remained very phenomenal. But the real breakthrough of the industrialisation came only after successful operation of the 2nd Five-Year Plan. During the Plan periods, a number of giant industrial establishments were set up mostly under public sector acting as the growth centres. Since then a number of industrial units have been located in different parts of the State. Bihar is fortunate in possession of wide range of raw materials, for example, minerals, forest, agricultural and live-stock produces. Consequently several types of industries have been established. On the basis of resource-base eight types of factory-industries can be identified[1] (Table 3.1) These industries are as follows :

(a) Agro-based industries,
(b) Forest-based industries,
(c) Livestock-based industries,
(d) Textiles,
(e) Mineral-based industries,
(f) Engineering industries,
(g) Chemical industries and
(h) Miscellaneous industries.

Figures 24 and 25 show district wise distribution of factories according to their size of employment. Eight bars proportionate to the employment for each of the above types of industries have been drawn. Among the eight types of industries, mineral-based industries account for 24.02 per cent of employment followed by agro-based industries 21.59 per cent, textile industries 15.98 per cent and forest-based industries 13.42 per cent. Employment in the remaining three industries together accounts for 14.19 per cent. Mineral-based industries occupy the first position according to employment strength in the districts of Singhbhum, Dhanbad, Shahabad, Hazaribagh, Muzaffarpur and Palamau and the last position is shared by Monghyr, Purnea and Bhagalpur districts. Agro-based industries occupy first position in order of employment in the districts of Monghyr, Champaran, Saran, Patna, Gaya, Darbhanga, Shahabad, Muzaffarpur and Purnea, and the last position is occupied by Ranchi, Dhanbad, Singhbhum and Hazaribagh districts. In the forest products Saharsa, Purnea, Palamau, Hazaribagh, Santhal Parganas, Champaran and Shahabad districts occupy the respective positions. Dhanbad and Singhbhum occupy the lowest positiou. The Engineering industries are very prominent in Ranchi district followed by Singhbhum and Monghyr districts. Chemical industries are important in Dhanbad district, only next to mineral-based industries.

A short description is presented here to high-light these industries in their spatial context.

Agro-based industries

Since agriculture is the mainstay of the state's economy, there

TABLE 3.1 : **Factories classified by types and size of employment, 1971**

Name of districts	Total pop. in factories/ industries (number)	Figures in percentage							
		I Agro-based	II Forest based	III Live stock based	IV Textiles	V Mineral based	VI Engine-ering	VII Chemi-cals	VIII Miscel-laneous
Patna	72,748	30.96	10.79	5.68	15.36	15.94	4.12	1.88	15.16
Gaya	63,243	26.83	13.87	3.67	20.71	19.35	5.78	0.84	8.95
Shahabad	65,797	25.71	16.10	3.23	12.89	27.72	4.66	0.82	8.89
Saran	45,528	31.60	11.04	2.77	20.25	19.98	2.68	1.48	10.20
Champaran	37,023	37.71	16.86	1.62	18.05	13.78	0.49	0.28	11.21
Muzaffarpur	47,452	23.20	16.81	3.40	16.79	23.33	2.06	1.18	13.23
Monghyr	76,644	37.83	12.53	2.44	10.27	10.30	15.60	4.43	6.60
Darbhanga	56,888	24.50	18.92	2.38	23.80	14.53	3.30	0.87	11.70
Bhagalpur	39,652	19.63	13.13	2.71	43.93	11.67	0.94	0.47	7.30
Saharsa	15,583	22.81	26.00	1.31	18.04	14.45	5.02	0.13	12.14
Purnea	39,588	20.91	23.18	2.46	25.87	10.74	4.45	0.72	11.67
Santhal Pargana	47,783	22.97	16.45	1.41	20.41	20.31	10.24	0.63	6.98
Palamau	14,574	18.00	18.13	5.29	16.89	22.68	10.12	0.55	8.34
Hazaribagh	36,030	11.42	17.96	2.06	13.88	32.20	5.96	4.72	11.80
Ranchi	58,463	5.37	11.35	1.39	12.63	18.06	42.38	0.63	8.19
Dhanbad	53,311	5.65	5.68	1.56	5.95	45.05	4.94	19.63	7.99
Singhbhum	1,15,887	7.80	6.08	0.56	4.60	49.36	26.52	1.28	3.80
Bihar	8,87,194	21.59	13.42	2.49	15.98	24.02	10.80	2.55	9.50

Source : Census atlas, Census of India, 1971, Bihar, series 4, part IX, p. 178.

is a good ground for the development of the agro-based industries. There are several already developed agro-based industries. They are food-grains and cereals, oil mills, sugar factories, backeries, beverages, tobacco etc. The Bihar Plain is the main region where these industries are highly concentrated.

Among the food-processing industries, milling of rice, dal, flour and oil are important. These industries mostly belong to the small scale group and have a wide spatial distribution. According to the annual survey of industries 1971, there were 40 major rice mills, 45 major flour mills and 75 cold storages to store potatoes in the state. Altogether, there were 353 food products industries mostly distributed in the plain areas of Patna, Monghyr, Purnea, Shahabad, Bhagalpur, Gaya and Saran districts.

Sugar industry : Sugar industry is the prime among the agro-based industries. This industry has remained one of the most important and has played a very dominant role in recasting state's economy. This is evident from the fact that more than five lakh cultivators are directly engaged in the sugarcane fields and nearly 35,000 workers are employed in all the 30 sugar mills of the State.[2] These sugar mills are widely distributed in the districts of Champaran, Saran, Muzaffarpur and Darbhanga in North Bihar; and Gaya, Patna and Shahabad in South Bihar. Fertile Plains, abundant labour, large markets and good transportation facilities are the main factors which have contributed their establishment and growth.

At present the condition of this industry is not very sound. More than five factories have been closed. In 1940 Bihar had 30 sugar factories only next to Uttar Pradesh. The same was the condition in production also. Now the State ranks fifth in production after Maharashtra, Uttar Pradesh, Tamil Nadu and Haryana, and third in numerical strength of factories after U.P. and Maharashtra. In the year 1971 Bihar produced about 2.93 lakh tonnes of sugar which was comparatively very low from 3.92 lakh tonnes produced in 1964-65.[3] This deterioration in the sugar production is caused by several factors. Lack of irrigation and transportation facilities, late payment of ready cash for sugarcane prices to the farmers, competition with cereals especially with wheat and rice, higher excise duty on sugar, higher prices of gur and khandsari in the open market and very old machineries in factories are some of the factors gagging the growth of the industry. Therefore, now incentives, protection from the government and modernization of the outdated machineries are essential to revitalize this declining industry.

Jute industry : There are only 3 Jute mills in Bihar, two located at Katihar and third at Muktapur in Darbhanga district. Nearly 7,000 workers are employed in these factories. The north-eastern portion of Bihar is climatically very ideal for jute cultivation. About 6.21 lakh tonnes jute is produced annually. Sacking bags, hessian cloth and twine are the chief products which have larger markets in Bihar. Thakurganj, Purnea and Kisanganj are centres where more jute mills are to be established.

Tobacco industry : There is only one large scale tobacco factory known as the M/s Imperial Tobacco Co. of India, at Monghyr which employs more than 2,000 workers. The rich tobacco growing areas of Diaras, either side of river Ganga provide a suitable site for this industry. A variety of cigarettes are produced here which bring a great income to the State.

Vanaspati industry : There are three Vanaspati factories in Bihar located one each at Dalmianagar, Rajgir and Samastipur. The factory at Dalmianagar is the largest one which produces about 25,000 tonnes of Vanaspati and employs nearly 500 persons. The "Hanuman" brand of product has greater demand through out the State.

Textile industry : Textiles, although grouped separately are essentially an agro-based industry. The industry, however, does not owe much importance in the State. There are only 6 medium-sized cotton mills located at Gaya, Patna (Phulwari Sharif), Mokameh, Dumraon, Buxar and Ormanjhi (Ranchi district). These mills produce only 3.2 per cent of total required cloths of the State. Nearly 2,700 workers are employed.

Forest-based industries

Bihar is fortunate to have forest economy to a considerable extent. Several industries for example, wood based industries, lac industry, silk industry, match industry, paper and pulp industry, biri industry etc. thrive on the forest products like timber, bamboos, sabai grasses, lac, tasar, kendu leaves etc. Except pulp and paper all could be classified as small scale.

Pulp and paper industry : Dalmianagar and Hayaghat are two places where paper factories are located. The Rohtas Paper Factory of Dalmianagar is one of the largest paper producing centres in the country. Here, the finest quality of paper, paper boards and printing papers are produced. It produces more than 60,000 tonnes of paper per year. About 2,000 workers are employed. The bamboo of Rohtas and Palamau forests, Sabai grass from Assam, Coal from Jharia and Bokaro, cheap labour from plain areas and wide market combined with the nodal location from transportation point of view are the main geographical considerations for its location at Dalmianagar. The Ashok paper mill at Hayaghat (Darbhanga) is the second unit which produces nearly 3,000 tonnes paper annually and nearly 900 workers are employed in this factory.

Match factory : During 1966-67 two match splint factories were located at Kodarma and Goelkera. These centres supply about 6,800 million splints to WIMCO annually. Another centre Bagaha in Champaran district is yet to start splint production.

Lac industry : Bihar is the greatest lac producer in India accounting for nearly 41 per cent of the country's lac output. There are more than hundred lac factories located in Ranchi, Singhbhum, Palamau and Hazaribagh districts which process stick lac into seedlac and shel lac. Only 17 factories are major lac producers which use power for crushing and washing the lac. Others are based on small scale. The Muri Lac Factory at Muri is the most modernised and fully mechanised factory which has been set up in German collaboration. This unit produces machine-made shellac through heating process and entire production is meant for export. The lac production has shown a decreasing trend from 22,898 tonnes in 1967-68 to 15,406 tonnes in 1967-70 on account of slack in world's markets. Nearly 1,500 persons are employed in this industry.[4]

Silk industry : The silk weaving industry of Bihar held a prestigious position in the country for many years, but now it has lost its importance to Madhya Pradesh. The silk weaving comprises of Tasar, eri and mulbury production but the former dominates. It is entirely carried on small scale, on handloom and power looms basis. Bhagalpur is the chief centre where washing, bleaching and finishing of silk fabrics are done.

Livestock-based industries

Such type of industries are varied in nature ranging from dairy farming, poultry farming, fisheries and leather industry and are widely distributed throughout the state mostly on small scale or household industry basis. Among all, leather industry is important to some extent.

Leather industry : There are only five leather factories in Bihar employing more than 1200 persons. Digha (Patna) and Mokameh along the river Ganga in Patna District are the main centres where varieties of boots, shoes and chappals are manufactured by the Bata Company. There is a small tannery at Gaya and two another leather works are located at Dehri.

Mineral-based industries

Mineral-based industries are the most dominant aspect of the industrial landscape of Bihar. The availability of huge amount of metallic and non-metallic minerals, combind with other economic and social infra-structures have acted as the 'seed-beds' for the establishment and growth of basic industries, like iron and steel, cement, aluminium, copper and several others. These industries are raw materials-oriented and thereby they have occupied the mineral zones of the Chotanagpur Highland Region.

Iron and steel industry : There are mainly two location-centres, i.e., Jamshedpur and Bokaro where massivesized iron and steel industries are located. The Tata Iron and Steel Co. Ltd. at Jamshedpur is the premier steel centre of the country. It produces 2 million tonnes of ingots and nearly 1.5 million tonnes of finished steel annually. About 40,000 persons are employed in this factory.[5]

The Bokaro Steel Plant is the most recent public enterprise and its full completion is yet to come. It has already completed the two phases out of the total four phases of growth. At present the plant is producing 4.0 million tonnes of ingot steel, hot and cold rolled coils and other structurals. Nearly 30,000 persons are directly employed in the Plant.[6]

Copper industry : M/s Indian Copper Corporation Ltd. at Moubhandar near Ghatshila is the only unit for copper production in India. The copper ore is brought from the Mosabani-Badia Mines through aerial ropeway which is only 10 kms. apart from the production centre. Other raw materials are zinc, pine oil etc. which are imported. 96,000 million tonnes of copper are annually refined and about 8,400 workers are engaged.[7] Nickel is also produced as by-product.

Aluminium industry : Muri near Ranchi is the single aluminium refiner-centre of the State. M/s Indian Aluminium Co. Ltd. at Muri obtains bauxite from the 'Pat' region near Lohardaga in Ranchi district. Coal is obtained from Jharia coal-fields. Bauxite is refined into alumina and transported to Hirakund (Orissa) and Alwaye (Kerala) for production of aluminium. Nearly 54,000 tonnes of alumina is refined annually with the help of nearly 1,500 persons as labourers.

Cement industry : There are 7 cement factories located at Dalmianagar (two), Banjari, Japla, Khelari, Sindri and Jhinkpani entirely in South Bihar. Since a variety of raw materials are used in the production of cement the location is widely diffused. The cement factories at Dalmianagar, Banjari, Japla and Khelari are mostly limestone based and hence their site of locations are near limestone belt of the Kaimur Plateau of Rohtas district. Only coal is brought from the coal-fields of the Upper Damodar basins. The cement factories at Sindri and Jhinkpani are entirely based upon the 'sludge' and 'slag', the waste materials from the Fertilizers and Iron and Steel factories respectively. The seven factories altogether have a capacity to produce 22.3 lakh tonnes of cement annually and produced nearly 18.7 lakhs tonnes in 1971. Above 8,000 persons are employed in these factories.[8] Besides several other new centres have been approved for cement production. Among these, Adityapur, Bokaro, Bhavanathpur (Palamau), Patratu, Latehar, Tilothu and Barauni are important and their location is based on the waste-products of the large enterprizes. Therefore, the prospect of this industry is very bright.

Mica processing industry : Mica processing, although mostly on the small scale, has got its national importance. There are altogether 140 factories employing 12,500 persons.[9] The industry is primarily concentrated in mica belt of Hazaribagh and Giridih districts. The chief producing centres are Kodarma, Jhumri Tilaiya, Giridih, Domchanch, Tisri and Chakai. The micanite factory at Jhumri Tilaiya is the most important and manufactures micanite through the modern technique under the supervision of foreign technicians. It produces micanite, mica/linen, mica silk, mica paper etc. all for export.

Glass industry : Bihar is again one of the leading Indian States in production and export of glass-sheet s During 1970-71 Bihar produced nearly 65 lakh square metres of glass and shared nearly 33 per cent of All India exports. There are 8 glass factories in which only two, one at Kandra in Singhbhum and another at Bhadarinagar near Bhurkunda are on large scale units. The Seraikela Factory at Kandra produces 35 lakh square metres while the Indo-Asahi Glass Works produces 55 lakh sq. metres annually.[10] Other glass producing centres are at Patna, Kumardhubi, Chirkunda, Chota Ambona and Ramgarh.

Refractory : Refractories have also developed at a considerable length on account of the proximity of the steel industry and occurrence of raw materials, like fireclay, bauxite, chromite, Sillimanite, Quartezite and Kynite etc. Refractories producing centres are Mugma, Dhansar, Nirsa Chatti, Jharia, Kumardhubi, Kharakaree, Dhanbad, Kusunda and Ramgarh. Except Ramgarh, all are in Dhanbad district. Nearly 6,55,255 tonnes of fire-bricks were produced in 1971.

Coal industry : Coal is the most important mineral constituent of the State which has given not only power but life to the industrial economy of the State. Coal contains several impurities and these impurities are mechanically separated through washery. Therefore, 14 coal-washeries have been set-up both in private and public sectors specially in the coal producing areas. These are Kargali, Dugda I, Dugda II, Bhojudih, Patherdih, Giddi, Kathra, Sawang, Jamadaha, West Bokaro, Londa, Sudamadih, Ramgarh and Gobindpur. The Kargali washery near Bermo is the largest in Asia and it washes nearly 22 lakh tonnes of coal per annum. These washeries serve the important metallurgical, engineering and other industries. Coal is also used in manufacturing of fertilizers at Sindri and several other chemical industries.

Engineering industries

After independence one of the special features of the industrial economy of the state has been the emergence of engineering industries. These industries, however, have precipitated the industrialisation by providing heavy machines, equipments and other transportational vehicles. Nearly one lakh persons are directly employed in these industries.

There are altogether 8 engineering centres in the state. The Heavy Engineering Corporation at Hatia near Ranchi, the Tata Engineering Co. at Jamshedpur, Kumardhubi and Jamalpur are the most important centres. The H.E.C. at Hatia constitutes three parts and produces numerous machineries, equipments and other heavy vehicles. Besides, a number of other engineering units have developed in Ranchi in which High Tension and Insulator Factory at Namkum, Electrical Equipment Factory, and the Usha Martine Black at Tati-Silwai, the Bharat Ball Bearing Co. Ltd. at Ratu and others are the important engineering units.

Jamshedpur is the second most important engineering centre of the State. The Tata Engineering Co., The Agrico, The Tata Foundary Co., The Jemco, The Indian Tube Co. and others are important engineering units at Jamshedpur which produce varieties of iron and steel structures.

The Kumardhubi Engineering Works established in 1917 produces 12,000 tonnes of machines per annum. It undertakes fabrication works like headgears, steel prusses, transmission posts and other structurals. Besides the repairing works of electric drills, coal cutting machines, haulages, pumps, steam plants etc., are also taken. The Eagle Rolling Mill Ltd. manufactures iron-bars, rods and light structurals. M/s Nally Bird Engineering Co., Ltd. manufactures cement, mill machinery, coal washing plant etc. The Barakar Engineering and Foundry Works at Nirsachatti is manufacturing coal tubes, steel structurals, haulages etc.

The Indian Railways have established big workshops at Jamalpur. This unit is one of the biggest locomotive repair workshop in the country which employs more than 14,000 workers. Samastipur, Chakradharpur and Sini are the centres of railways workshops for repairs and construction of rolling stocks.

Apart from these centres, there are more than hundred medium-sized engineering and metal-based industrial units scattered throughout the State. Chaibasa, Chakulia, Dhanbad and its suburb, Sindri, Dalmianagar, Mokameh, Muzaffarpur, Jhajha, Gomoh, Deoghar are important among them.

Chemical industries

Bihar holds a good ground for the establishment and growth of chemical industries. Its vast resources of coal, pyrites, petroleum refinery, industrial alcohol, industrial gases etc. are now utilised as the major inputs for chemical industries. Bihar has already started manufacturing the sulphuric acid, soda-ash, caustic soda and calcium carbide.

Fertilizers : The importance of fertilizers is great in Bihar where agriculture and agricultural activities dominate. The State has two important fertilizer producing centres, one at Sindri in Dhanbad district and the other at Barauni. The former is the largest fertilizer producing centre in the country. Here, varieties of fertilizer products like amonium sulphate, urea, double salt, triple superphosphate, amonium nitrate etc. are produced. The total producing capacity of the factory is 3,55,000 M/T per annum and employs 7,744 persons.[11] The Bihar Superphosphate Factory at Sindri near Chasnalla is the state governments enterprize which produces 25 tonnes sulphuric acid per day and 10 tonnes superphosphate per hour.

The Fertilizer Corporation of India has established another fertilizer factory at Barauni which utilizes oil refinery gases and neptha as the major input. The factory has a capacity to produce 1,52,000 tonnes of nitrogen. The factory is still in its initial stage and therefore, it has to break certain constraints in the way of expansion.

The Bihar Government has already proposed to establish another fertilizer centre at Giddi (Hazaribagh) on coal and at Amjhore in Rohtas on Pyrites.

Industrial chemicals : The chemical plant of Rohtas Industries at Dalmianagar produces a variety of industrial chemicals like sulphuric acid, ferric alum, caustic soda, liquid chloric acid, bleaching powder, synthetic hydrochloric acid and sodium sulphate. This unit is of medium-sized and employs more than 500 persons. The state government has started construction of chemical units at Daltonganj (Palamau) and Bokaro, near steel factory, where coke oven will provide several by-products of the chemicals.

The Indian Explosive Factory at Gomia is designed to produce about 7,000 tonnes of blasting explosives per annum.

Miscellaneous industries

Some important industries which have not been included in the above categories are now being considered under this subhead.

Oil refinery at Barauni : The Indian Oil Refinery located at Barauni is the joint venture of the Indian and the Russian Governments. Nearly 3 million tonnes of refined petroleum and petroleum products are produced annually from Barauni. The crude oil is piped from Assam and also from Haldia port to this centre. Again refined petroleum is supplied through pipelines from Barauni to Calcutta and another from Barauni to Kanpur and Delhi. The by-products and waste products of petroleum has laid the establishment of several other petrochemical industries in the vicinity of the refinery.

Among other industries, lead smelting and refining at Tundoo near Katrasgarh, Ceramics plant at Ranchi, Bermo, Jharia and Dhanbad are important.

In this way the spatial concentration of these industries in different parts of the state has led to the formation of several industrial landscapes. These are : industrial landscape of Singhbhum, Ranchi, upper Damodar Basin, South Bihar Ganga Plain and North Bihar Ganga Plain. But before description of the growth and regional pattern of industrial complexes, it is imperative to delimit them for proper analysis and understanding. The following section deals with the delimitation of such region.

DELIMITATION OF AN INDUSTRIAL REGION

The distribution map of industries of Bihar shows an uneven pattern. Though industrial centres are developed in various parts of the State most of the industrial activities are confined to a few regions forming industrial pockets. These pockets are dominated by giant industrial establishments which have formed nucleus and around which several other large medium and small ancillaries have grown up. Indeed, these units have established linkages on the principle of coexistence. An attempt therefore, is made to locate those giant nucleus or industrial complexes on the basis of some scientific criteria.

To delimit an industrial complex, like an industrial region is very difficult as accepted by Pounds,[12] Buchanan[13] and Jarrett.[14] The difficulties lie mainly in data collection, and fixation of criteria. Miller[15] has, however, suggested a few criteria for measuring manufacturing activities. These are : (i) number of establishments, (ii) number of employees, (iii) number of production workers, (iv) percentage of the labour force, (v) value added, (vi) power consumption and (vii) physical output. But he is satisfied with none because of difficulty in operationalization. It is quite difficult to obtain data on various criteria. The first two criteria, number of units and number of employees, are considered to be the most important because data can be easily obtained and analysed also.

Several attempts have been made to measure the level of industrial concentration. For example, De Geer,[16] a Swedish scholar considered persons employed in American manufacturing as an index for measurment. The work of Wright[17] is based on "the value added by manufacturing" and has delimited the manufacturing districts of the United States. Strong[18] applied "power consumption" by each industrial centre as an index of measuring concentration. Jones[19] adopted a new method known as "multiple criteria" and prepared three maps on the basis of workers employed, power consumed, and value added by manufacturing. Further he superimposed the map to demarcate the level of concentration and also studied the regional characteristics of industries. Hartshorne's[20] attempt is based on the percentage of persons employed in manufacturing to the total employment of any centre and thus obtained intensity of manufacturing. Thompson[21] has used 'multi-criteria' method and has taken six variables in his study. These variables include persons employed in manufacturing, salaries and wages, value added by manufacturing, ratio of all employees in manufacturing to total employed in all industry groups, ratio of all employees in manufacturing to total population and ratio of value added by manufacturing to total population. Similarly, Alexander[22] has used several methods to delimit the manufacturing regions taking number of establishments and number of employees into account. He used several statistical methods like location quotient, index of diversification, index of concentration etc. to arrive at scientific conclusions.

In this respect Indian works, barring a few are less analytical and less contributory. A few studies made by Karan and Jenkins[23] and Karan[24] are worth mentioning. In these works the basis rest on the employment statistics. Indian industrial regions demarcated by Sinha is an appreciable attempt who based his conclusions on average daily factory employment.[25] Mandal attempted to demarcate the manufacturing regions of North Bihar with the help of manufacturing intensity formula which is as follows :[26]

$$\left(\frac{X + Y}{2}\right)$$

$$\text{Where } X = \frac{\text{No. of factories in a block X 100}}{\text{No. of factories in North Bihar}}$$

$$\text{and } \quad Y = \frac{\text{No. of persons employed in manufacturing in a block}}{\text{No. of persons employed in manufacturing in North Bihar}}$$

It is quite clear that the author has given equal weightage to factory and a worker in his formula. Had there been an additional weightage on factory, the study would have been a good portrayal of industrialisation in North Bihar instead of manufacturing regions.

In this study two variables, that is, number of employed workers and number of industrial units are taken into consideration. These two methods are although classical but seem to be necessary. This is purely based on availability of data therefore is selected for the purpose. No empirical work has yet been done in the case of Bihar, therefore, this seems to be a novel attempt.

Delimitation on the basis of employed workers

In the first instance number of workers[27] engaged in manufacturing other than house-hold is collected anchalwise. There are 595 anchals in 17 districts of Bihar. On the basis of workers engaged in non-household industries, data is tabulated and four maps have been prepared accordingly. Fig. 26 shows the distribution pattern by simple dot method. The heavily concentrated area is demarcated in Fig. 27.

The demarcation is categorised into seven groups showing areas of high to low concentrations. This map shows that two anchals, Golmuri in the Singhbhum district and Namkum in the Ranchi district are the areas of higher concentrations Two other anchals, namely, Patna Sadar in Patna district and Jharia-cum-Jorapokhar-cum-Sindri in Dhanbad district are areas of high concentration, comparatively lesser in comparison to the two anchals. The third order of concentration includes anchals of Chas and Nirsa-cum-Chirkunda in Dhanbad district and Dehri in Shahabad district. Kanke Anchal in Ranchi district and Jamalpur Anchal in Monghyr district are in the fourth order of succession. The fifth order comprises of Jagdishpur Anchal in Bhagalpur district, Monghyr Anchal in Monghyr district, Gaya Town Anchal in Gaya district and Adityapur Anchal in Singhbhum district. In the sixth order includes anchals of Dhanbad-cum-Kenduadih-cum-Jagta and Baghmara-cum-Katras in Dhanbad district; Chakradharpur in Singhbhum district; Ratu in Ranchi district; Katihar and Forbesganj in Purnea district; Arrah Sadar, Rohtas and Nawhatta in Shahabad district; Jhajha, Begusarai-I and Barauni in Monghyr district; Jamtara in Santhal Pargana district; Musahari in Muzaffarpur district; Darbhanga Sadar and Samastipur in Darbhanga district; Danapur-cum-Khagaul, Mokameh and Bihar (Nalanda) in Patna district; and Patratu in Hazaribagh district. The rest of the anchals come in the last order.

The distribution pattern is further tested by a method known as 'Location Factor' or 'Location Quotient' as initially used by

Florence.[28] Location quotient is an index to show the degree of concentration and is actually a ratio of ratios.[29] When the proportion of any characteristics in an area is studied in relation to its proportion in the region, the ratio used is known as the location quotient. It gives the relative picture of such proportions.[30]

The index of location quotient is the true indicator. When the location quotient is 1.0 it means a region has neither more or less concentration. When it is higher than 1.0, it means a relatively high concentration and when it is less than 1.0, it indicates that an industry is less developed in the region than manufacturing in general.

The same anchalwise data is analyzed to find out the L.Q. of each and every anchal of Bihar on the basis of the following formula :

$$\text{L. Q.} = \frac{\dfrac{\text{Non-household industrial workers in a block/anchal}}{\text{Total workers in a block/anchal}}}{\dfrac{\text{Non-household industrial workers in Bihar}}{\text{Total workers in Bihar}}}$$

The location quotient of each anchal is noted on the anchal map of Bihar and is finally divided into five groups. (Fig. 19.28) The map indicates that Namkum Anchal in Ranchi district and Nawhatta Anchal in Shahabad district contain the highest location quotient. Rohtas Anchal in Shahabad district; Nirsa-cum-Chirkunda and Chas Anchals in Dhanbad district; and Golmuri Anchal in Singhbhum district contain higher order of location quotient. Similarly, anchals of Jharia-cum-Jorapokhar-cum-Sindri in Dhanbad district; Ratu and Kanke Anchals in Ranchi district; Adityapur Anchal in Singhbhum district; Katihar Anchal in Purnea district, Jagdishpur Anchal in Bhagalpur district; Gaya Sadar Anchal in Gaya district; Bettiah in Champaran district and Bihar in Patna district contain high location quotient. The anchals of Lohardaga, Burmu, Ormanjhi, Silli and Jaldega in Ranchi district; Gobindpur, Baliapur, Dhanbad-cum-Kendudih-cum-Jagta and Baghmara-cum-Katras in Dhanbad district; Jhinkpani in Singhbhum district; Hazaribagh, Kodarma, Gumia, Jagdish, Ramgarh, Mandu, Patratu, Giridih and Bermo in Hazaribagh district; Daltonganj and Hussainabad in Palamau district; Jamtara, Dumka, Deoghar,

Madhubani, Suhilganj, Paljhari, Pakur in Santhal Pargana district; Manpur in Gaya district; Arrah town, Sasaram and Dehri in Shahabad district; Danapur-cum-Khagaul, Phulwari, Fatwa, Rahui and Mokameh in Patna district; Monghyr, Jamalpur, Jhaja in Monghyr district; Nathnagar, Sultanganj in Bhagalpur district; Forbesganj, and Kishanganj in Purnea district; Darbhanga, Samastipur, Kalyanpur, Dalsinghsarai, Madhubani and Pandaul in Darbhanga district; Musahari, Hajipur, Bairgania, Riga in Muzaffarpur district; Chapra, Manjhi, Marhaura, Dighwara, Siwan, Hussaingunj, Guttand, Mairwa, Pachrukhi and Uchkagaon in Saran district; and Motihari, Chakia, Raxaul, Ramnagar, Narkatiaganj, Lawriya and Chanpatia in Champaran district are the anchals having average location quotient. Rest of the anchals have less than 1.0/L.Q. and therefore these are less industrially marked.

It is important to point out that the map has correctly represented the reality. Anchal with even single industry has been marked out. Even the most centralised anchals have been represented. It seems that the map needs some corrections. For example, Barauni and Begusarai-I the most important industrial centres have obtained L.Q. less than 1.0. Similarly, Nawhatta and Rohtas Anchals in Shahabad district have L.Q. more than the most industrialised anchals like Golmuri, Chas and others. In other words, Golmuri having the highest number of workers in the whole state has been graded into higher rank with less L.Q. in comparison to Namkum in Ranchi, Chas in Dhanbad, Nawhatta and Rohtas in Shahabad. The result seems to be somewhat misleading has after all it is a ratio of ratios. Again anchals having only industrial workers of more percentage of total workers, naturally, their L.Q. is higher than the anchals whose percentage of industrial workers are less due to the development of tertiary activities. Golmuri is the case where the development of tertiary activities has lowered down the industrial percentage. It means industrialisation is more pronounced in Golmuri/Anchal than other areas. Nawhatta and Rohtas are the anchals where industrial workers dominate over total workers whereas in Dehri it is overdoomed by tertiary workers. In Namkum it is also the same but Barauni and Begusarai anchals are over-run by large population percentage.

The comparison of two maps (Fig. 27 and Fig. 28), one based on numerical value and the other on L.Q. gives more or less the similar result. On the basis of these maps industrial areas of high concentrations are discernible. They are Golmuri Anchal in Singhbhum; Namkum Anchal in Ranchi; Chas, Nirsa-cum-Chirkunda and Jharia-cum-Jorapokhar-cum-Sindri Anchal in Dhanbad; Gaya Sadar and Manpur Anchals in Gaya district; Dehri Rohtas, Nawhatta, and Arrah town Anchals in Shahabad; Patna Sadar, Phulwari, Danapur-cum-Khagaul Anchals in Patna disrtict; Monghyr and Jamalpur Anchals in Monghyr district; Jagdishpur and Nathnagar in Bhagalpur district; Dumka, Deoghar, and Jamtara Anchals in Santhal Parganas; Katihar Anchal in Purnea; Darbhanga and Samastipur Anchals in Darbhanga district; Masahari Anchal in Muzaffarpur; Motihari Anchal in Champaran; and Marhaurah and Siwan Anchals in Saran district.

Now it seems pertinent to correlate areas of industrially high concentrations with the number of industrial units. Before making a correlation a study of areas of concentration has to be done on the basis of industrial units.

Delimitation on the basis of industrial units

There are 89,061 factories and workshops in the state engaged in manufacturing, processing or servicing in the non-household sector according to the Census of 1971.[31] These factories and workshops are classified into five groups according to the number of workers employed as shown in the Table 3.20. This also indicates that factories and workshops employing less than 5 persons account for more than 87 per cent, 5 to 19 persons 10.25 per cent, 20 to 49 persons 1.52 per cent, and factories employing more than 50 persons and 0.40 and 0.70 per cent respectively (Table 3.20). It means large and medium scale industries are comparatively few in the state.

Since the study is basically regional in approach, the industries having regional impact are taken into consideration. The small scale, cottage, handlooms, khadi etc. although constitute a major share in numerical strength are not considered in this study. This is because : firstly, such type of industries are

TABLE 3.20 : **Distribution of factories and workshops by size of employment, 1971**

Name of district	Total no. of factories and workshop in person	Size of employment in percentage (number of persons)				
		1—4	5—19	20—49	50—99	100+
Patna	9,220	85.23	12.02	1.79	0.47	0.50
Gaya	6,762	90.31	7.09	0.58	0.16	1.86
Shahabad	7,009	92.38	6.06	0.76	0.20	0.61
Saran	6,656	91.30	7.26	0.77	0.15	0.53
Champaran	4,803	90.28	7.79	0.98	0.33	0.62
Muzaffarpur	6,877	88.77	9.31	0.95	0.31	0.67
Darbhanga	7,995	91.17	7.36	0.81	0.26	0.40
Monghyr	6,501	86.13	11.17	2.23	0.28	0.20
Bhagalpur	3,746	81.87	14.76	2.43	0.35	0.59
Saharsa	1,826	90.25	8.11	0.71	0.44	0.49
Purnea	5,369	88.77	9.95	0.75	0.28	0.32
Sathal Pargana	3,847	80.95	14.19	3.43	0.81	0.62
Palamau	2,588	93.47	5.91	0.46	0.04	0.12
Hazaribagh	4,910	81.85	14.20	1.92	0.79	1.24
Ranchi	3,686	84.02	13.16	1.60	0.68	0.54
Dhanbad	3,598	81.52	13.87	2.25	1.00	1.36
Singhbhum	3,578	72.97	19.09	5.70	0.87	1.37
Bihar	89,061	87.13	10.25	1.52	0.40	0.70

Source : Census Atlas, Census of India, 1971, Bihar, Series 4, Part IX, p. 178.

widely distributed (Fig. 29); secondly, their nature is 'footloose' and hence no specific locational criterion is fixed up and thirdly, if the units are too small or too unwieldy, the efficiency of the industry in general and its competitive power in particular may be seriously empaired.[32] It is expected that it may generalise the whole result into confusion if taken into account.

Table 3.21 clearly indicates that there are 197 large and medium-sized industrial units in Bihar. On the basis of this table three maps are drawn. The first map (Fig. 24) shows the distribution of factories and factory types. The second map (Fig. 31) shows industrial centres with factory size on the basis of labour employment. The third map (Fig. 30) shows the concentration of industrial units. On the basis of these maps, the areas of concentration or clustering of industrial units are

TABLE 3.21 : **Large and medium scale industries of Bihar, 1971**

Districts	Industrial central	No. of units.	No. of workers
1	2	3	4
Patna	1. Patna	8	1,500
	2. Bihta	1	1,039
	3. Mokameh	3	1,000
	4. Rajgir	1	800
	Total	13	4,339
Gaya	1. Gaya	2	1,700
	2. Warsaligaj	1	1,000
	3. Guraru	1	1,200
	Total	4	3,900
Shahabad	1. Dalmianagar	12	13,000
	2. Dumraon	2	440
	3. Buxar	2	923
	4. Banjari	1	1,260
	Total	17	15,623
Saran	1. Marhowrah	5	2,019
	2. Pachrukhi	2	1,350
	3. Siwan	2	1,675
	4. Sasamusa	1	767
	5. Mirganj	2	905
	Total	12	6,716
Muzaffarpur	1. Muzaffarpur	4	800
	2. Motihari	1	1,371
	3. Goraul	1	700
	4. Belsund	1	1,200
	Total	7	4,071
Darbhanga	1. Samastipur	4	3,000
	2. Hasanpur	1	726
	3. Sakri	3	3,681
	4. Darbhanga	1	901
	Total	9	8,308

BIHAR
DISTRIBUTION OF INDUSTRIES
1971
32 16 0 32
KMS.
WEST BENGAL
INDEX
S SUGAR MILLS
C CEMENT
A ALUMINIUM
F FERTILIZER
Ch CHEMICALS
CW COAL WASHERIES
P PAPER
E ENGINEERING
G GLASS
R REFRACTORY
V VANASPATI
T TEXTILES
J JUTE
SL SILK
L LEAD SMELTING
CO COPPER
M MATCH FACTORY
TB TOBACCO
OIL REFINERIES
IRON & STEEL
AGRICULTURE IMPLIMENTS
EX EXPLOSIVE

FIG. 24

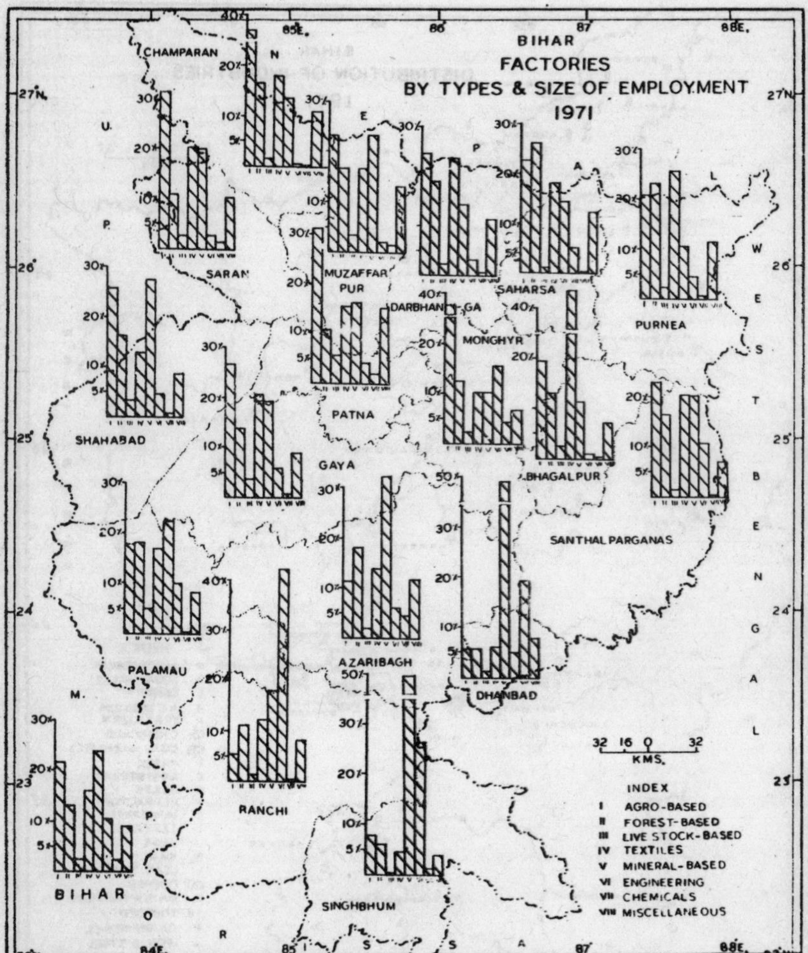
BIHAR
FACTORIES
BY TYPES & SIZE OF EMPLOYMENT
1971
CHAMPARAN
SARAN
MUZAFFARPUR
DARBHANGA
SAHARSA
PURNEA
SHAHABAD
PATNA
MONGHYR
GAYA
BHAGALPUR
SANTHAL PARGANAS
PALAMAU
AZARIBAGH
DHANBAD
RANCHI
SINGHBHUM
BIHAR
INDEX
I AGRO-BASED
II FOREST-BASED
III LIVE STOCK-BASED
IV TEXTILES
V MINERAL-BASED
VI ENGINEERING
VII CHEMICALS
VIII MISCELLANEOUS
32 16 0 32
KMS.
WEST BENGAL
U. P.
M. P.
ORISSA
NEPAL

FIG. 25

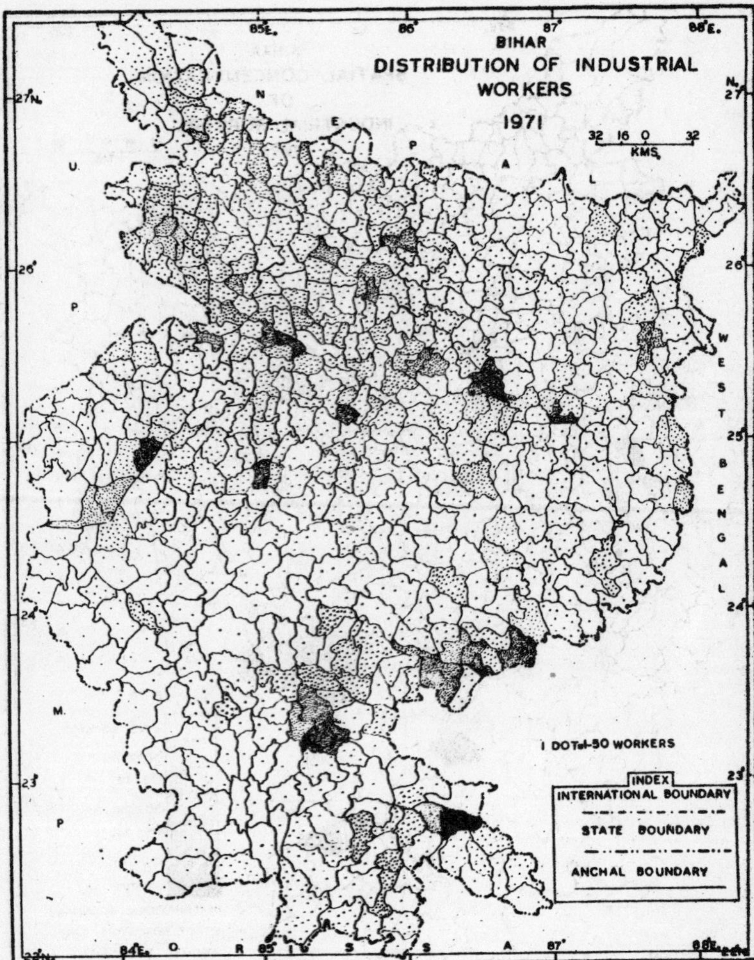

BIHAR
DISTRIBUTION OF INDUSTRIAL WORKERS
1971
32 16 0 32
KMS.
N E P A L
U. P.
M. P.
W E S T B E N G A L
O R I S S A
1 DOT=1-50 WORKERS
INDEX
INTERNATIONAL BOUNDARY
STATE BOUNDARY
ANCHAL BOUNDARY

FIG. 26

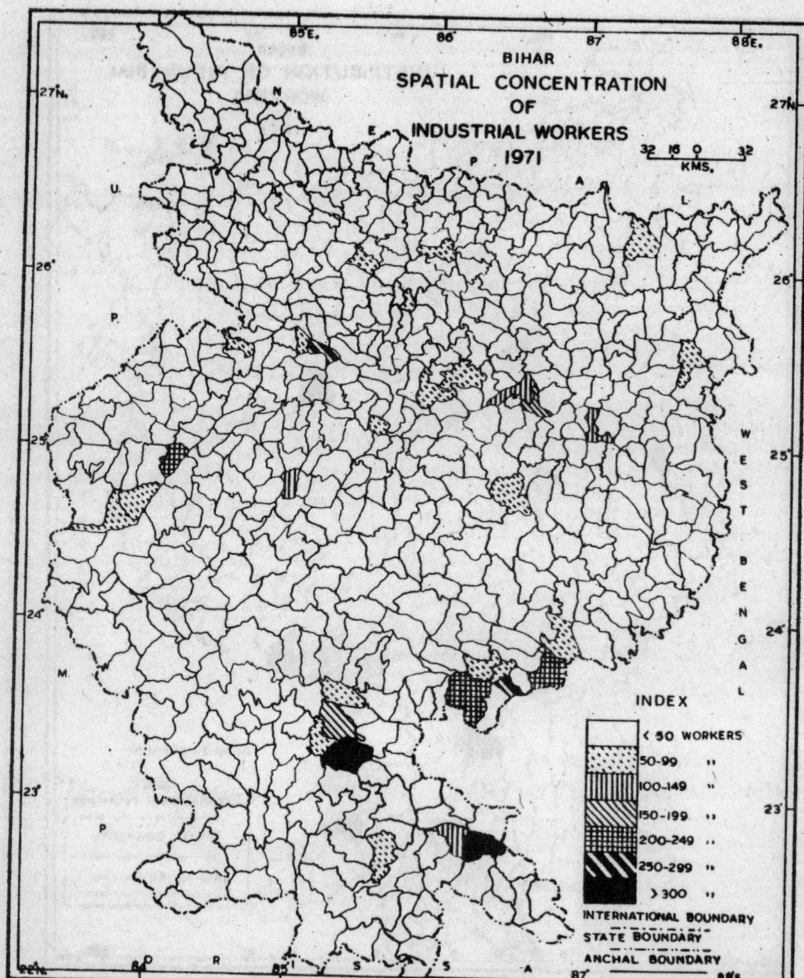
BIHAR
SPATIAL CONCENTRATION
OF
INDUSTRIAL WORKERS
1971
32 16 0 32
KMS.
N E P A L
U. P.
M. P.
O R I S S A
WEST BENGAL
INDEX
< 50 WORKERS
50-99 "
100-149 "
150-199 "
200-249 "
250-299 "
> 300 "
INTERNATIONAL BOUNDARY
STATE BOUNDARY
ANCHAL BOUNDARY

FIG. 27

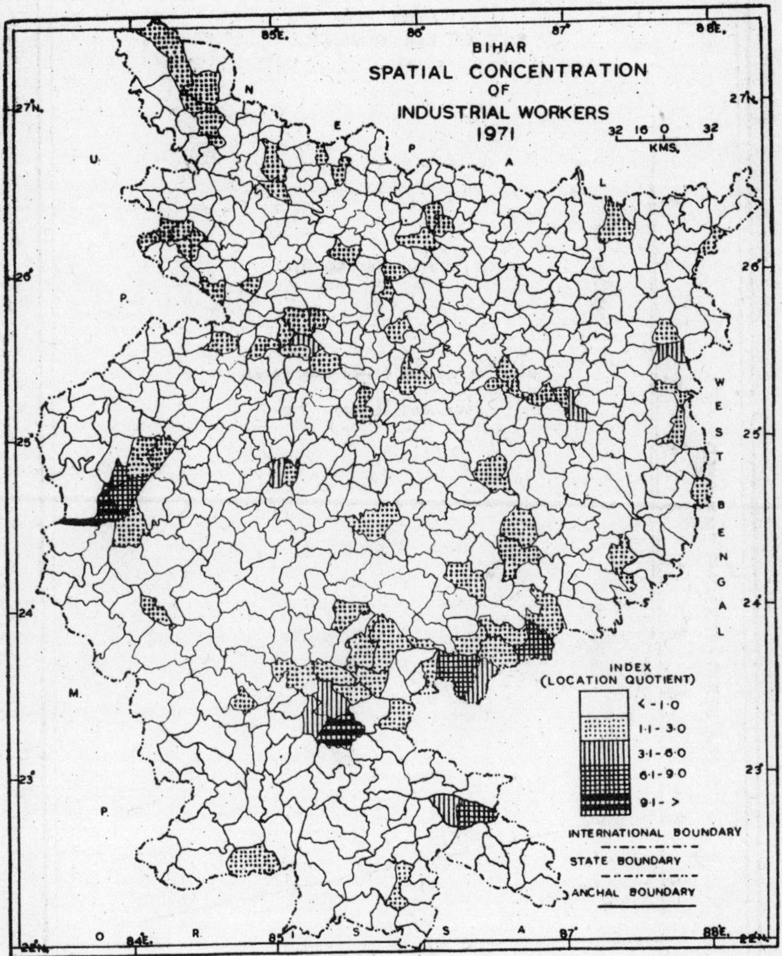
BIHAR
SPATIAL CONCENTRATION OF INDUSTRIAL WORKERS 1971
32 16 0 32
KMS.
INDEX (LOCATION QUOTIENT)
< - 1·0
1·1 - 3·0
3·1 - 6·0
6·1 - 9·0
9·1 - >
INTERNATIONAL BOUNDARY
STATE BOUNDARY
ANCHAL BOUNDARY
N E P A L
U. P.
M. P.
O R I S S A
W E S T B E N G A L
84°E. 85°E. 86° 87° 88°E.
27°N. 26° 25° 24° 23° 22°N.

FIG. 28

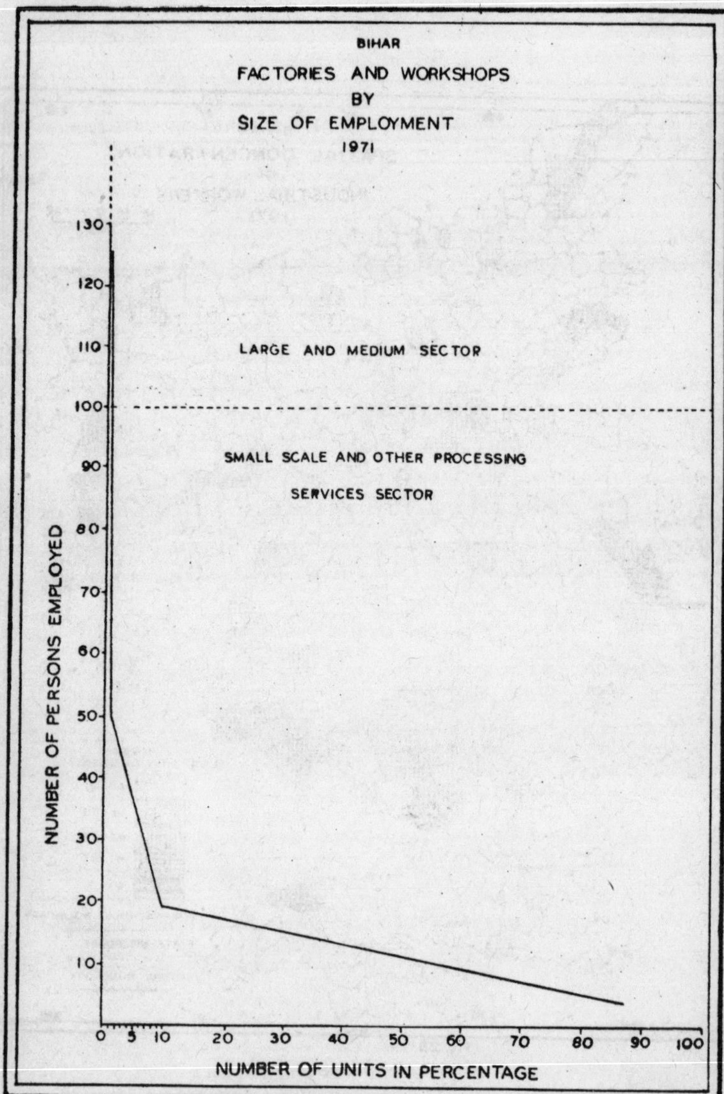
BIHAR
FACTORIES AND WORKSHOPS
BY
SIZE OF EMPLOYMENT
1971
LARGE AND MEDIUM SECTOR
SMALL SCALE AND OTHER PROCESSING
SERVICES SECTOR
NUMBER OF PERSONS EMPLOYED
130
120
110
100
90
80
70
60
50
40
30
20
10
0
5
10
20
30
40
50
60
70
80
90
100
NUMBER OF UNITS IN PERCENTAGE

Fig. 29

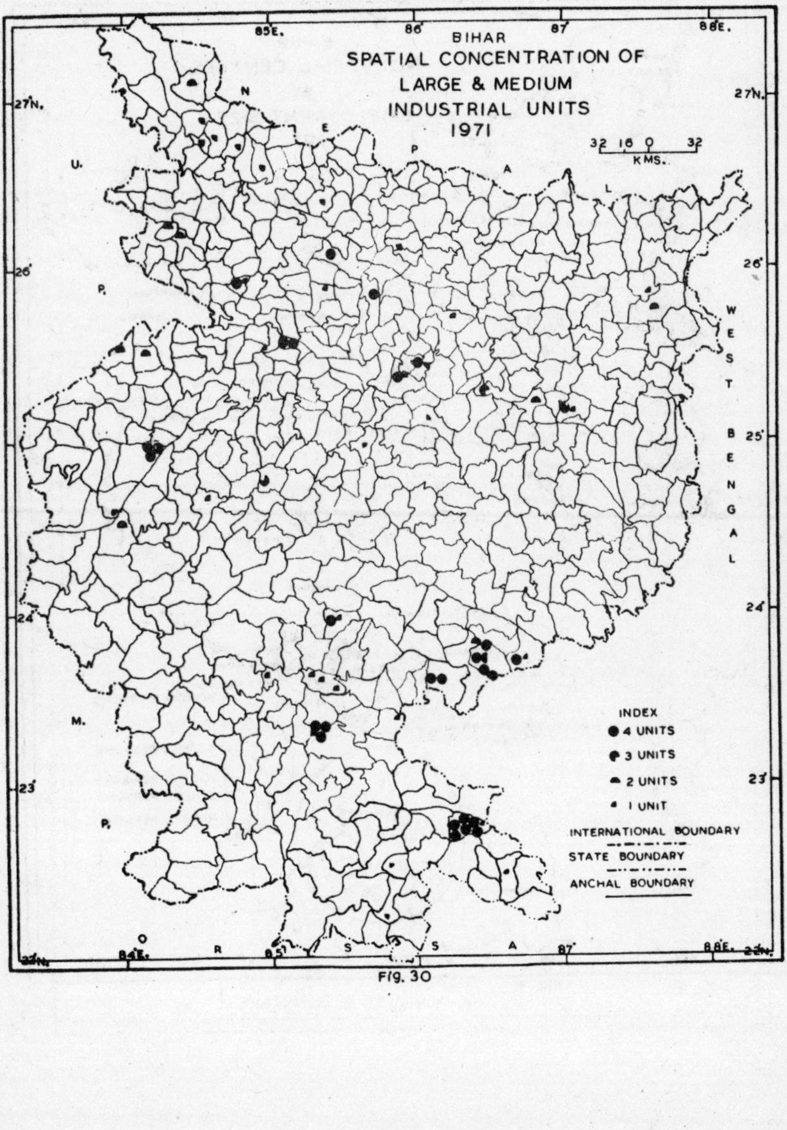
BIHAR
SPATIAL CONCENTRATION OF
LARGE & MEDIUM
INDUSTRIAL UNITS
1971
32 16 0 32
KMS.
NEPAL
U. P.
WEST BENGAL
M. P.
ORISSA
INDEX
4 UNITS
3 UNITS
2 UNITS
1 UNIT
INTERNATIONAL BOUNDARY
STATE BOUNDARY
ANCHAL BOUNDARY
85°E.
86°
87
88°E.
27°N.
26°
25°
24°
23°
22°N.
84°E.
85°
87°
88°E.

Fig. 30

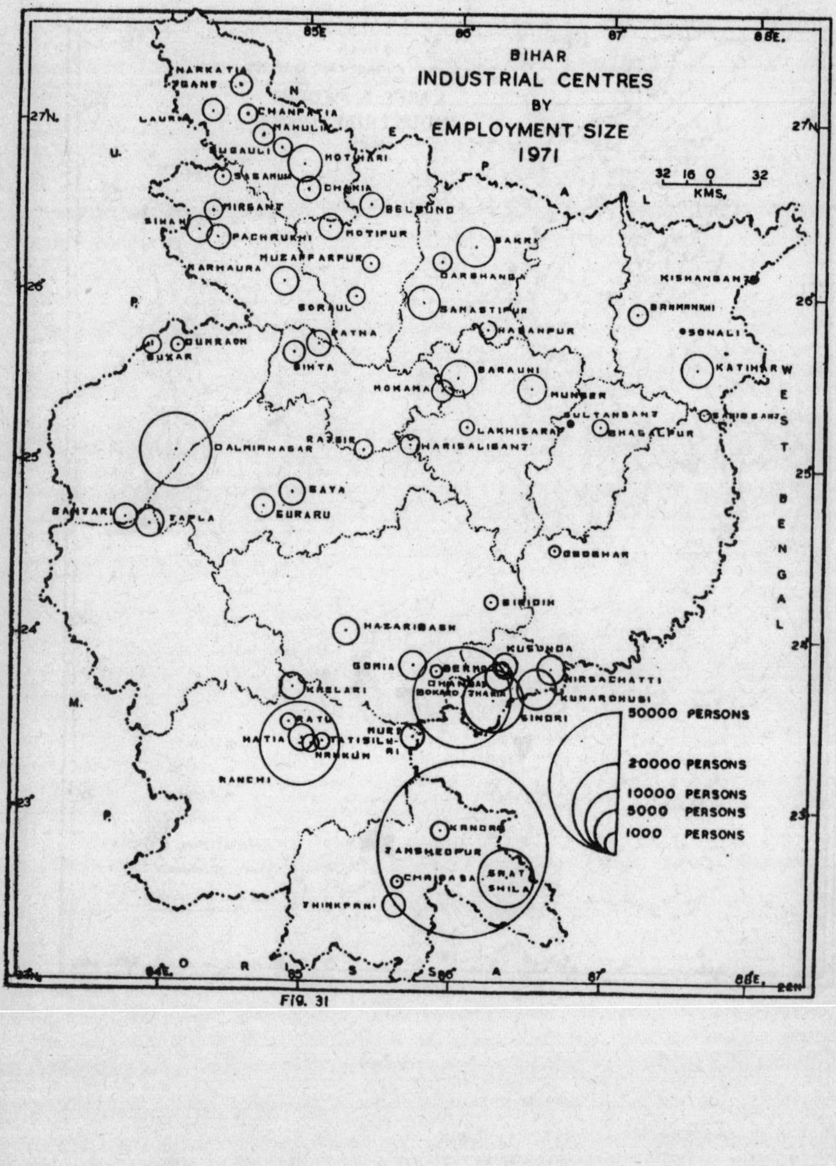
BIHAR
INDUSTRIAL CENTRES
BY
EMPLOYMENT SIZE
1971
32 16 0 32
KMS.
50000 PERSONS
20000 PERSONS
10000 PERSONS
5000 PERSONS
1000 PERSONS
WEST BENGAL
CHANPATIA
MOTIHARI
BELSUND
MUZAFFARPUR
SAMASTIPUR
PATNA
BIHTA
DUMRAON
BUXAR
DALMIANAGAR
GAYA
GURARU
BARAUNI
MOKAMA
MUNGER
LAKHISARAI
SULTANGANJ
BHAGALPUR
KATIHAR
DEOGHAR
GIRIDIH
HAZARIBAGH
KUSUNDA
SINDRI
RANCHI
HATIA
JAMSHEDPUR
CHAIBASA
THINKPANI

FIG. 31

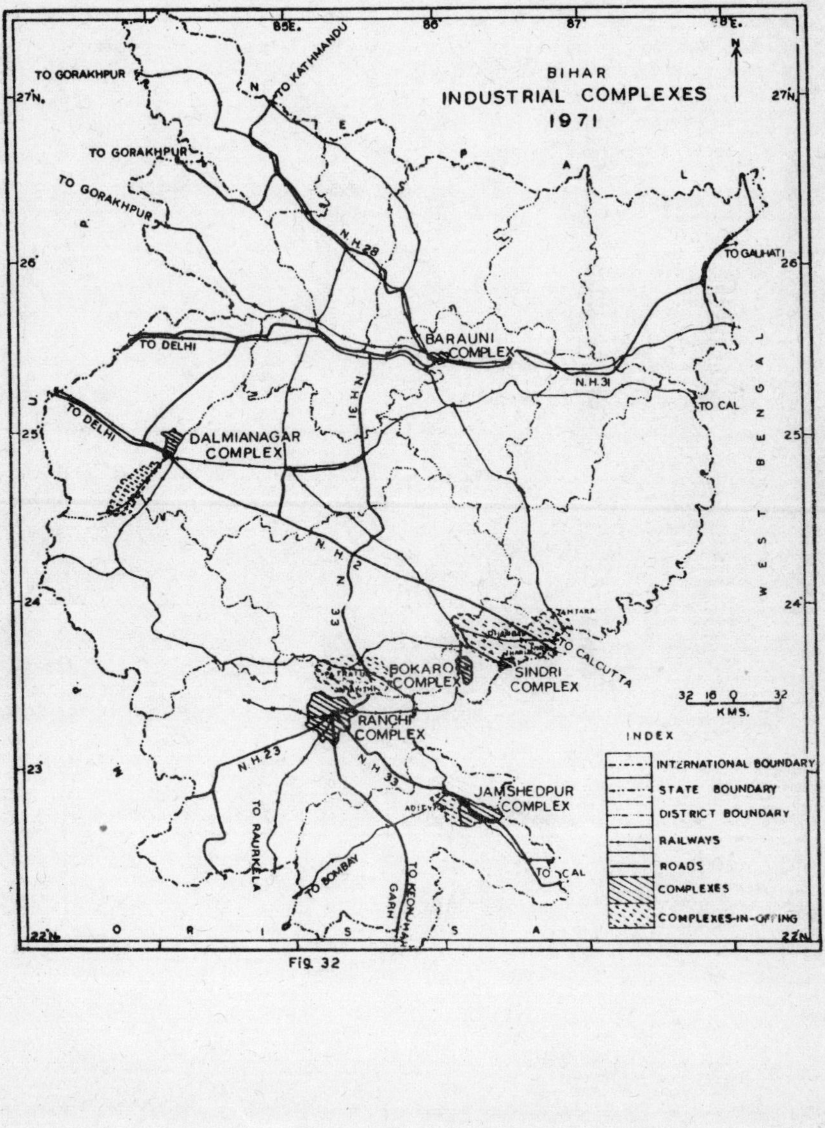
BIHAR
INDUSTRIAL COMPLEXES
1971
TO GORAKHPUR
TO GORAKHPUR
TO GORAKHPUR
TO KATHMANDU
N E P A L
N.H.28
TO GAUHATI
BARAUNI
COMPLEX
TO DELHI
TO DELHI
N.H.31
N.H.31
TO CAL
DALMIANAGAR
COMPLEX
W E S T B E N G A L
N.H.2
N.H.33
BOKARO
COMPLEX
SINDRI
COMPLEX
TO CALCUTTA
RANCHI
COMPLEX
N.H.23
N.H.33
JAMSHEDPUR
COMPLEX
TO RAURKELA
TO BOMBAY
TO KEONJHAR GARH
TO CAL
O R I S S A
KMS.
INDEX
INTERNATIONAL BOUNDARY
STATE BOUNDARY
DISTRICT BOUNDARY
RAILWAYS
ROADS
COMPLEXES
COMPLEXES-IN-OFFING

Fig. 32

TABLE 3.21 (*contd.*)

1	2	3	4
Bhagalpur	1. Bhagalpur	5	609
	2. Sultanganj	2	100
	Total	7	709
Munger	1. Barauni	5	2,371
	2. Munger	3	2,172
	3. Lakhisarai	1	422
	Total	9	5,825
Saharsa		—NIL—	
Purnea	1. Sonali (Purnea)	1	30
	2. Kisanganj	1	50
	3. Katihar	2	2,604
	Total	4	2,684
Santhal Parganas	1. Deoghar	1	350
	2. Sahebganj	4	250
	Total	5	600
Champaran	1. Mahaulia	1	1,000
	2. Chakia	1	1,123
	3. Chanpatia	1	908
	4. Narkatiaganj	2	1,033
	5. Narayanpur	1	900
	6. Sugauli	1	833
	7. Motihari	3	3,151
	Total	10	8,948
Singhbhum	1. Jamshedpur	25	74,878
	2. Ghatshila	4	8,400
	3. Jhinkpani	1	1,217
	4. Kandra	1	815
	5. Chaibasa	1	250
	Total	32	85,560
Hazaribagh	1. Giridih	1	423
	2. Gomia	1	1,910
	3. Hazaribagh	5	1,650
	4. Bermo	1	250
	Total	8	4,233

TABLE 3.21 (*contd.*)

1	2	3	4
Ranchi	1. Ranchi	3	1,700
	2. Hatia	7	16,000
	3. Namkum	1	800
	4. Ratu	1	622
	5. Tatisilwai	1	600
	6. Muri	1	1,200
	7. Khalari	1	1,541
	Total	15	22,503
Dhanbad	1. Sindri	7	9,338
	2. Jharia	6	1,935
	3. Dhanbad	6	1,509
	4. Kumardhubi	5	3,894
	5. Nirsachatti	4	2,000
	6. Bokaro	5	25,000
	7. Kusunda	3	500
	Total	44	48,342
Palamau	1. Japla	2	1,796

Source : Industrial Directory of Bihar, 1973, pp. 6-36.

demarcated. Jamshedpur in Singhbhum district, Dalmianagar in Shahabad district, Hatia in Ranchi district, Sindri, Jharia, Dhanbad, Kumardhubi and Bokaro Steel City in Dhanbad district, Barauni in Monghyr district, Bhagalpur in Bhagalpur district are industrial centres where clustering of industrial units are pronounced. Other centres are characterised by single industrial unit. They are located on principle of industrial location in isolation. They have not developed linkage among themselves and therefore, these centres are not discussed here.

The correlation of two series of maps, one based on the workers employed and the other based on industrial units provides some common results. The anchals of high concentration are also the regions of greater number of industrial units. For example, Golmuri, Namkum, Chas, anchals of Dhanbad district; Dehri and others are regions of greater agglomeration of industries centred at Jamshedpur, Hatia, Bokaro Steel City, Sindri, Kumardhubi and Dalmianagar respectively. Therefore, these centres are the only centres of industrial agglomerations (Table 3.22).

Delimitation of an industrial complex

The delimitation of industrial complex is an important aspect of this study which comes next after the delimitation of manufacturing regions. It is important to emphasize the definition of an industrial complex as "a set of activities occurring at a given location and belonging to a group of (sub-system) activities, which are subject to important production, marketing or other inter-relations".[33] This definition states three most important characteristics of an industrial complex. These are : (a) a set of industries belonging to a group of activities, (b) there should be inter-relationships or linkages or interdependency among the units and (c) geographical proximity on these parameters, the manufacturing regions and their industrial establishments are already demarcated.

Table 3.22 shows the structure of important industrial centres of the state with their nucleus units and also their essential nature of production. This justifies the three parameters essential for an industrial complex.

The first characteristic that an industrial complex must have a set of industries becomes clear. The iron and steel industry, fertilizer industries, oil refinery and heavy engineering come to this group. Iron and steel industry is a set of so many subsystems of production forming a complex in itself. The similar is the case with fertilizers and oil refineries and also with engineering industries. Therefore, the industrial centres of iron and steel, engineering, fertilizer and refinery, for example, Jamshedpur, Bokaro Steel City, Hatia, Sindri and Barauni qualify as industrial complexes. No other centres from a set. Dalmianagar also presents a set of activities. For example, limestone is converted into lime, lime is used in cement factories and in other chemical industries. Again from cement, asbestus cement, and other cement products like hume pipes etc.; are manufactured. 'Bagasse' the waste product of sugar industry is used in paper and pulp factories. From paper several card-boards and other packing papers are manufactured. All this proves a set of activities but not as strong as in the case of iron and steel and fertilizers. Moreover, Jharia to Ramgarh and Patratu, coal activities in the form of coal mining and coal washeries

TABLE 3.22 : **Structure of important industrial centres, 1971**

Name of the centre	Location in anchal & district	Year of establishment	Number of units	Nucleus plant	Total labour employed	Production stems	Total areal expansion in kms
1	2	3	4	5	6	7	8
Jamshedpur	Golmuri, (Singhbhum)	1907	25	TISCO	75,000	Metallurgical Goods	64 sq. kms.
Ranchi	Namkum, Ratu & Kanke, (Ranchi)	1958	13	HEC	25,000	Heavy Engineering	200 sq. kms.
Sindri	—Sindri, Dhanbad	1947	7	The Indian Fertilizers and Chemicals Ltd.	10,000	Fertilizer and Cement	12 sq. kms.
Kumardhubi	Kumardhubi-Nirsachatti, (Dhanbad)	1917	5	Kumardhubi Engineering Works.	4,000	Engineering Goods	5 sq. kms.
Dhanbad	Dhanbad	—	6	Various	1,500	Fireclay, Potteries	5 sq. kms.
Jharia	(Dhanbad)	—	6	Hindustan Mallable	2,000	Coal and Coal based Products	8 sq. kms.
Hazaribagh	Hazaribagh	—	5	Indian Fire works Insulators	1,600	Refractories	—

(*Contd.*)

TABLE 3.22 : (*Contd.*)

1	2	3	4	5	6	7	8
Bokaro Steel City	(Dhanbad)	1965-69	8	Iron and Steel Products	20,000	Steel and Steel Products	40 sq. kms.
Dalmianagar	Dehri (Shahabad)	1933	12	Rohtas Industries, Ltd.	12,000	Cement, Sugar, Paper, Chemicals, etc.	8 sq. kms.
Patna Town	(Patna)	—	8	—	15,000	Various	20 sq. kms.
Barauni	(Mugulsarai) (Monghyr)	1964	5	Indian Oil Refinery	3,500	Oil and Fertilizer	30 sq. kms.
Jamalpur	(Monghyr)	1862	3	Railway workshop	2,400	—	5 sq. kms.
Bhagalpur	(Bhagalpur)	—	5	Silk industries	500	Tasar Silk	—
Maraurah	(Saran)	1904	3	Sugar mill	2,000	Sugar	3 sq. kms.

Source : Compiled by the author.

have developed forming a coal-complex. But no industrial centre is credited to be called a complex because no set of industries are visible. In the future several chemical fertilizer and cement industries are yet to develop. Therefore, Jharia to Ramgarh and Patratu are industrial complex in offing. Nawhatta and Rohtas where Pyrites are mined at Amjhore, the industrial activities based on pyrites are yet to develop and, therefore, this is also an industrial complex in offing.

An industrial complex is best adjudged on the basis of linkage phenomena. But it is regretted that due to non-availability of data on linkages, the study is seriously handicapped. Only the generalised discussions are set forth.

Jamshedpur has the highest number of large and medium units in its close proximity. The Tata Iron and Steel Co., Ltd. (TISCO) is the nucleus plant which provides iron and steel and other structurals as raw materials for other ancilleries. These units produce engineering goods, vehicles and other structurals which are oftenly required by the mother plant. All these units in close association with TISCO form a large iron steel and other steel produce-consumption centres of the region.

Bokaro Steel Centre also contains several units and other ancilleries are yet to come. This is the most recent enterprise and, therefore, other infra-structures are still in offing.

H.E.C. at Hatia is a giant engineering enterprise where three main parts of one body exist on principle of coexistence. The similar is the case with Sindri, Barauni and Dalmianagar. Dalmianagar is the best industrial complex which has developed on the basis of interdependence. Twelve units are closely interlinked on the input-output matrix.

Kumardhubi, Nirsachatti, Jharia, Dhadbad, Jamalpur and other centres are the centres of industrial units. These units are developing in isolation based on the utilisation of various raw materials readily available. No linkage phenomenon has developed and, therefore, they are not considered as industrial complex.

From the above discussion it, therefore, emerges that there are only six industrial complexes in Bihar. These complexes are the following:

1. The Jamshedpur Complex in Singhbhum district.

2. The Ranchi Complex (Hatia) in Ranchi district.
3. The Bokaro Complex in Dhanbad district.
4. The Sindri Complex in Dhanbad district.
5. The Dalmianagar complex in Shahabad district.
6. The Barauni Complex in Monghyr district.

Besides these, Kumardhubi to Nirsachatti, Jharia-Dhanbad-Katras, Ramgarh, Patratu and Amjhore near Rohtas are the industrial regions where industrial complexes are in offing (Fig. 32).

Mukherjee[34] pointed out five complexes in Chotanagpur, for example, Dehri-Amjhore Complex, Ramgarh-Patratu Complex, Bokaro Complex, Ranchi Complex and Jamshedpur-Adityapur Complex. She attempted to establish these complexes on the basis of their material and product linkages. She, however, overstressed the industrial interactions in Ramgarh-Patratu Complex and Dehri-Amjhore Complex which according to her has the greatest spatial dimension. But certainly she has ignored other testing parameters like "a set of activities". These set of activities related to coal and coal chemicals are yet to come. Again she has understressed Sindri as a complex where an apparent linkage phenomena exists between fertilizer plant and cement plant located in close proximity.

This author[35] in previous studies demarcated six industrial complexes in Bihar on the basis of units clustered at a given location. This also corroborates the present result.

REFERENCES

1. Das, B.L. (1971), *Census Atlas, Census of India*, 1971, Bihar, Series 4, Part IX, pp. 172-178.
2. Industrial Directory of Bihar, Patna, 1973, pp. 6-36.
3. Prasad, J.M. (1976), "Sick Sugar Industry of Bihar", *The Indian Nation*, Patna, April, 18, p. 4.
4. *The Bihar Information*, Patna, January 26, 1974, p. 50.
5. *Tata Steel, Change and Response* (1981), Calcutta, p. 12.
6. *From Ore to Steel at Bokaro*, Bokaro, 1980, p. 17.
7. *Industrial Directory of Bihar*, Patna, 1973, p. 84.
8. *Industrial Directory of Bihar*, Patna, 1973, pp. 10-36.

9. Sinha, R.P. (1974), "Development of Industries in Bihar : Achievements and Prospects", *Bihar Information*, Jan. 26, p. 45.

10. *Industrial Directory of Bihar*, Patna, 1973, p. 32.

11. *Industrial Directory of Bihar*, Patna, 1973, p. 31.

12. Pounds, N.J.G. (1951), "Rurh Area : A Problem in Definition", *Geography*, Vol. 36.

13. Buchanan, R.O. (1959), "Some Reflections on Agricultural Geography", *Geography*.

14. Jarrett, H.R. (1977), A Geography of Manufacturing, op. cit., p. 147.

15. Miller, E.W. (1962), "*A Geography of Manufacturing*" Prentice Hall, London, pp. 13-16.

16. De Geer, Steem (1927), "The American Manufacturing Belt", *Geografiska Annaler*, 4, pp. 233-259.

17. Wright, Alfred, J. (1938), "Manufacturing Districts of the United States", *Economic Geography*, 14, pp. 195-200.

18. Strong, H. (1937), "Regions of Manufacturing Intensity in the United States", *Annals of the Association of American Geographers*, 27, pp. 23-43.

19. Jones, C.F. (1938), "Areal Distribution of Manufacturing in the United States", *Economic Geography*, 14, pp. 217-222.

20. Hartshorne, R. (1936), "A New Map of Manufacturing Belt of North America", *Economic Geagraphy*, 12, pp. 45-53.

21. Thompson, J.H. (1955), "A New Method for Measuring Manufacturing", *Annals of the Association of American Geographers*, 45, pp. 416-436.

22. Alexander, J.W. (1977), *Economic Geography*, Prentice Hall of India, New Delhi, pp. 404-426.

23. Karan, P.P. and Jenkins, W.M. (1959), "Geography of Manufacturing in India", *Economic Geography*, Vol. 35.

24. Karan, P.P. (1964), "Changes in Indian Industrial Location", *Annals of the Association of American Geographers*, Vol. 54, pp. 336-54.

25. Sinha, B.N. (1972), *Industrial Geography of India*, Calcutta, p. 19.

26. Mandal, B. (1971), "Manufacturing Regions of North Bihar", *The National Geographical Journal of India*, Varanasi, [Vol. XVII, Part I, pp. 50-62.

27. Census 1971, District Census Handbook, Bihar Series 4, Part X-B (Other than Household Industry Vb).

28. Florance, S. (1948), *Investment Location and Size of Plant*, op. cit., p. 34.

29. Alexander, J.W. (1977), *Economic Geography*, op. cit., p. 406.

30. Mahmood, A. (1977), *Statistical Methods in Geographical Studies*, Rajesh Publications, New Delhi, p. 104.

31. *Census Atlas*, *Census of India*, 1971, Bihar, Series 4, Part IX, p. 178.

32. Gupta, N.S. and Singh, A. (1978), *Industrial Economy of India*, New Delhi, p. 31.

33. Isard, W. (1960), op. cit.

34. Mukherjee, M. (1970), "Aspects of Recent Industrialisation in Chotanagpur", *The National Geographical Journal of India*, Vol. 16, pp. 101-109.

35. Singh, R P. (1980), "Industrial Complexes of Bihar", *The Geographical Review of India*, Vol. 42, pp. 229-237.

4

REGIONAL CHARACTERISTICS OF INDUSTRIAL COMPLEXES

A GEOGRAPHER is interested primarily in three aspects of manufacturing, that is, its pattern of distribution, its relationships to other elements (physical, economic and cultural) within its region of location, and its relationships to other regions.[1] The relationships both within the region of location and with other regions are observable in terms of physical setting and regional setting. The former is associated with the natural phenomena, necessarily not the result of man's doing. This includes site and situation, surface configuration, climatic conditions, raw materials and power resources, etc. The regional setting, on the other hand, is associated with the cultural elements resulting from man's activities, e.g., markets, labour supply and means of transportation, etc.

The first aspect, that is, the distributional pattern of industries of Bihar has already been discussed in the previous chapter. On the basis of some selected parameters six industrial complexes were also identified. These are Jamshedpur, Ranchi, Sindri, Bokaro, Dalmianagar and Barauni complexes. This chapter, however, attempts to analyse the regional characteristics of each complex,[2] and to establish their types and character in relation to regional perspectives. Finally zones of influence are demarcated on the basis of raw materials, labour supply (unskilled) and markets to affix the intra-regional (local), sub-regional (state level), inter-regional (national) and extra-regional (international) character of the complexes. This is done to prove the relationship within its region of location and its relationships to other regions.

JAMSHEDPUR COMPLEX

Jamshedpur (4,38,781)[3], the premier Steel city of India, is among the largest iron and steel producing centres of the world. The present township expanded around a single integrated industry—iron and steel, and a number of other heavy, medium and light industries, which made the centre one of the biggest industrial complexes of the country with more than twenty-five industrial units and above 1,00,000 workers. Administratively, Jamshedpur is the headquarters of Dhalbhum subdivision and Singhbhum district. It has a very high concentration of population in the eastern region of the country, next to that of Calcutta, Patna and Ranchi.

Geographically, Jamshedpur extends between 22°44′45″ N. to 22°50′15″ N. Lat., and 86°9′0″ E. to 86°16′30″ E. Longitudes. Thereby, it falls under the Tropics of Cancer limit, exhibiting all tropical climatic character with higher temperature (44°C maximum-May, 8.8°C minimum-January) and good rainfall (between 1200-1400 mm.). However, it is in the modified form due to its hilly character.

Jamshedpur occupies an attractive site at the confluence of the Subarnarekha and the Kharkai rivers. Its situation in the middle of the rugged terrain of south-eastern Chotanagpur Plateau of Bihar adds natural beauties. The landscape is undulating. The increase in elevation is more apparent in the north where the Dalma Hills rise up to 3036′. The terrain slopes down in east and towards south-east directions along with the flow of the master stream, the Subarnarekha. The valley slightly flattens there with a general height of 532′ above the sea level, (Fig. 33).

Geologically, Jamshedpur belongs to a region which is characterised by its distinctive richness in metallic mineral deposits. It is a part of the Singhbhum anticlinorium of the pre-cambrian period which has been reduced today to a peneplain. A traverse along the Subarnarekha valley from west to east, shows the abundance of hornblende schists closely interbedded with mica-schist plain upto Ghatsila. The soils vary from eroded scarp soil in the east to heterogeneous soil and red soil in the west.[4]

Jamshedpur is an unique creation of both the Nature and the man. Nature has provided ample raw materials, power and other resources. Man has been tapping them with the help of advanced technology. This has led to the location of heavy industry and its associated manufacturing activities. The 130-160 kms. radius area from the city of Jamshedpur contains the huge iron-ore, manganese ore, copper ore, limestone, dolomite, coking coal and refractories. These huge resources can feed Jamshedpur industries for centuries to come in addition to their supply to other industries of the region.[5]

Tatanagar, the main railway junction of Jamshedpur is located at the Calcutta-Bombay main railway line, connects the two giant consumers of steel and steel products in the country. It is located about 1550 km. from Delhi, 1700 km. from Bombay, 1580 km. from Madras, 250 km. from Calcutta and 480 km. from Patna. Moreover, Ranchi, Dhanbad, Asansol, Kharagpur, Nagpur and several other industrial and urban centres are directly connected with Jamshedpur (Fig. 34).

Similarly the road transportation has well knitted the vicinity of Jamshedpur and has become complementary to railways. The centre is mainly served by the National Highway No. 32 and 33.

The geographical closeness of Calcutta as the largest market of steel and steel products and the greatest canurbation and the biggest port for in and out transhipments has credited a number of advantages to Jamshedpur.

Thus, all the essential factors like raw materials, market, labour force, transportation facilities and other varied richness of the surroundings have made the centre aptly suitable for steel production. But primarily it is a raw material oriented centre where all the necessary raw materials like coking coal, iron-ore, manganese, limestone, dolomite, fireclay etc. are obtainable within a circumference of less than 200 km. " . . . . Jamshedpur is representative of a location which is central in relation to coking coal and iron-ore as well as other raw materials, though at the same time it is indicative of a shift towards ore, ..."[6] From the south-west direction iron-ore moves from Noamundi (company's largest supplier), Gurumahisani, Badampahar, Sulaipat and Joda; manganese-ore from Joda mines (Keonjhar); limestone from Hatibari, Birmitrapur and Gangpur; dolomite from Panpash and Gomardih; and fireclay from Belpahar. Likewise, from the north-west direction coking coal is supplied from Jharia and west Bokaro and washed coal from Jamadeba and west Bokaro coal washeries (Table 4.1).

TABLE 4.1 : **Annual requirements and sources of principal materials used at Jamshedpur, 1972**

Source of supply	Annual requirement	Approximate distance from Jamshedpur km.
1	2	3
Raw materials		
(a) Coal	2.5 million tonnes	188.29
(i) Jamadaba		
(ii) Sizua		
(iii) Malkera		
(iv) Bhelaland		
(v) Chaitodih		
(b) Iron ore	2.6 million tonnes	
(i) Noamundi		130
(ii) Gurumahisani		145
(iii) Badampahar		153
(iv) Joda		160
(c) Manganese ore		
(i) Joda	90,000 tonnes	160
(d) Limestone	0.6 million tonnes	
(i) Birmitrapur		189
(ii) Hatibari		
(e) Dolomite	0.3 million tonnes	
(i) Panposh		169
(ii) Gomardih		192

1	2	4
Water		
(i) Dimna Lake (ii) Subarnarekha river.	8030 million gallons for plants only	12
Power		
Own captive thermal power plant and D.V.C.	88 million watts	—

Source : Baby, J. (1972), "Development of Iron and Steel Industry in India", unpublished Ph.D. Thesis, Calcutta University, Calcutta, p. 48.

To bring together, coal, iron-ore and flux necessary to make one ton of big iron, Jamshedpur requires 534 ton-kms. against 966 ton-kms. of Pittsburgh, 1658 ton-kms. for Gary and 2403 ton-kms. in Fontana in the U.S.A. Even within the country compared with other steel plants, the location of Jamshedpur (except Bokaro) is the most ideal and economical.[7] Table 4.2 justifies this statement.

TABLE 4.2 : **Cost structure of the movement of raw materials for various steel plants in India (tonne-km. of raw materials moved per tonne of steel ingot)**

Location	Iron-ore	Coal	Lime-stone	Total
TISCO				
Jamshedpur	145	199	190	534
IISCO				
Burnpur	435	60	217	712
Durgapur	477	90	284	851
Rourkela	80	610	130	820
Bhilai	100	1,485	10	1,595
Bokaro	348	30	70	448

Source : M.N. Dastur and Co., August, 1972, p. 38.

It is fact, however, that the pull of raw materials has determined the locational choice at Jamshedpur in the beginning but market and labour supply have never played secondary role. TISCO, being the pioneer steel plant, was the major supplies of iron and steel products in the country till the erection of other steel producing plants under the public sector at Durgapur, Rourkela and Bhilai. Its importance was again affected by Bokaro Steel Plant the most recent one. But still 'Tata Quality' is quite popular in the country. Thus, its market as well as labour supply zones are ever perennial which have made the centre raw material-cum-market oriented location.[8]

The role of water in the site selection at Jamshedpur has never remained a less significant factor. In respect of raw materials and transport facilities any place from Manoharpur to Ghatsila on the Howrah-Nagpur Railway line would have been equally suitable for steel works, but "the superiority of the Jamshedpur site results from the fact that adequate water can be obtained at a point about midway, between the sources of coking coal, iron-ore and flux".[9] The Dimna Lake (about 12 kms. north) a great reservoir of fresh water and the Subarnarekha river are the main sources of water supply for the factories and township. Similarly, 88,000 Kw. of power is met from the adjacent captive thermal power plants. A little power is also supplied from the D.V.C.

The total number on the pay roll of TISCO is nearly 73,000 of which 40,000 are employed in the TISCO plant, while the rest are engaged in the mines and sales offices.[10] Most of the unskilled labour are drawn from the adjacent regions of Bihar, Bengal, Orissa, Madhya Pradesh and Uttar Pradesh. The skilled labour force is of secondary nature coming from far and wide.

Riding on the crest of such a rich natural and regional environs, Jamshedpur commands excellent potentialities for further industrialization. Initially, Jamshedpur's major economic base was the production of steel only. But subsequently along with the steel came a galaxy of other large, medium and small industries huddled within a territory of 64 sq. kms., where TISCO 'the locus',[11] has acted as the 'mother plant' providing all economic and social infra-structures to them. Among these units the Indian Steel and Wire Products Co., the Tin-plate Co. of India, the Humepipe Co., The Indian Cable Co., The Tata Engineering and Locomotive Co., Ltd. (TELCO); the Tata Engineering and Machine Manufacturing Co. (JEMCO), The

Agrico, the Tata Foundary Co. and several others are important. TELCO is the largest and the far-famed unit only next to TISCO. It manufactures nearly 33,000 commercial vehicles, 100 excavators and crawler cranes annually. It is one of the biggest heavy engineering complexes of the country, playing a vital role in the Indian economy by producing a substantial part of the national output of essential goods, and by developing more than 7000 big and small ancillary suppliers on a countrywide basis. It has employed more than 33,000 people directly and generates additional employment for 12 persons for each truck put on the road.[12] The Jemco and the Agrico stand next after TISCO and TELCO in order of importance. These units interlink themselves on the basis of 'input-output model' and thus, provide one of the best examples of 'vertical and horizontal combinations in heavy industries'.[13]

The morphology of township presents a well planned industrial city which expands over 64 sq. kms. in a compact fashion in all directions from the original nucleus of TISCO formed in 1911 (Fig. 36). Jamshedpur is neat, open and uniform with substantial buildings, broad roads, a number of green spots (Jubilee Park, 200 acres), and notable differentiation of functional zones.[14] The principal industrial section covering an area of about 4 kms. is occupied by TISCO with two cooling tanks. The other steel using industries like, Telco, Jemco, Agrico, Tinplate, Indian Cable and wire are located in the eastern portion of the city. The administrative and residential areas are in the north around Sakchi with a rectangular street pattern. The business-marketing section lies in Bistupur, which is traversed by the Sakchi boulevard—the widest urban street in Bihar.[15] On the either side of this road lie the planned Tata's officials bungalows and markets. The length of roads in the city totals to 438 kms.

The city of Jamshedpur is well equipped in many respects—in the standard of its civic services, in its educational and recreational facilities and in its cultural and social lives. Jamshedpur is a highly cosmopolitan city. Since its very inception, people from all parts of India and abroad with their different religious beliefs are working and living together. Even the Adivasi folk with their traditional tribal heritages traverse the whole urban system without any restrictions. Tata steel not only provides them with a secular living but has also taken pains to integrate them into an urban community without any damage to their traditional pattern of living.

Moreover, to avoid congestion in the existing spread of the city several satellite towns, for example, Jugsalai, Mango and Adityapur have been developed leading to the emergence of Greater Jamshedpur. Jugsalai is a small thickly-built residential-cum-commercial area on the south of the railway line. Mango on the north of the steel city across the Subarnarekha river has come into Jamshedpur urban folds only after the new extension of N.H. 33. Adityapur is the name of one of a group of villages on the west of the steel city across the river Kharkai. Until 1960, it was completely cut off from the steel city; but after the completion of a road bridge, this physical barrier was overcome and since then it is treated as a part of Jamshedpur (Fig. 35).

Thus, Jamshedpur establishes a perfect spatial interactions within its region of location and also with other regions of raw materials, markets and labour pool.

RANCHI COMPLEX

Ranchi (4,87,485) with the far farmed H.E.C. (Hatia) and several other industrial units, is a major modern industrial complex of the country. Even from the administrative point of view it holds an important position being the headquarters of Ranchi district and South Chotanagpur Division. It is also the summer capital and second largest town of Bihar only after Patna.[16]

Ranchi is located between 23°23 'N Lat. and 85°23 'E. Long. The Tropic of Cancer passes from its northern side. Its climate is more guided by its altitude which provides a pleasant, healthy and attractive climatic conditions with moderate temperature (23°C mean annual) and rainfall (1400 mm.).

Ranchi occupies the central location in the heart of the Ranchi Plateau, the most important part of the Chotanagpur Highland (Fig. 37). It is a rejuvenated peneplain along with the bounding scarps to the north, east and south. The general elevation ranges from 1800 feet to 2200 feet from the sea level.

The important rivers like the Subarnarekha and its tributaries, e.g. the Hinoo, the Harmu, the Karma, the Jhumar, and other rivers like the Kanchi, the Karo and tributaries of the South Koel radiate from a point of Ranchi-Ladma site forming a radial pattern of drainage.[17] The land slopes down in the eastward and southward directions. Ranchi is a place of tanks where more than 30 tanks of considerable size are scattered in different parts of the town. The largest one is the Ranchi Lake which covers an area of 50 acres. Likewise, there are several residual hillocks, e.g., Ranchi Hill, Morabadi or Tagore Hill and Gonda Hill. They are relics of hard granitic rocks. Gneisses and granites are the basic rocks and minerally these are unimportant. Some chromite and galena occur near Silli and Silwai.

The pattern of industrial location in the Greater Ranchi is influenced by its inherent topographical features. Besides the availability of ample non-agricultural land around Ranchi, the stable land formed of granite and basalt of Precambrian Era is the most suitable for the erection of Heavy Engineering Plants. Moreover, the stable land of Ranchi is quite free from seismic disturbances also.[18]

Water is a great determinant of industrial location in the Chotanagpur. The underground water-table is quite uneven due to faulting and igneous intrusions. Secondly, due to steep slopes the drainage is swift. The site of Ranchi on the Subarnarekha with its tributaries was prompted by this consideration in the initial period of its growth. The site has proved all the more advantages when large industrial plants were located around Ranchi.[19]

The nodal location of Ranchi in respect of rail and road communications has also stimulated industrial growth (Fig. 38). The trunk roads radiate from Ranchi in all directions connecting other industrial and urban centres like Hazaribagh, Bokaro, Dhanbad, Patna, Jamshedpur, Purulia, Chaibasa, Rourkela, Lohardaga and Daltonganj. "It is a typical highway oriented town depending entirely on road transport for both its external and internal interchange".[20] The city has rail communications with Calcutta, Patna, Bombay and Delhi. The Chandrapura-Rourkela railway line passes through Ranchi. This line is meant for carrying coal from Damodar Basin to the steel plants of Rourkela and Bhilai. While coming for coal the wagons are loaded with pig-iron and other steel products for the engineering plants of Ranchi and for Bokaro Steel Plant. This has made the transportation of raw materials very economical.

In regional context, too, Ranchi enjoys a very favourable situation. It is centrally located between the coal fields of the Damodar Basin in the north and mineralised belt of Singhbhum district in the south. Similarly, it is also almost in the middle of all important iron and steel factories of Jamshedpur, Bokaro, Burnpur, Rourkela and Bhilai.[21] This location is advantageous for both Ranchi as well as all the steel producing centres. For example, Bokaro's 70 per cent machines are the product of the H.E.C. Similarly, Bhilai's expansion has been done on the H.E.C.'s equipments. All the powers required for industrial work at Ranchi are supplied from Patratu Thermal Power Station, the Damodar Valley Corporation and the Subarnarekha Hydel Projects.

India is a demand area for heavy machines and tools. The H.E.C., the only heavy machinery supplies enterprize, utilizes the opportunities. If the nation claims to be self-reliant in engineering products, it is only due to H.E.C. A host of important work orders have been complied with—Mishra Dhatu Nigam, Salem Steel Plant (Tamil Nadu), Visakhapatnam Steel Plant (Andhra Pradesh), Bokaro's third sintering plant and 6th Coke Oven Battery, 18 Excavators for Coal India, Rotary Wagon Tippler Complex and Stacker-cum-reclaimer for the Thermal Power Project at Bongaigaon (Assam), Bhilai's four million tonne expansion including the 3600 plate mill, sophisticated drilling machines for oil exploration, materials for shipbuilding industries at Visakhapatnam and Cochin and several others at the national level.[22] Even around the industrial landscape of Ranchi a rich market is available for the H.E.C. All the iron and steel plants, new as well old, fertilizer plants at Sindri for its modernization, setting of chemical complex at Barauni, cement factories in the Damodar and the Son valleys, coal washeries in the coal-belt, coal, iron ore and other mining centres of eastern India, engineering industries of Bihar, Bengal and Orissa require machineries and equipments from the H.E.C.

for construction, addition and replacements.[23] The performance of the H.E.C. on the export front has also been laudable. The H.E.C. has received export orders for more than Rs. 78 crores so far out of which equipments worth over Rs. 28 crores have already been supplied to countries like Yugoslavia, Turkey, Bulgaria, Egypt, Hungary, Sri Lanka, Bangladesh, Cuba, U.S.S.R. etc.[24]

Ranchi complex expands over an area of more than 200 kms and presents a diversified industrial pattern. The industrial undertakings are scattered all sides from the main town along the radiating roads. Hatia, Ratu, Namkum, Tatisilwai and Muri are the important industrial centres with Ranchi as the hub of the activity.[25]

There are about a dozen large and small industrial units, but the HEC is the only largest unit. The Heavy Engineering Corporation Ltd. at Jaganathpur (Hatia) is single integrated engineering complex of its type in the world, where three giant plants, the Heavy Machine Building Plant (HMBP) the Foundary Forge Plant, (FFP) and the Heavy Machine Tool Plant (HMTP) work together on horizontally and vertically linkages basis under a monomighty complex.[26] These plants are indigenous in nature and provide employment for nearly 30,000 working population of various kinds. Other industrial units at Ranchi and its surroundings are of medium-sized and produce varieties of products in response to the regional demands.

The morphology of Ranchi is multi-functional. (Fig.39). Residential, commercial, educational, industrial, administrative and several other types of services have influenced the functional character. The internal structure of the city is closely associated with its road pattern. The hub of the town centres at the convergence point of four main streets, e.g. the Chaibasa road, the Hazaribagh road, the Jail road and the Kanke road.[27] The main retail business is located southwards on the either side of Chaibasa, Hazaribagh and Church roads. The wholesale market is located along the main road in the northern part known as the Upper Bazar. The residences are aligned strictly along the various other streets. The Ranchi University Campus lies in the open Morhabadi Maidan on the north of court. Thus, the city has assumed a characteristic star shape.[28]

The outer marginal part of the township is characterised by sectoral zones covered by military area, industrial area, aerodrome area, etc. Kanke, Ratu, Tati silwai, Doranda Hatia and Jaganathpur are the suburb areas comprising the Greater Ranchi.

The industrial section of Ranchi is divided into two groups, unplanned and planned. The former associated with small scale industries is scattered haphazaradly in the residential, commercial and educational areas. The latter are located in three areas, e.g. Jaganathpur (HEC), the Kokar area and the Namkum-Tatisilwai locality.

The H.E.C. near Hatia is located at Jaganathpur covering an area of about 15 sq. kms. It lies between the Subarnarekha in the south and Hinoo river in the north. The planned township has been emerging with residential rows, markets and heavy industrial plants. This town has metalled roads with 12 to 40 metres of width. The roads run at right angles to each other and are provided with shady trees on either side.

In Kokar area most of the industries are concentrated within a triangle formed by the old Hazaribagh Road and the Ranchi Distillery Industrial area. Industries in this area are more varied from small scale to medium type. Industries like distillery, Hume pipe, small engineering concerns, saw mills, limo and brick clins have developed on account of infrastructural facilities.

The Namkum-Tati silwai area is characterised by sporadic industrial pockets along the Purulia Road. The Insulator Factory, the Usha-Martin Rope-Wire Industry, and Vaux-Pol concern are the main industrial units, which have developed between Purulia Road and the Muri-Ranchi railway line. South of this railway line are located the Vaccine Institute, Lac Research Institute and Glass Factory. A Solar Energy plant is to be established in this area to convert sunlight into electricity first of its kind in the country.[29]

The industrial development has changed the social structure of the city. It has become cosmopolitan city with different nodes of living. Except for a small indigenous aboriginal population, Ranchi has a large external population drawn from South and North Bihar, Bengal, Marwar (Rajasthan), Punjab and other parts of the country. They form their own homogenous colonies, like, Bengali colony, Marwari Tola, Sikh colony and Muslim colonies. The Adivasis, which have now mostly adopted Christianity, occupy the fringes of the urban sprawls. They live in 'tolis' (small settlement), like, Karamtoli, Chutia, Seramtoli, Dangratoli and Kantatoli.

Thus Ranchi complex has displayed a better areal interaction and its relationship within the region and with other regions.

SINDRI COMPLEX

Sindri (70542) is a chief fertilizer town in the country. Its township is the outcome of fertilizer complex, which is the first of its type in the whole country. It was commissioned in October, 1951. This premier plant has given the birth of several ancillery units like cement, coke, triple superphosphate plant, etc., turning whole into a functional combination of industrial complex.

Sindri extends between 23°34′N latitude and 86°30′E longitude. It is located 25 kms. south of Dhanbad in the Dhanbad district along the left bank of river Damodar in the belt of Jharia coal field.

The physical set up of Sindri is complicated one. The land on which it is situated has gone through several processes of evolution in different ages, and each age has left behind some unique features. The topography is quite undulating. The land is rugged and dissected by small nala in the south eastern part. The land rises between 400 to 600 ft. from the sea-level and the land slopes towards south and south-east direction. The rocks are hard, crystalline and metamorphosed. Coal is the only economic resource on which its industrial face has been decorated (Fig. 40). The Damodar river flows from west to east and supplies all required water for industries and township. The climate of the town is very pleasant during winter, but summer is very hot and scorchy. The temperature varies between 26°C in January to 44°C in May. The average annual rainfall is 1250 mm.

The main economic base of the town is its industries, and especially the fertilizer plant. The location of the factory is coal-oriented where pyrites from Amjhore (Rohtas district) and gypsum from Bikaner and Jodhpur mines of Rajasthan move to the centre. In the initial stage the over-riding factor in favour of Sindri was a constant traffic of coal wagons from the Jharia coalfield to upper India which return to the coal-fields empty and which could be economically utilized for bringing gypsum from Rajasthan.[30] For the coal and coke, Jharia and Raniganj coal fields are situated nearby. All the mines are connected with each other by various loops and branches of the Eastern Railway. They are also connected with Sindri, Bejdih, Methani (Raniganj coal-fields), Lodna and Loyabad collieries of the Jharia coal-field. Pyrites from Amjhore move to the centre for Sulphuric acid plant. On this basis several chemical complexes are proposed to set up around Sindri.

It is important to mention that fuel has guided the location of fertilizer factories at Sindri but communication links are also considerable. Sindri lies between the two main railway lines of Eastern Railway bifurcating at Gomoh towards east, one leading to Calcutta via Dhanbad and Asansol and another to Kharagpur via Bankura. Unfortunately, Sindri does not stand on the direct main line although this deficiency had been mitigated by constructing numerous branch lines and roads. At present Sindri is linked with the rest of the region by an all weather good roads known as Dhanbad-Sindri Road on the south-west and Gobindpur-Baliapur Road on the east. A new Highway is under construction which will connect Sindri to Dhanbad on north and then to link National Highway No. 2 (Fig. 41).

Regionally, Sindri sets itself in the midst of Bihar and Bengal, the two agricultural states. For the better efficiency in production fertilizers are of great demand in these states. Naturally, the importance of Sindri becomes most significant. Both these states are the main markets of fertilizer and also the main source of labour supply.

Sindri gets power by the D.V.C.'s sub-station located at Sindri. This sub-station releases 3600 Kw. and is entirely used by factories and its township.

The industrial landscape of Sindri is dominated by the fertilizer plants and its associery cement factory. The fertilizer factory is the biggest one and produces ammonium sulphate, double salt (Nitrate) and Urea. Besides, it produces calcium carbonate (Sludge) as the waste raw material which is used in the cement factory located nearby. The superphosphate factory of Bihar is another unit located on Dhanbad-Sindri Road. Thus, Sindri presents an example of more compact and vertical linkage than horizontal.

The planned township of Sindri is primarily industrial and residential spreading over an area of 8 sq. kms. along the Dhanbad-Sindri Road. The total area occupied under the residential use is 1589 acres which is about 11 per cent of the total town area. The residential areas have been developed by various manufacturing agencies, such as F.C.I., A.C.C. and B.I.T. to provide housing to their employees (Fig. 42).

Industrial land occupies 460 acres which constitutes only 3.1 per cent of the total area. The Fertilizer Factory itself occupies the major chunk of this industrial land.

Educational area is very limited covering only 37 acres of land mostly occupied by Birla Institute of Technology. The land under commercial area includes 22 acres which is a small fraction of the total area. The main reason for this insufficient development is the nearness of Jharia and Dhanbad commercial centres. The further growth of township will be solely dependent on the location of new industries or the expansion of these industrial units for which the area is potentially suitable.[31]

BOKARO COMPLEX

Bokaro Steel City (220,907), a new industrial town of Bihar is located in Dhanbad district at a distance of 260 kms. from Patna and nearly 300 kms. from Calcutta. The Bokaro Steel Plant, the fourth among the integrated steel plants under the public sector, is located at Bokaro Steel City. This plant is a massive enterprise which is to be completed into four phases. Two phases have already been completed, and when completed fully, the plant would be the largest in Asia. This is a monotype steel complex with six blast furnaces (four already started). The city extends between 23°48′N. lat. and 86°2′E. long. and lies in the middle Damodar Valley. The topography is undulating and often interrupted by Gondwana residuals (Fig. 40).

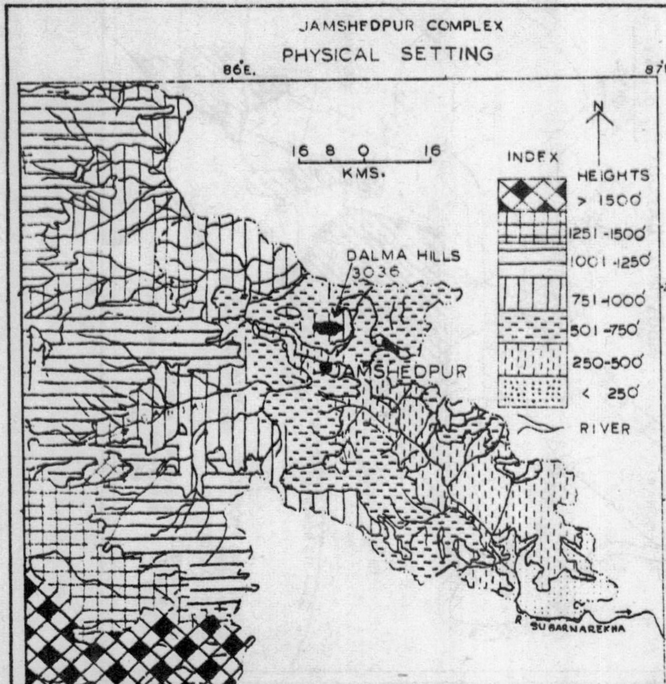
JAMSHEDPUR COMPLEX
PHYSICAL SETTING
86°E.
87°E.
16 8 0 16
KMS.
INDEX
HEIGHTS
> 1500'
1251 -1500'
1001 -1250'
751 -1000'
501 -750'
250-500'
< 250'
RIVER
DALMA HILLS
3036
JAMSHEDPUR
R SUBARNAREKHA
23°
22°N

Fig 33

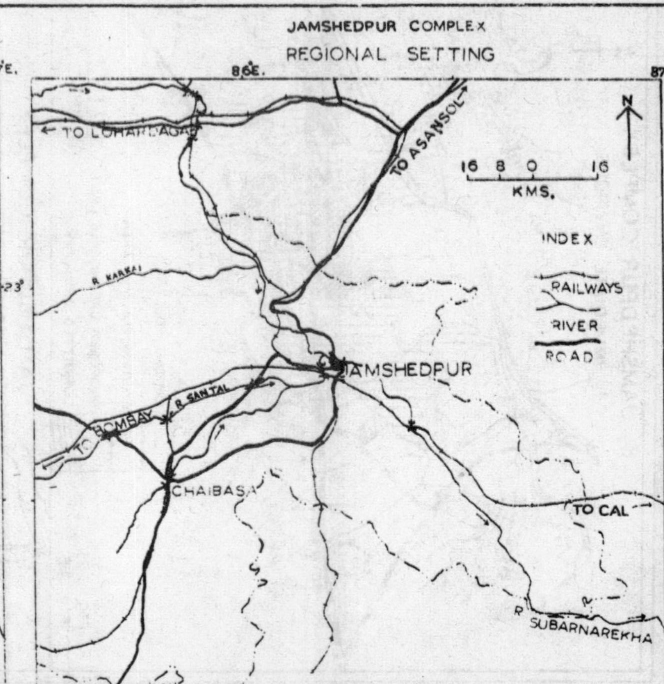
JAMSHEDPUR COMPLEX
REGIONAL SETTING
86°E.
87°
16 8 0 16
KMS.
INDEX
RAILWAYS
RIVER
ROAD
TO LOHARDAGA
TO ASANSOL
R KARKAI
JAMSHEDPUR
R SANJAL
TO BOMBAY
CHAIBASA
TO CAL
R SUBARNAREKHA

Fig. 3·4

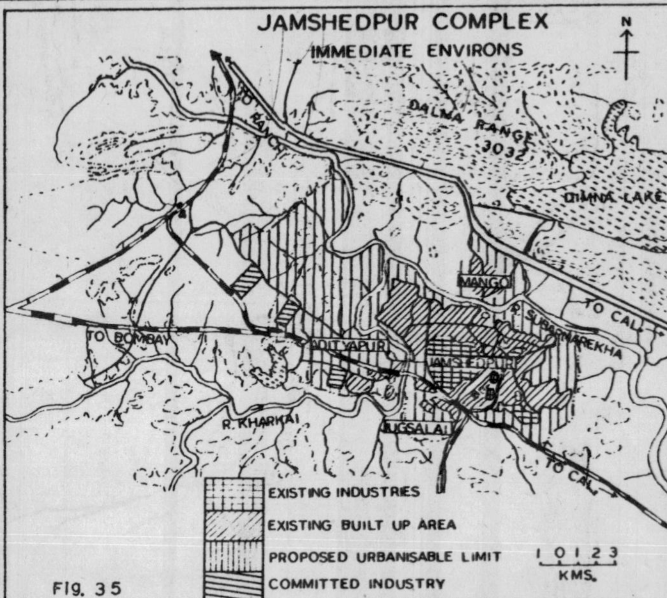
JAMSHEDPUR COMPLEX
IMMEDIATE ENVIRONS
N
DALMA RANGE
3032
TO RANCHI
DIMNA LAKE
MANGO
TO CAL.
R. SUBARNAREKHA
TO BOMBAY
ADITYAPUR
JAMSHEDPUR
R. KHARKAI
JUGSALAI
TO CAL.
EXISTING INDUSTRIES
EXISTING BUILT UP AREA
PROPOSED URBANISABLE LIMIT
COMMITTED INDUSTRY
1 0 1 2 3
KMS.

FIG. 35

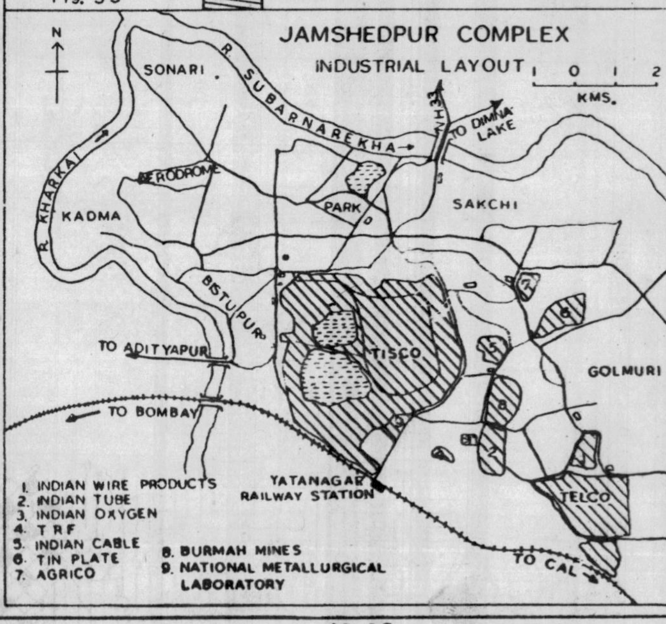
JAMSHEDPUR COMPLEX
INDUSTRIAL LAYOUT
N
1 0 1 2
KMS.
SONARI
R. SUBARNAREKHA
NH 33
TO DIMNA LAKE
R. KHARKAI
AERODROME
KADMA
PARK
SAKCHI
BISTUPUR
TO ADITYAPUR
TISCO
GOLMURI
TO BOMBAY
YATANAGAR RAILWAY STATION
TELCO
TO CAL
1. INDIAN WIRE PRODUCTS
2. INDIAN TUBE
3. INDIAN OXYGEN
4. TRF
5. INDIAN CABLE
6. TIN PLATE
7. AGRICO
8. BURMAH MINES
9. NATIONAL METALLURGICAL LABORATORY

FIG. 36

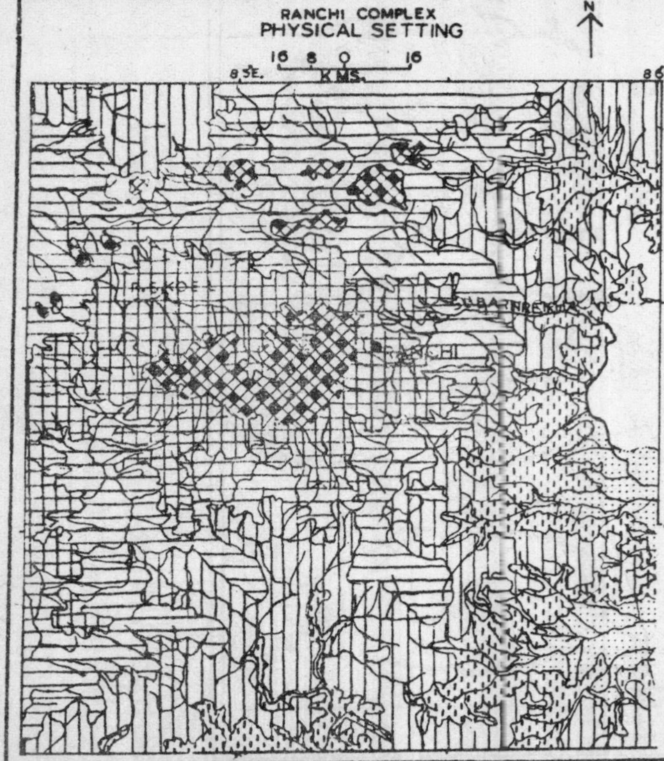
RANCHI COMPLEX
PHYSICAL SETTING
16 8 0 16
KMS.
85E.
86E.
24N.
23N.
R. KOEL
SUBARNREKHA
RANCHI
N

Fig. 37

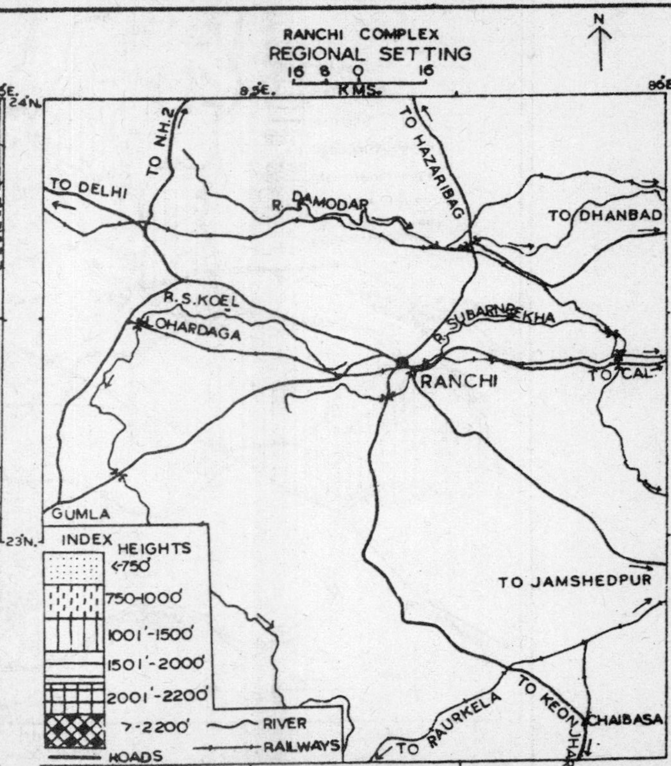
RANCHI COMPLEX
REGIONAL SETTING
16 8 0 16
KMS.
85E.
86E.
N
TO N.H.2
TO DELHI
R. DAMODAR
TO HAZARIBAG
TO DHANBAD
R. S. KOEL
LOHARDAGA
R. SUBARNREKHA
RANCHI
TO CAL.
GUMLA
TO JAMSHEDPUR
TO RAURKELA
TO KEONJHAR
CHAIBASA
INDEX
HEIGHTS
<750'
750-1000'
1001'-1500'
1501'-2000'
2001'-2200'
>2200'
ROADS
RIVER
RAILWAYS

Fig. 38

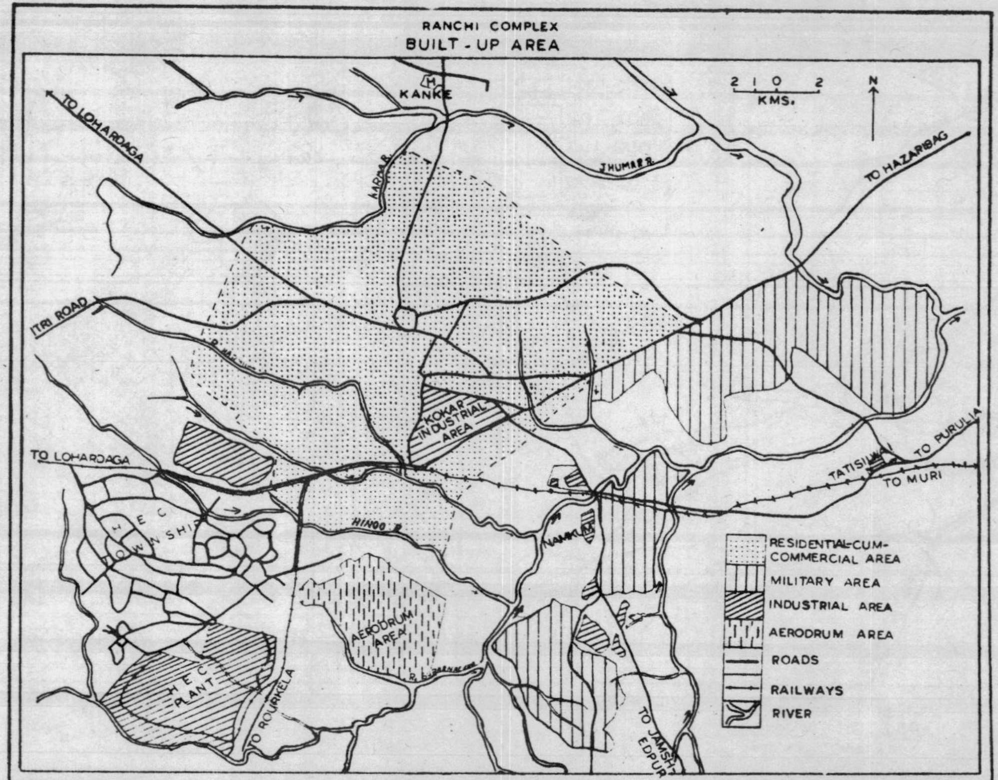
RANCHI COMPLEX
BUILT - UP AREA
2 1 0 2
KMS.
N
KANKE
TO LOHARDAGA
TO HAZARIBAG
JHUMAR R.
ITRI ROAD
KOKAR INDUSTRIAL AREA
TO LOHARDAGA
TATISILWAI
TO PURULIA
TO MURI
HINOO R.
NAMKUM
AERODRUM AREA
H E C TOWNSHIP
H E C PLANT
TO ROURKELA
TO JAMSHEDPUR
RESIDENTIAL-CUM-COMMERCIAL AREA
MILITARY AREA
INDUSTRIAL AREA
AERODRUM AREA
ROADS
RAILWAYS
RIVER

Fig. 39

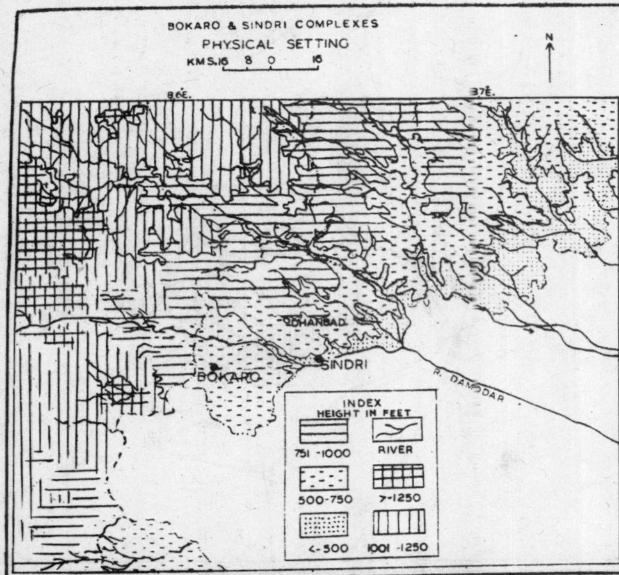

BOKARO & SINDRI COMPLEXES
PHYSICAL SETTING
KMS.16 8 0 16
N
86°E.
87°E.
24°N
23°N
DHANBAD
SINDRI
BOKARO
R. DAMODAR
INDEX
HEIGHT IN FEET
751 -1000
RIVER
500-750
7-1250
<-500
1001 -1250

Fig. 40

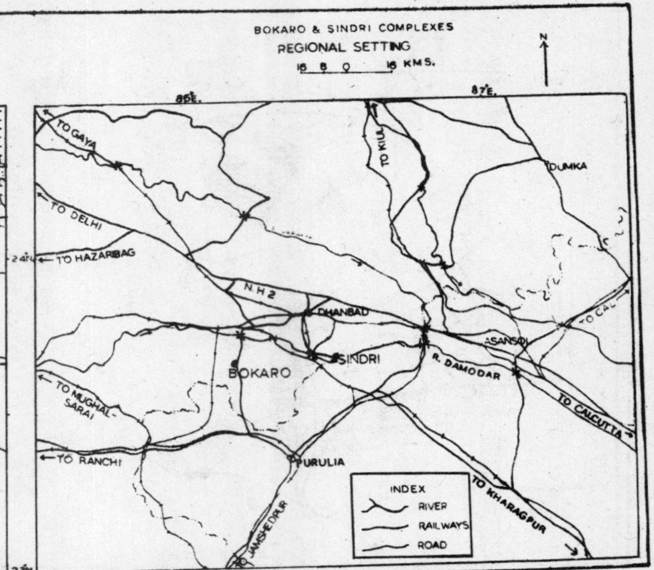

BOKARO & SINDRI COMPLEXES
REGIONAL SETTING
16 8 0 16 KMS.
N
86°E.
87°E.
TO GAYA
TO KIUL
DUMKA
TO DELHI
TO HAZARIBAG
N.H 2
DHANBAD
SINDRI
BOKARO
ASANSOL
TO CAL
R. DAMODAR
TO CALCUTTA
TO MUGHAL-SARAI
TO RANCHI
PURULIA
TO JAMSHEDPUR
TO KHARAGPUR
INDEX
RIVER
RAILWAYS
ROAD

Fig. 41

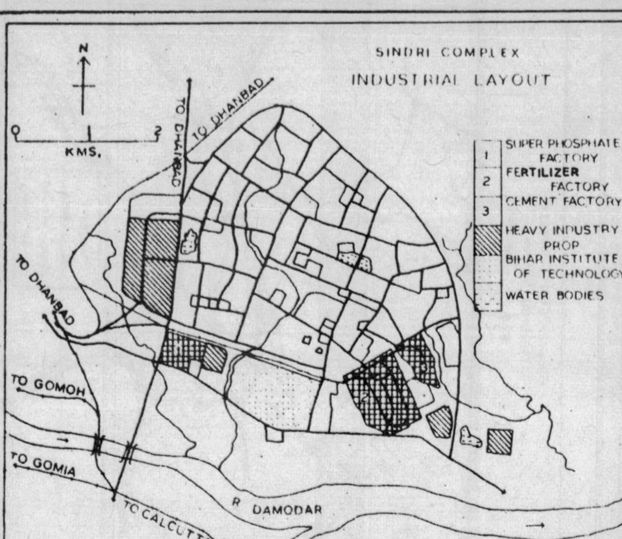
SINDRI COMPLEX
INDUSTRIAL LAYOUT
N
0
1
2
KMS.
TO DHANBAD
TO DHANBAD
TO DHANBAD
TO GOMOH
TO GOMIA
TO CALCUTTA
R. DAMODAR
1 SUPER PHOSPHATE FACTORY
2 FERTILIZER FACTORY
3 CEMENT FACTORY
HEAVY INDUSTRY PROP
BIHAR INSTITUTE OF TECHNOLOGY
WATER BODIES

Fig. 42

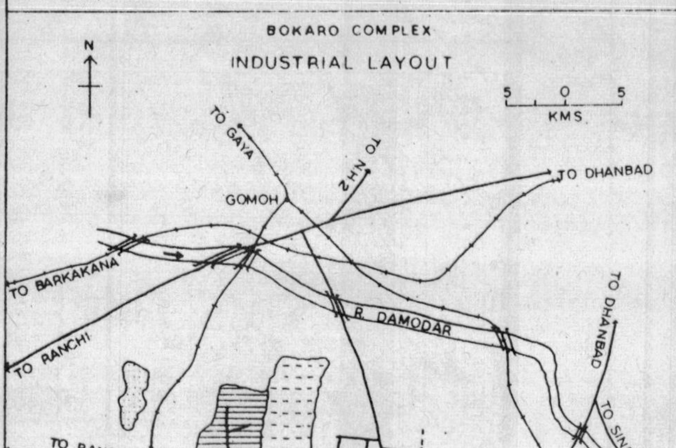
BOKARO COMPLEX
INDUSTRIAL LAYOUT
N
5
0
5
KMS.
TO GAYA
TO N.H.2
TO DHANBAD
GOMOH
TO BARKAKANA
TO RANCHI
R. DAMODAR
TO DHANBAD
TO SINDRI
TO RANCHI
R.S.
B. S. CITY
TO CALCUTTA
CHAS
TO MURI
N.H.32
TO PURULIA
TO PURULIA
TO ADRA
BSP AREA
SITE FOR ANCILLARIES
WATER BODIES

Fig. 43

Fig. 44

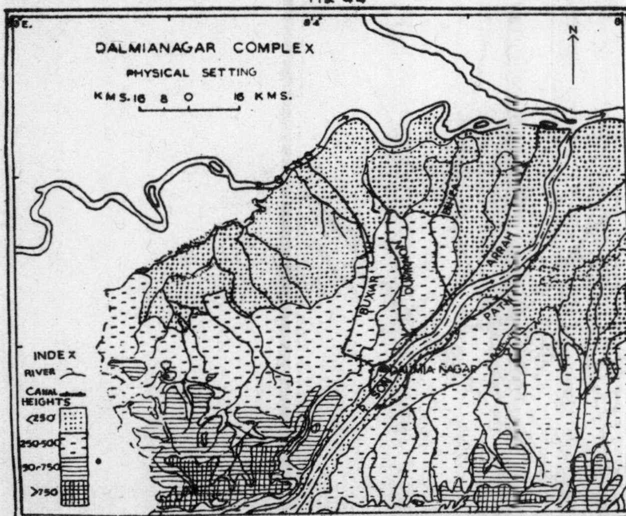
DALMIANAGAR COMPLEX
PHYSICAL SETTING
KMS. 16 8 0 16 KMS.
N
INDEX
RIVER
CANAL
HEIGHTS
<250'
250-500'
500-750'
>750'
BUXAR
DUMRAON
ARRAH
PATNA
SON
DALMIA NAGAR
25°N.

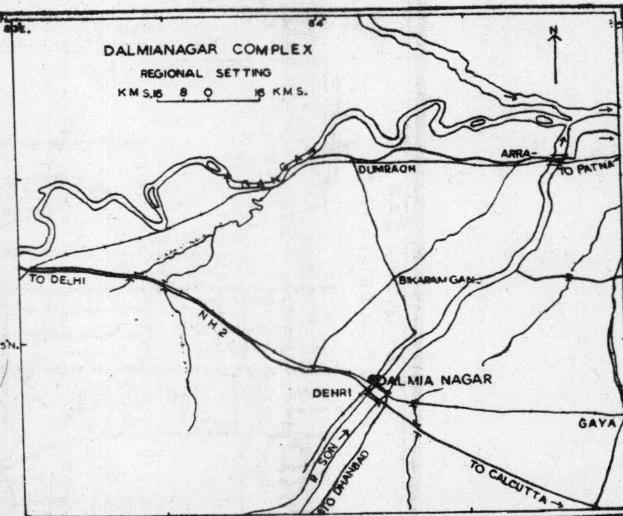
DALMIANAGAR COMPLEX
REGIONAL SETTING
KMS. 16 8 0 16 KMS.
N
DUMRAON
ARRA
TO PATNA
TO DELHI
BIKARAMGANJ
NH 2
DALMIA NAGAR
DEHRI
GAYA
SON
TO DHANBAD
TO CALCUTTA

Fig. 45

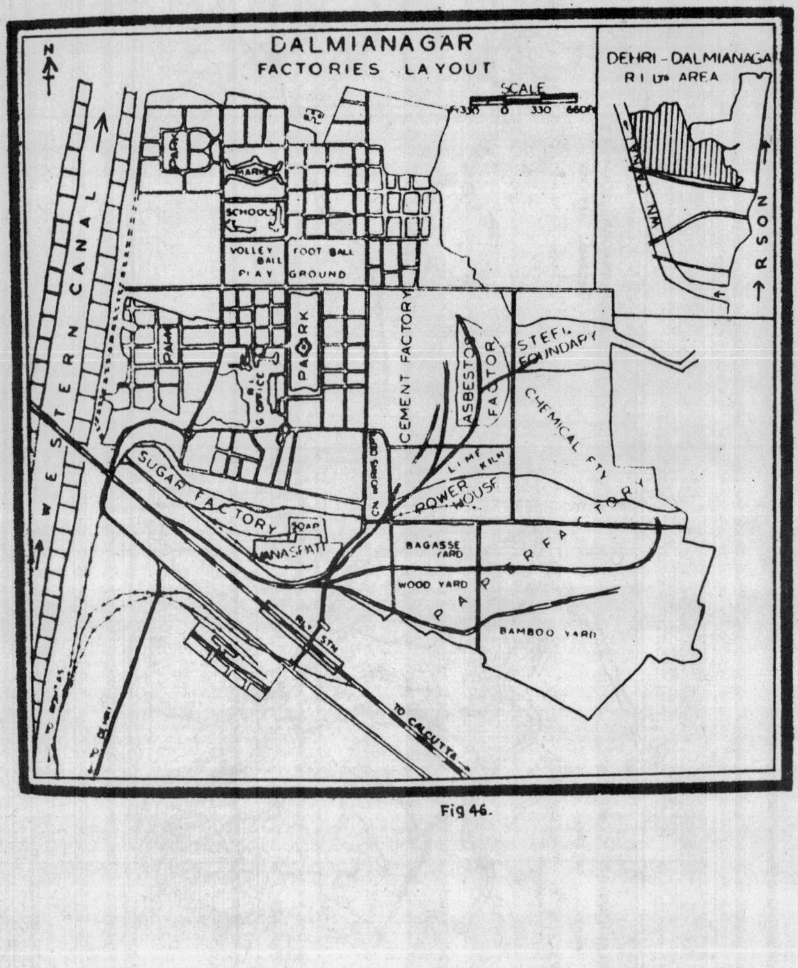
DALMIANAGAR
FACTORIES LAYOUT
SCALE
DEHRI - DALMIANAGAR
WESTERN CANAL
PARK
MARKET
SCHOOLS
VOLLEY BALL
FOOT BALL
PLAY GROUND
PARK
CEMENT FACTORY
ASBESTOS FACTORY
STEEL FOUNDARY
CHEMICAL FTY
SUGAR FACTORY
LIME KILN
POWER HOUSE
SOAP
VANASPATI
BAGASSE YARD
WOOD YARD
PAPER FACTORY
BAMBOO YARD
TO CALCUTTA
R SON
Fig 46.

Fig. 47

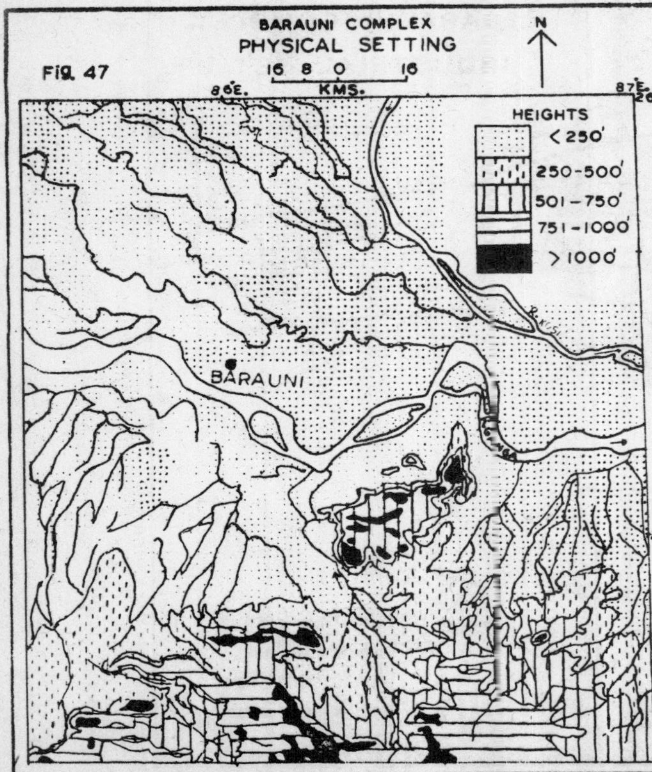
BARAUNI COMPLEX
PHYSICAL SETTING
16 8 0 16
KMS.
N
86°E.
87°E.
26°N.
25°N.
HEIGHTS
< 250'
250-500'
501-750'
751-1000'
> 1000'
BARAUNI
R. KOSI

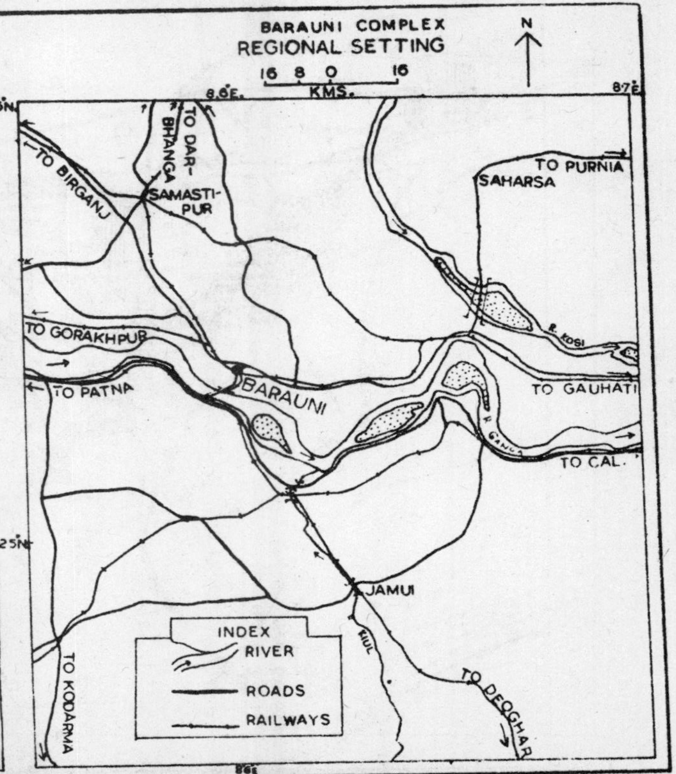
BARAUNI COMPLEX
REGIONAL SETTING
16 8 0 16
KMS.
N
86°E.
87°E.
TO DAR-BHANGA
TO BIRGANJ
SAMASTI-PUR
TO PURNIA
SAHARSA
TO GORAKHPUR
TO PATNA
BARAUNI
R. KOSI
TO GAUHATI
TO CAL.
JAMUI
KIUL
TO KODARMA
TO DEOGHAR
INDEX
RIVER
ROADS
RAILWAYS

Fig. 48

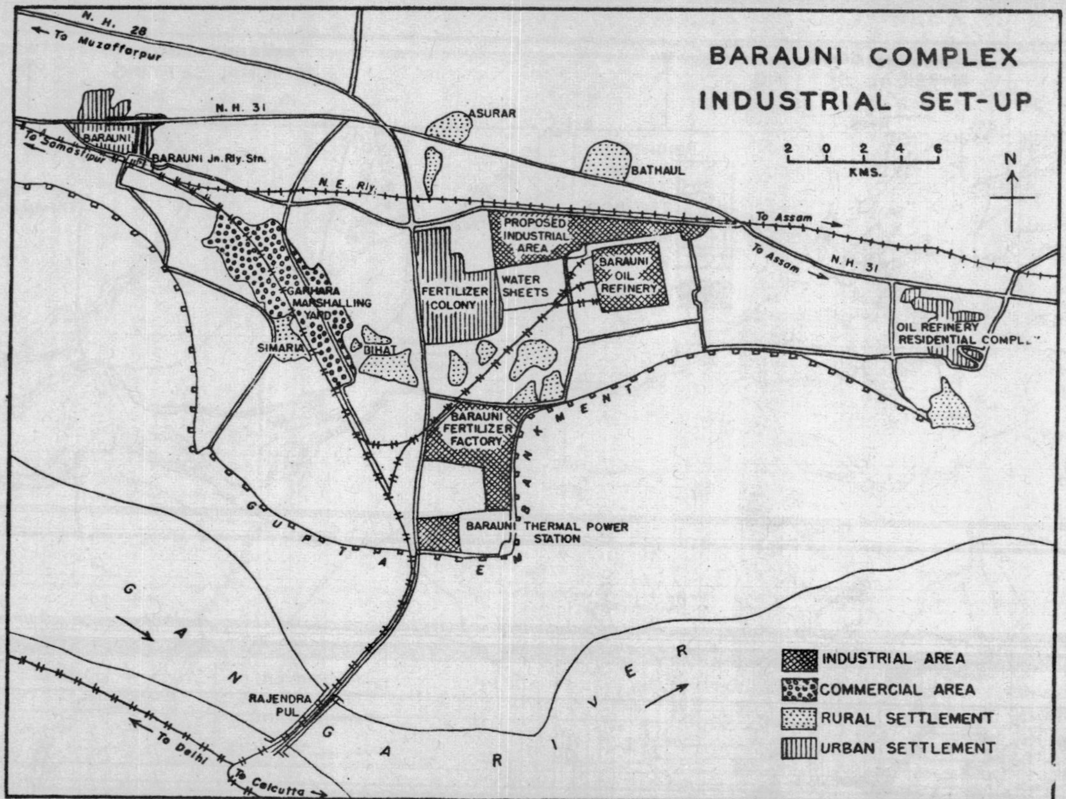
BARAUNI COMPLEX
INDUSTRIAL SET-UP
N. H. 28
To Muzaffarpur
N. H. 31
BARAUNI
To Samastipur
BARAUNI Jn. Rly. Stn.
ASURAR
BATHAUL
2 0 2 4 6
KMS.
N
N. E. Rly.
To Assam
To Assam
N. H. 31
PROPOSED INDUSTRIAL AREA
BARAUNI OIL REFINERY
WATER SHEETS
FERTILIZER COLONY
GARHARA MARSHALLING YARD
SIMARIA
BIHAT
OIL REFINERY RESIDENTIAL COMPL...
BARAUNI FERTILIZER FACTORY
GUPTA EMBANKMENT
BARAUNI THERMAL POWER STATION
GANGA RIVER
RAJENDRA PUL
To Delhi
To Calcutta
INDUSTRIAL AREA
COMMERCIAL AREA
RURAL SETTLEMENT
URBAN SETTLEMENT

FIG. - 49

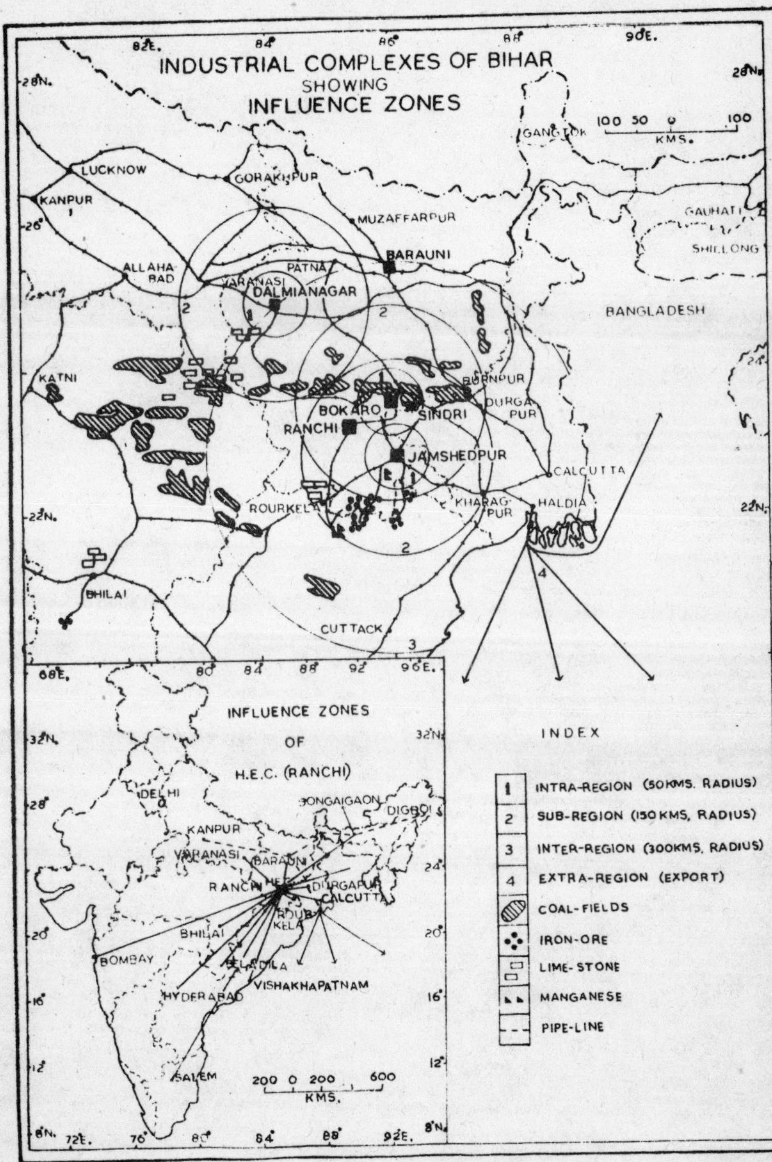

INDUSTRIAL COMPLEXES OF BIHAR
SHOWING
INFLUENCE ZONES
100 50 0 100
KMS.
LUCKNOW
KANPUR
GORAKHPUR
MUZAFFARPUR
GANGTOK
GAUHATI
SHILLONG
ALLAHABAD
VARANASI
PATNA
BARAUNI
DALMIANAGAR
BANGLADESH
KATNI
BURNPUR
DURGAPUR
BOKARO
SINDRI
RANCHI
JAMSHEDPUR
CALCUTTA
ROURKELA
KHARAGPUR
HALDIA
BHILAI
CUTTACK
INFLUENCE ZONES
OF
H.E.C. (RANCHI)
DELHI
KANPUR
VARANASI
BARAUNI
BONGAIGAON
DIGBOI
RANCHI
HEC
DURGAPUR
CALCUTTA
ROURKELA
BHILAI
BOMBAY
BAILADILA
VISHAKHAPATNAM
HYDERABAD
SALEM
200 0 200 600
KMS.
INDEX
1 INTRA-REGION (50KMS. RADIUS)
2 SUB-REGION (150KMS. RADIUS)
3 INTER-REGION (300KMS. RADIUS)
4 EXTRA-REGION (EXPORT)
COAL-FIELDS
IRON-ORE
LIME-STONE
MANGANESE
PIPE-LINE

Fig. 50

The Gondwana Sedimentaries (lower) contain shales and sandstone, under which coal deposits lie.[32] Fire-clay is another important mineral. The unproductive nature of soil and stable land-base had also added to the consideration of plant location. The mean annual temperature fluctuates between 30° to 32°C and rainfall occurs between 1200 to 1400 mm.

The Bokaro Steel Plant is located on the southern bank side of the Damodar river along the Dhanbad-Ranchi highway (Fig. 41). On the opposite bank of the river are Chandrapura Thermal Power Station and Dugda Coal washery. Bounded on the west by the Ranchi-Gomoh railway line, Bokaro is hardly 51 kms. from Dhanbad which is on the main Delhi-Howrah railway line. Ranchi, Bokaro and Jamshedpur form three points of a triangle, each about 145 kms. equidistant from the other. The setting up of a giant steel complex in this location has lep to a tremendous pace of activity. This indicates a bright future for the region which has fixed itself on the industrial map of India within a short span of a decade.[33]

Bokaro has a strong raw materials base. It is in close proximity to coal mines and washeries. Washed coal is supplied from Dugda, Kathara, Giddi and Kargali washeries, and coal from Jharia coal fields. Nearly 50 per cent of the required coal is obtained from the Kargali coal seams of Bokaro coal fields, 35 per cent from the Dugda washeries of Jharia about 12 kms. away by an aerial ropeway and the remainder from Giddi of South Karanpura field.

Iron-ore is obtained from the Kiriburu and Meghahatuburu mines of the Bonai-Keonjhar range on Bihar-Orissa border, 400 kms. south-west of Bokaro. Limestone of blast furnace grade is brought from captive mines of Bhawanathpur in Palamau district. Limestone is obtained from Kuleshwar mines of Katni (M.P.) about 400 kms. Dolomite—the other flux material is supplied by captive Tulsidamar mines close to Bhawanathpur. Manganese-ore is purchased from the Barajamda mines of Singhbhum district (Bihar).

All the essential machineries and equipments are indigenous and are transported from the Heavy Engineering Corporation Ltd. of Hatia (Ranchi) ". . . . the Bokaro Steel Plant between the Ea st Bokaro and Jharia coal fields, is based essentially on consideration of transport economy, on the profitable utilization of wagons which carries coking coal from Bokaro and Jharia to Rourkela and Bhilai and brings ore (and limestone etc.) from Durg and Rourkela to Bokaro on their return journey".[34] Therefore, the locational site of the Bokaro Steel Plant is coal and transport oriented, where the per tonne km. transport cost is lowest in India[35] (see Table 4.2)

The requirement of water for the steel plant is supplied from the Tenughat Dam constructed on the river Damodar. The water flows by gravity along a 40 kms. long canal and is stored in a reservoir close to the plant. A definite advantage of this site is that the configuration of the terrain has facilitated the construction of a gravity canal, a unique contribution to this site. All power supply to the Bokaro plant are met from Chandrapura Thermal Power Station and also from its own captive plants (Table 4.3).

The country is fast building up a sizeable industrial base for the domestic manufacture of industrial machinery, transport and electrical equipment and a modest range of consumer goods. Progress in this direction calls for the increasing use of flat rolled products. Bokaro is designed to supply this rising demand for flat products so that country's industrial diversification is not held back by the shortage of flat products.[36] Therefore, Bokaro covers a large extent of markets and labour supply areas. From Bokaro pig-iron has been exported to U.S S.R , Japan, South Korea, Poland, etc. and order for export of slabs to Yugoslavia was completed in time. Hot Rolled coils have been exported to U.S.A. Kuwait, Iran, Pakistan, and other Asian countries. The first lot of cold rolled sheets produced has been exported to the U.S.S.R. Therefore, home as well as foreign markets are well received by Bokaro Steel Plant.[37] The Bokaro Steel Plant has already achieved a production target of 40 lakh tonnes of steel annually. Four blast furnaces, five coke ovens, one sintering plant, slabbing mills, Hot Strip Mills (HSM), Cold Rolling Mills (CRM), and Lime and Dolomite Calcining Plant are the main units of the one-steel plant. Numerous ancillery units based on the by-products of this massive plant are still in offing.

TABLE 4.3 : **Annual raw materials consumption for the Bokaro Steel Plant, 1980**

Raw materials	'000 tonnes		Source region	Approx. distance from BSC (in Km.)
	1st stage (1.7 MT)	2nd stage (4.0 MT)		
Coking coal				
Raw+Washed	3,344	5,573	Bokaro, Jharia, & S. Karanpura	12-58
Iron-ore	4,170	7,557	Kiriburu, Megha-hataburu (Bihar-Orissa)	400
Manganese-ore	140	256	Barajamda (Bihar)	325
Limestone				
(i) Blast furnace	1,185	1,906	Bhawanathpur, Palamu (Bihar)	90
(ii) SMS	443	1,067	Kuleshwar (M.P.)	400
Dolomite	57	139	Tulsidamar (Palamu)	100
Water	53	. 105 (Cusecs)	Tenughat Dam	40
Power	121	240 W.	Chandrapura & own plants	10

Source : Compiled by the author.

Thereby, at present the Bokaro Steel Complex presents only the vertical-combination of linkages. If horizontally expanded in future, this will move from compact to diversified nature of complex.

Bokaro Steel City with well planned industrial and residential sectors and other amenities has been growing fast. Today the township spreads over an area of 167.25 sq. kms. with a population of 220,907 (1981 Census) (Fig. 43).

The Maraphari area in the Chas Anchal is mainly occupied by the steel plants and its units. It occupies more than 40 sq. kms. of area. The state government of Bihar has set up an Industrial Development Authority at Bokaro, just in the north-western part of the township, for developing the ancillery industries. The residential complex of the city is located almost 5 kms. east of the plant area.

The general plan of Bokaro steel city provides for about 30,000 dwelling units and is based on primary and secondary school district concept. It embodies the principle of organising the pattern of human settlement in a city on the basis of a hierarchy of functions, essential to provide the necessary environment for promoting social welfare. The self-contained sectors aim at bringing homes, schools, shopping centres and other daily necessities of life, just to add a proper spatial relationship between residence and work place. Six sectors have developed since its start and consist of about 21,700 houses of different types apart from a few other non-residential buildings. The township has been planned to have primary schools, a community centre, shopping areas and a Higher Secondary Sechool in each sector as well as one Health Centre to a group of sectors. A modern hospital with 500 beds is already functioning. Indeed, the Bokaro steel city is in the initial stage of its long morphological evolution which is yet to develop in course of time.

DALMIANAGAR COMPLEX

Dalmianagar (90,132)[38] is an important industrial centre of the state where a number of factories are located. These factories form a major agglomerated industrial complex and have reoriented the outlook of the entire Son valley. It actually compensates the industrial inefficiency of the whole western section of the South Bihar Plain region.[39]

Dalmianagar is located at 24°54′N. lat. and 84°11′E. long. on the western bank of the Son river in the Rohtas district. It is not far away from the tropics. It experiences a transitional and moderate type of climate because of its central location in the Great Northern Plain of India (Fig. 44).

Dalmianagar has developed on a relatively sandy and non-alluvial plain. The plain is long, level and wide in the centre of the lower Son valley, where the Kaimur Plateau abruptly ends and gives way to the Ganga Plain. The northern face of the Kaimur escarpment is, however, rough and undulating. The plain area is about 355 feet above mean sea level and is free from floods. Because of vast alluvial tract and reverine deposites recent origin the region is devoid of minerals. The Kaimur Plateau, on the other hand, belongs to the Vindhyan Group of deposits which is characterised by sandstones, limestones, pyrites, dolomite and shales. The horizontally bedded limestone is of immense value as it is used in the cement and lime manufacturing of the region.[40]

From the point of view of transportation, the town lies on the nodal point of communication.[41] The N.H.2 connects it to the great cities like Calcutta (580 kms.) and Varanasi (145 kms.). It is also connected by metalled roads to towns like Buxar, Dumraon, Arrah and Patna. Likewise, it is also located at the junction of the Eastern Railway of Howrah-Delhi line. The Dehri-Rohtas Light Railway links it with Rohtas which is the main source of most of raw materials (Fig. 45).

Dalmianagar has its own region of influence. The source region of the city may be delimited on the north by the river Ganga and on the south by the outskirts of the Kaimur Plateau. The eastern and western boundaries are less clearly defined. This region is densely populated and provides a source of cheap labour. Besides, larger markets, good communication facilities and cheap labour source, the Kaimur Range provides ample limestone for cement manufacturing. The Rohtas forest is a rich source of bamboos for the paper factory. The flat and fertile Gangetic plain furnishes sugarcane for the sugar factory. And finally the inexhaustible wealth of water in the Son river has induced the industries to be located here.[42] These basic factors have led to the establishment of more than a dozen medium-sized industries in a very limited space making the centre an industrial complex. The main industries are, the sugar factory (closed since a long period), the paper factory, the cement factories and several other industries like, Vanaspati (hydrogenated oil), soap, lime, asbestos, chemicals and a host of other engineering works. All these factories based on different resource bases, present the best form of a horizontally-linkage system.

The present township of Dalmianagar has developed over an area of more than 8 kms. It is a small but well-planned township. The industrial and residential sections are separately built-up on the modern lines providing all facilities to the urban dwellers (Fig. 46). Dehri, nearly 2 kms. south of Dalmianagar is the main commercial and business centre. Dehri-Dalmianagar separated by cultural mark of the railway line is fully inter-dependent upon one another and is a good example of 'twintownship'.[43]

BARAUNI COMPLEX

Barauni (67,898) stands among the major industrial towns of Northern India. It is the single industrial complex in North Bihar which breaks the agricultural monotony of the whole region. It lies on the northern bank of the river Ganga in the Begusarai district. With its oil refinery, fertilizer factories, Thermal Power Plant, dairy farm and other expanding ancillary and allied industries, it is bound to progress as a significant river side industrial town of state.[44]

Barauni extends between 25°30'N. lat. and 85°58'E. long. Climatically it lies in the extra-tropical zone. It experiences hot summer, humid monsoon and dry and cold winter.

Barauni is the main industrial-cum-urban centre of the Gandak-Kamla interfluvial region (Fig. 47). The area is almost a dead level alluvial plain composed of relatively the recent sedimentary rocks. The geography of this region is the geography of rivers. Frequent visits of flood have left their marks. Every year the rivers bring enormous silts to deposit in their courses enriching the soils of the region. Rich soil together with timely monsoonal rains make the region a granary centre of Bihar.

Barauni has got an ideal location in view of transportational facilities. Both the metre-gauge and broad-gauge rail lines aligned in the same direction of the Ganga river connect the town from east to west and north to south from different cities of Northern India. Similarly, the National Highway No. 31 and 28 connect the centre with Assam across West Bengal and again Raxaul via Muzaffarpur. The Rajendra Rail-cum-Road Bridge (Mokameh) has connected with other cities and towns, e.g. Patna, Gaya, Bokaro, Ranchi and Jamshedpur (Fig. 48).

The choice of location of the Indian Oil Refinery at Barauni has no relation to its raw material-source, rather it is at the regional consideration on market vertex. Its location is almost in the middle of raw material source region of the upper Assam in the east, and consumers urban-agglomerations of Kanpur and Delhi in the west. Its link with Haldia port in the south-east direction has added another favourable point of consideration. The transportation of crude and refined oil through pipe-lines has minimised the transportation value of rail and road. The first pipe line, 1152 km. long, carries crude oil from Naharkatiya to Barauni via Moran and Noonmati. This pipe line has a rated capacity to carry 4 million tonnes of crude oil. Another pipe line starts from Barauni and goes 1200 km. west to Kanpur. It carries refined oil only. This line carried about 8 million tonnes of oil during 1970-71. The Barauni-Haldia pipe line is designed to carry refined products of Haldia and through another pipe crude oil to Barauni. Recently, the Oil India Ltd. has taken up a scheme of Rs. 40 crores to expand the Naharkatia-Barauni pipe-line system to receive further 2.25 million tonnes of crude oil per year for Barauni Refinery as well as for the proposed Bongaigon Refinery Centre of the Lower Assam Valley.[45]

Barauni has several industrial units, but the Indian Oil Refinery, the Thermal Plant and the Fertilizer Plant are the major units. The oil refinery and its associaries are the main establishments which have influenced the industrial landscape of Barauni. The units have developed on the basis of oil and oil products. Two atmospheric and vaccum units, two kerosene oil units, two petroleum coking units, two Bitumen and phenol extraction and two dewaxing and contact filtration units are there. The Indian Oil refines upto 3 million tonnes of petroleum annually and a host of other bye-products also. The bye-products like Napthe, gases, diesel oil, kerosene oil, lubricating oil and petroleum coke have acted as a basement for the establishment of various other units like, fertilizer, cement and other petro-chemical complexes. The fertilizer factory has already started production of Urea. Therefore, the Barauni complex with oil refinery and fertilizer plant has attained a pattern of vertical and horizontal linkages in which the former is more apparent.

The Thermal Power Plant with an installed capacity of about 145 MW is the main power source for the major industrial units at Barauni. The Plant was commissioned in 1969 in order to compensate the regional deficiency of power in North Bihar. There are three sub-units of this plant and each has a capacity of 50 MW.

Barauni spreads over an area of about 30 sq. kms. The Oil Refinery, the Fertilizer Plant and the Thermal Plant have been located separately. About 900 acres of land are under the oil refinery, 350 acres under fertilizer plant, and about 15 acres of land under the thermal plant. Besides, the state government has established an Industrial Estate on 3,600 acres of land for a tractor factory, a creamery, a nylon plant, a steel rolling mill, a state soil testing laboratory and several other ancillery industries.

The refinery plant colony is a model town on the road to Begusarai (Fig. 49). Barauni has a planned railway colony and an extensive railway yard Teghra, another town located a few kms. north-west of Barauni, may provide ground for future urban expansion of the present township.

Thus, the following conclusions may be derived from the above analysis. Firstly, Jamshedpur, Ranchi, Sindri and Bokaro are located in the Chotanagpur mineral zones. Dalmianagar and Barauni occupy the plain and non-mineral region of the Bihar plain. Secondly, all the complexes have river-side locations. Thirdly, the Damodar Basin provides coking coal and other coal to all industrial centres. Fourthly, Jamshedpur, Ranchi and Bokaro are the largest integrated complexes which influence wider range of areas. Fifthly, Ranchi, Bokaro, Barauni expand on larger tracts of land producing scattered pattern while Jamshedpur, Sindri and Dalmianagar expand relatively a smaller areas producing a compact pattern, leaving very little scope for future expansion. Sixthly, Jamshedpur, Ranchi and Barauni complexes are characterised with vertical and horizontal linkages, Sindri and Bokaro only vertical, whereas Dalmianagar is more horizontally agglomerated. Finally, Jamshedpur is ore oriented, Bokaro and Sindri coal oriented whereas Dalmianagar is raw materials oriented centre.

INDUSTRIAL COMPLEXES AND THEIR ZONES OF INFLUENCE

An industrial town acting as a growth foci always begins to

grow on a regional perspective.[46] This becomes more stronger when the centre specializes in heavy industries like, Iron and Steel, Heavy Engineering and Fertilizer, etc. In such cases, a strong relation between the plant site and the feeder areas develops. These feeder areas provide accommodational facilities, supply raw materials, labour and also act as the consumer centres. In returns, the feeder areas, too, are fed by the growing towns in several respect. Thus, functional linkage or an interdependence between the centre and the region is established. This relation, however, stands on various considerations, among which raw materials, markets and labour are important. These materials form their own regions of occurrences, e.g., raw material region, market region, etc. It is also known as 'Zones of Influence'. Thereby, each industrial centre, large or small must have its own zones of influence. These zones of influence may be intra-regional, sub-regional, inter-regional and even extra-regional depending up on the magnitude of the plants. If the plant is heavy, integrated and large scale producer, its zone of influence would be more extensive and intensive. If the plant is small or medium-sized, its zone of influence would be extensive only upto the level of intra-regional, sub-regional or also inter-regional to a limited extent. If the plant is old and stable, its zone of influence would be well established and clearly defined, and in contrast, when it is new and unstable, the zone of influence will also vary accordingly.

The analysis of the industrial complexes of Bihar on the basis of their zones of influence is relevant to this study. Jamshedpur, Ranchi and Bokaro are among the largest massive enterprizes of basic industries in the country. Naturally, their impact may be quite extensive covering intra-regional, sub-regional, inter-regional and extra-regional influences (Fig. 50). These zones of influence have been determined on the basis of local consideration, raw materials, market and labour supply. All complexes show almost the same result. This is so because all centres are located in close proximity to another near the raw materials, either on ore or coal or in between the two. The markets and labour supply areas are also common covering all the states of Eastern India. Calcutta, the greatest market and the largest port, is located at an equal distance. These complexes are highly important since their products are widely received by country's like Yugoslavia, Russia, Turkey, Egypt, Cuba, other African countries, Sri Lanka, Bangladesh, Iran and other Asian countries (Table 4.4). Among these three, the H.E.C. has stronger influence at the inter-regional or national level in comparison to Jamshedpur and Bokaro. The H.E C. is the single supplier of machineries and equipments in the country whereas Jamshedpur and Bokaro steel producers have limited influence markets to the Northern and Eastern India level. But TELCO, again supplies locomotives to all parts of the country, widening the national influence zone of Jamshedpur more than Bokaro.

TABLE 4.4 : **Extra-regional influence (export) of complexes**

Industrial complex	Products	Rs. in crores	Places of export
Jamshedpur complex	Steel products (TISCO)	55.5 (1970)	U S.A., Egypt, Yugoslavia,
	Vehicles & automobiles (TELCO)	250.0 (1980)	Egypt, Iran, China, Bangladesh & several others.
Ranchi complex (H.E.C.)	Equipments	28.0 (1980)	Yugoslavia, Turkey, Bulgaria,
		250.0 (Order)	Egypt, Hungary, Sri Lanka, Bangladesh, Cuba, U.S.S.R. etc.
Bokaro complex	Steel and steel products	12.3 (1978)	*Pig Iron* U.S.S.R., Japan,
		26.0 (1980)	S. Korea, Poland. *Slabs* Yugoslavia. *Hot Rolled Coils* U.S.A., Kuwait, Iran, Phillippines, Pakistan, Hong-kong, Thailand, Indonesia. *Cold Rolled Sheets* Russia.

Source : Compiled by the author.

TABLE 4.5 : **Industrial complexes and their zones of influence**

Intra-regional	Sub-regional	Inter-regional	Extra-regional
Jamshedpur	Jamshedpur	Jamshedpur	Jamshedpur
Ranchi (HEC)	Ranchi (HEC)	Ranchi (HEC)	Ranchi (HEC)
Bokaro	Bokaro	Bokaro	Bokaro
Sindri (partially)	Sindri	Sindri (partially)	—
Dalmianagar	Dalmianagar	Dalmianagar (partially)	—
—	—	Barauni (partially)	—

Source : Arranged on the basis of their influence by the author.

Other three complexes, Sindri, Dalmianagar and Barauni project intra-regional, sub-regional and to a limited extent intra-regional influence, since these are medium-sized and basically dependent upon the local demands (Table 4.5).

One interesting point emerges from Fig. 50 that zones of influence overlap. This indicates that all the essential mineral materials like iron-ore, coal, limestone are limited in their geographical space and these complexes are located adjacent to each other to economize the freight rate. Wagons coming for coal in the Damodar Coal Basin bring iron-ore, manganese-ore, limestone and other steel products from the one region and distribute them to the industrial centres located on the same rail-road route upto Bokaro. From there coal is carried by these wagons touching industrial centre and distributing coal to Rourkela and Bhilai. This provides a unique pattern of movement of coal and iron as practised in the Great Lakes Region of the U.S.A.

Thus, it may be concluded that Jamshedpur, Ranchi and Bokaro are three facets of one national integration of economic polarisation whereas Sindri, Dalmianagar and Barauni are the supporting wings of major goal of economic achievement which is equivalent to the Russian terminology the territorial production complexes.

REFERENCES

1. Miller, E.W. (1962), *A Geography of Manufacturing*, op. cit., p. 1.

2. Discussions based on the author's paper—"Industrial Complexes in Bihar", *The Geographical Review of India*, Calcutta, Vol. 42, Sept. 1980, pp. 229-237.

3. Lal, B.B. (1981), *Census of India*, op. cit., p. 6.

4. Singh, R.P. and Kumar, A. (1970), op. cit., p. 187.

5. Dutt, A.K. (1960), "Jamshedpur and Its Upland : A Study in Urban Geography'' Unpublished Ph.D. Thesis, Patna University, Patna, p. 3.

6. Dayal, P. (1964), "Aspects of Industrial Location in India". *Transactions of the Indian Council of Geographers*, Patna, Vol. I, p. 2.

7. *Jamshedpur, The Steel City*, Calcutta, 1974, p. 2.

8. Mukherjee, M. (1967), "Manufacturing Towns of Bihar", *Transactions of the Indian Council of Geographers*, Patna, Vol. 4, p. 36.

9. Brush, J.E. (1952), op. cit., pp. 44-45.

10. '*Tata Steel' Challange and Response*, Calcutta, 1980, p. 7.

11. Dutt, A.K. (1960), op. cit., p. 49.

12. 'TELCO' Issued by the P.R.D. Jamshedpur, Sept. 80, pp. 3-4.

13. Ram, L.N. (1968), "Industrial Belts in South-east Chotanagpur", *Transactions of the Indian Council af Geographers*, Vol. 5, p. 83.

14. Karan, P.P. (1977), "Perception of Environmental Pollution in Chotanagpur Industrial Area, India", *The National Geographer*, Vol. 12, p. 19.

15. Ahmad, E. (1965), op. cit., p. 392.

16. On the basis of 1981 Census Report (Provisional) Ranchi has outnumbered Jamshedpur.

17. Sing, R.P. and Kumar, A. (1970), op. cit., p. 184.

18. Pandey, P. (1970), op. cit., p. 197,

19. *ibid.*

20. Singh, J. (1964), Transport Geography of South Bihar, Varanasi, *National Geographical Society of India*, p. 191.

21. Pandey, P. (1969), "Industrial Landscape of Greater Ranchi", *Geographical Outlook*, vol. 6, p. 41.

22. Chinoy, P.D. (1981), *H.E.C. News* (edited), Ranchi, pp. 1-10.

23. Sinha, R.P. (1973), "Industrial Landscape of Ranchi, India", *Journal of Geography*, Jabalpur, Vol. 4, p. 25.

24. Chinoy, P.K. (1981), op. cit., p. 9.

25. Ram, L.N. (1968), op. cit., p. 87.

26. Sinha R.P. (1974), "Development of Industries in Bihar : Achievement and Prospects", *The Bihar Information*, Patna, Jan., p. 41.

27. Mukherjee, B. (1956), "Ranchi : A Study in Urban Morphology", *The National Geographical Journal of India*, Vol. 11, p. 99.

28. Singh, J. (1964), op. cit., p. 191.

29. *The Indian Nation*, Patna, 19th April, 1982, p. 4.

30. *District Gazetteers*, (Dhanbad), 1964, Chap. V, p. 206.

31. Dhanbad-Jharia-Sindri-Draft Master Plan, L.S.G. Department, Bihar, Patna, 1966-1986, p. 107.

32. Ahmad, E. (1965), op. cit., p. 372.

33. *From Ore to Steel*" a booklet published from B.S.C. Plant and obtained from the P.R.O. 1980, p. 1.

34. Dayal, P. (1964), op. cit., p. 6.

35. Sinha, R.P. (1974), op. cit., p. 39.

36. Mukherjee, M. (1967), op. cit., p. 40.

37. *From Ore to Steel*, op. cit., p. 9.

38. The Population figure is combined with Dehri, 1981 Census.

39. Singh, R.P. (1974), "Dalmianagar : A Study of the Industrial Complex", Indian Geog. Studies, *Research Bulletin* No. 2, p. 36.

40. Dayal, P. (1953), *Bihar in Maps*, Patna, Kusum Prakashan, p. 10.

41. Goswami, S.B. (1956), "The Regional Setting of Dalmianagar", *Geographical Outlook*, Vol. 1, p. 29.

42. Singh, R.P. (1968), "Industrial Geography of Dalmianagar", Unpublished Master Thesis, Patna University, Patna, p. 16.

43. Singh, K.N. (1959), "Morphology of the Twin-Township of Dehri-Dalmianagar", *The National Geographical Journal of India*, Vol. 3, p. 169.

44. Singh, R.P. and Kumar, A. (1970), p. 164.

45. *The Indian Nation*, Patna, October 3, 1975, p. 1.

46. Qaiyum, A. (1981), "Role of Steel Towns in the Regional Development", in L.R. Singh's (ed.) *New Perspectives in Geography*, Allahabad, p. 41.

5

GROWTH OF INDUSTRIAL COMPLEXES

THIS chapter presents a chronological study of the growth of industries and industrial complexes of Bihar. In the industrial literature growth is a sequential development of an industrial unit or a region which accounts in terms of time, space and dimension. Time relates to the temporal study through which the growth trend is ascertained. Space is related to the spatial expansion mostly, vertically or horizontally or both and even diagonally also. Dimension includes various aspects like production, employment, decennial population variations, etc. These three are related to one another and determine the upward, downward or stability of growth. A model is developed accordingly and tested to ascertain the growth pattern of industrial complexes of Bihar. This is as follows :

(i) $T^{+1}+S^{+1}+D^{+1}=G+$

(ii) $T^{+1}+{}^{+}S^{0}+{}^{+}D^{0}=G\pm$

(iii) $T^{+1}+S^{-1}+D^{-1}=G-$

Where (i) $(\text{Time}+\text{Space}+\text{Dimension})^{+1}=$ Growth, upward

(ii) $(\text{Time}+\text{Space}+\text{Dimension})^{+0}=$ Growth, Stable or no growth.

(iii) $(\text{Time}+\text{Space}+\text{Dimension})^{-1}=$ growth downward

Before testing this model it is essential to present a brief discussion of industrial conditions of the state and the growth trend as well. The industrial growth periods of Bihar is divided into three phases. The first phase includes period before AD 1900, second phase between 1901-1950, or pre-independence condition and the third phase after 1951, or the plan periods.

BEFORE 1900 PERIOD

The industrial economy of Bihar dates back to antiquity. Bihar is a dominant agricultural region and hence the industrial economy was also based on agricultural products. Before 1900 the industries related to agricultural base was the only feature of industrial landscape. Therefore, this landscape was mostly concentrated in the plain region only. The industries were mostly of cottage and small scale type. Organised industries were absent. Salt petre and opium were very much popular during the 17th and 18th centuries. English, French and Dutch people were keenly interested in the trade of these articles. Chapra, Patna and Singhia were the main trade centres. The districts of Saran and Champaran were the main regions of opium cultivation. About 4.643 mounds of opium was exported from Champaran through the river traffic the main source of transportation in 1876.[1] But during the second half of the nineteenth century due to China's supermacy in opium trade, the Indian trade of opium was badly smashed. This slackness of trade compelled the farmers to shift from poppy cultivation to indigo and sugarcane cultivation. In the beginning sugarcane was taken on priority basis, but later on it was overtaken by indigo, because indigo was paying more and quick money in comparison to the former. Therefore, salt petre and indigo were the important commercial items. The indigo, however, as industry ruled the economy of the region and sugar was lagging behind till the beginning of 1900. In South Bihar cereal trading was important in Shahabad, Patna and Gaya districts.

The Chotanagpur Plateau Region, "A Little known Province of the Empire"[2] was under the 'Jungle Rule' with a very poor economy of primitive cottage industries. Tandwa in Hazaribagh district was the centre of iron-smelting in 1863. Coal was already in practice in the form of power, the Giridih coal field was opened in the year 1851 but it attained commercial importance only after the extension of a branch railway line from Madhupur to Giridih in 1875. It was the first railway line to reach the coal fields. The arrival of the railways, however, marked a turning point in the coal industry. After that the chord line reached Dhanbad in 1894 from Sitarampur on the Howrah-Delhi Main line and it was further extended westward to Mughalsarai in 1900. But the mining of coal on the commercial line started only after the opening of the Jharia coalfield in 1891. The real progress of coal industry was recorded when this coal mine was connected with Calcutta and Mughalsarai in 1900.[3] The lack of transportation facilities was the main constraint in the growth of industrial economy of the region. And uptil 1900 this hurdle was to some extent loosened out due to the extension of many railways and roads in the region.

AFTER 1900 ONWARDS TO 1950

The year 1900 is landmark in the industrial history of Bihar from where modern trend of industrialization started. The old fashioned industries like salt petre and indigo began to decay rapidly from their economic decadence. There were mainly two reasons for it. Firstly, these industries began to pay less to the farmers in comparison to sugarcane and cereals. During this period sugarcane was the most important commercial crop for the farmers. Secondly, these industries were associated with foreigners, especially the English people. On the eve of the national movement for independence the Indian farmers totally disregarded the production of indigo, opium and salt-petre to frustrate and make financially weak to the English people. The dominance of sugarcane overwhelmed the fertile plain region of North Bihar and on account of this, the first sugar factory came into operation at Marhowrah in Saran district in 1904. It was followed by Lauriya and Barachukia in Champaran district in 1905 and 1906 respectively. The growth trend continued rapidly with opening of another sugar factories at Ryam and Lohat in 1914 and Siwan in 1918. The indigo industry was still a greater competitor. During 1911 indigo industry with 78 factories and more than 27000 workers was the leading industry in the state. But after three decades in 1941 there were only 4 factories with 250 workers. It was declining rapidly due to the growth of sugar industry, a more money giving industry.[4]

The Chotanagpur region was also humming with the industrial activities. The region's centuries obsecurity was broken with the establishment of the first large scale, the Tata Iron and Steel Co. Ltd. at Sakchi in 1907. This enterprise heralded the modern industrial age in India[5] and represented an industrial 'breakthrough' for the economically backward countries of the world.[6] The coal of Jharia and iron-ore from newly discovered iron-ore mines of Singhbhum-Mayurbhanj Iron Series[7] gave strong footing to TISCO. From here a new trend of industrialization broke out. Kumardhubi in 1907 with Fireclay and Silica works, the Ranchi Distillery in Ranchi in 1908 and the copper refinery at Maubhandar in 1911 followed the suit (Table 5.1.) The TISCO's first ingot streamed out in December 1911 and since then it has long marched on the way of prosperity.

The First World War (1914-18) gave an impetus to the industrial progress of the region. The war interrupted the commercial link between India and England. Naturally, shortage of imported goods compelled the business men to start many enterprises around Jamshedpur, where many infra structural conditions were available. Even TISCO launched its expansion programme. Many metallic and non-metallic minerals were exploited for the establishment of engineering, firebricks, refractories, copper and melting, mica processing, coal washeries, glass factories and various other works. In North Bihar several sugar factories were located.

Between 1920 and 1930 the pace of industrialization was slackened due to the economic depression caused by war. The government of India, after realising the hard fact, granted tariff protection. Railways freight rates on the indigenous industrial products were heavily reduced. Those concessional measures gave a new filling to the industrial growth. A number of sugar factories were located in the districts of Saran, Champaran, Muzaffarpur and Darbhanga. In South Bihar Ganga Plain these factories were located at Bihta (Patna), Dalmianagar (Shahabad), Guraru and Warsliganj in Gaya district. At Dalmianagar near Dehri, cement, paper, chemicals and engineering workshop were established almost the same time. Cement factories at Japla, Khelari, Jinkpani were established. Jamshedpur became the hub of the industrial locations where more than a dozen industrial units flourished in and around the mother plant, TISCO.

The Second World War (1939-45) again stimulated the growth of industries in Bihar. Already established units expanded their production capacity. Several new units were also established. The iron products, cement, refractories and sugar were greatly benefited. The old locomotive and automobile units were revived at Jamshedpur by the name of Telco. Kumardhubi, Jharia, Dhanbad, Giridih, Dalmianagar, Jamalpur, Monghyr, Bhagalpur, Muzaffarpur, Darbhanga etc. were the centres of industrial activities. Jamshedpur and Dalmianagar were already developed as industrial complexes.

Then came independence. The new economic measures in the form of Five Year Plan was executed in 1951. During the First Plan Period (1951-56) the emphasis was laid on the agriculture and agricultural associated activities. The first fertilizer complex was established at Sindri in 1947 and production started from 1951. All the older units were facilitated with expansion programmes. In 1955, a cement factory was also located at Sindri.

In the Second Five Year Plan (1957-62) which was primarily for industrial renovation and relocation, all the units were revitalized. Exploitation of resources and minimisation of regional economic disparities by setting massive capital intensive plants were mooted out. The H.E.C. Ltd. at Hatia was the result of that planning. The location of H.E.C. Complex was a tremendous attempt which changed the whole landscape and brought the pride and prestige to Bihar.

During the Third Five Year Plan (1963-68), establishment of large scale oil refinery at Barauni was another achievement of glory. In succession of this the second fertilizer plant was established in the vicinity of oil refinery at Barauni. Besides, a number of other new units came up in different parts of the State.

In the Fourth Five Year Plan (1968-1973) another prestigeous massive steel plant came into existence at Bokaro. By the establishment of this Steel Complex Bihar surpassed all other Indian States. The plant was established in 1968 and production started in 1972. This plant is still under construction and when finally completed this would be one of the largest enterprises in the world. After that no new addition came to the State, but the expansion and modernization programmes are going on to maintain the efficiency of the established plants.

Thus, from the beginning of 1900 to 1980 is a progressive story of industrial achievements as shown in Fig. 51. The pre-independence industrial growth is characterised by the wider distribution of industrial units on larger area while the post-independence growth is marked with the great concentrations of industries at regional climaxes at a few nuclei. Moreover, in the pre-independence period, the location of industries was mostly in the private sector while the post-independence location of industries was almost in the public sector.

TABLE 5.1 : **Industrial units with their years of establishment**

Name and location of factories	Year of Establishment and commissioning	Year of closure
1	2	3
The Opium, the Salt-Petre and the Indigo Industries, Champaran, Saran & Patna.	From the 17th to the beginning of 20th century.	Decayed
Giridih Coal Mines Giridih, Hazaribagh Dist.	1851	
The Eastern Railway Workshop, at Jamalpur, Monghyr	1862	
The Cn. Railway Workshop at Chakradharpur, Singhbhum Dist.	1872	
Jharia Coal Mines, Jharia, Dhanbad District.	1891	
The Indian Rifle Factory at Monghyr, Monghyr District.	1898	
After 1900 :		
M/s Cawnpure Sugar Works Ltd., Marhowrah, Saran	1904	
M/s S.K.G. Sugar Ltd., Lauria, Champaran.	1905	
M/s Champaran Sugar Co. Ltd., Barachakia, Champaran.	1906	

1	2	3
The Tata Iron and Steel Co., Sakchi (Jamshedpur) Singhbhum.	1907	1911
Fire Clay and Silica Works, Kumardhubi, Dhanbad.	1907	
The Peninsular Tobacco Co., Monghyr.	1907	
The Ranchi Distillery, Ranchi.	1908	
The Cordoba Copper Co. (Indian Copper Corpn. Ltd.) Maubhandar, Ghatsila, Singhbhum.	1911	
M/s Darbhanga Sugar Co. Ltd., Lohat, Darbhanga.	1914	
M/s Ryam Sugar Co. Ltd., Darbhanga.	1914	
Kumardhubi Eng. Works, Kumardhubi, Dhanbad.	1917	
M/s S.K.G. Sugar Ltd., Siwan, Saran.	1918	
The Indian Cable Co., Jamshedpur.	1920	
Tinplate Co. of India, Jamshedpur.	1920	
M/s Samastipur Sugar Co. Samastipur (Darbhanga)	1920	
M/s Jessop Ared Co. Jamshedpur.	1921	
The Indian Steel & Wire Products Co., Jamshedpur.	1921	
The Bihar Sugar Works Pachrukhi, Saran	1922	
The Japla Cement Factory, Japla, Palamau	1922	
The Agrico, Jamshedpur.	1923	
M/s Arther Butler Co., Ltd., Muzaffarpur.	1923	
The Tobacco Co. of India, Monghyr.	1924	
The Indian Hume Pipe Co., Jamshedpur.	1926	
The Tata Foundary Co.	1927	
The Eagle Rolling Mill Ltd., Kumardhubi, Dhanbad.	1927	
Sixteen Sugar Factories, located in Bihar out of which 6 in Cham-	1933	

1	2	3
paran districts—Majhaulia, Motihari, Narkatiaganj Chanpatia, Narayanpur and Sugauli; 3 in Saran district—Sasamussa, Mirganj & Sidhawalia; 2 in Muzaffarpur district—Motipur and Goraul; 1 Darbhanga district, Sakri; 1 Patna District, Bihta, 1 Shahabad district, Dalmianagar, 2 Gaya District, Guraru and Warsaliganj.	1933	1968
The A.C.C. Cement Factory, Khelari (Ranchi).	1935	
The Indian Oxygen & Acetylene Co. Ltd., Jamshedpur.	1935	
The Jemco, Jamshedpur.	1936	
M/s R.I. Cement Factory at Dalmianagar, Shahabad.	1937	
The Aluminium Corporation of India, Muri, Ranchi.	1937	
The Cotton and Jute Mills, Gaya.	1937	
The R.I. Paper Factory, Dalmianagar	1938	
The R.I. Chemical Factories, Dalmianagar.	1939	
The Mahabir Glass Works Ltd., Chirkunda, Dhanbad.	1941	
The R.I. Asbestos Cement Factory, Dalmianagar.	1943	
The Khandelwal Glass Works, Ambora, Dhanbad.	1943	
The R.I. Vanaspati Factory, Dalmianagar.	1944	
The Telco, Jamshedpur.	1945	1950
Jharia Glass Factory, Jharia, Dhanbad.	1945	
Refractories Co. Nirsachatti, Dhanbad.	1946	
M/s Cement Works Ltd., Banjari, Shahabad.	1946	
After Independence, 1947		
The Sindri Fertilizer and Chemicals Ltd., Sindri.	1947	

1	2	3
The A.C.C. Cement Factory, Jhinkpani, Singhbhum	1947	
Glass Factories at—Bhurkunda (Hazaribagh)	1947	
Kandra (Singhbhum)	1947	
Daltonganj (Palamau)	1947	
Jharia (Dhanbad)	1947	
M/s R.I. Cement Factory, Dalmianagar.	1950	During the First Five Year Plan 1950-51 to 1955-56
The Indian Tube Co., Jamshedpur	1953	
R I. Vulcanised Fiber Plant, Dalmianagar.	1954	
The A.C.C. Cement Factory Ltd., Sindri.	1955	
M/s Ashoka Cement Ltd., Dalmianagar	1956	
M/s Reliance Firebricks and Pottery Co., Chircunda.	1957	
The Indian Explosive Factory, Gomia, Giridih.	1958	
The Heavy Engineering Corporation Ltd., Hatia, Ranchi.	1959	1962-63
M/s Bihar Phosphate Factory, Sindri.	1960	
The Ashoka Paper Mills, Darbhanga	1960	During the Second Five Year Plan (1956-57 to 1961-62).
The High Tension Insulator Plant, Namkum, Ranchi.	1960	
The Minimax Ltd., Kokar, Ranchi.	1960	
The Bharat Ball Bearing Co. Ltd. Ratu, Ranchi.	1961	
The Usha Martin Black Ltd., Tatisilwai, Ranchi.	1962	
The Waxpol Industries Ltd., Tatisilwai, Ranchi.	1962	
The Tata Robins Frazer Ltd., Jamshedpur.	1962	
R.L. Soap Factory, Dalmianagar.	1964	
The Indian Oil Refinery, Barauni (Monghyr).	1964	
The Fertilizer Factory of India, Barauni.	1965	

1	2	3
Tata Yodoguwa Ltd., Adityapur, Jamshedpur.	1968	
Bokaro Steel Plant, Bokaro Steel City, Dhanbad.	1968-72	
Three Jute Mills, two at Katihar and one at Darbhanga	1969	
Sugar Factory at Banmankhi (Purnea)	1970	
M/s Asiatic Oxygen and Acetylene, Ltd., Barauni.	1973	
M/s Usha Alloys Ltd., Adityapur, Jamshedpur.	1974	

Source : Compiled by the Author.

A list of important industrial establishment with their years of commission is prepared to show the trend of industrial growth in Bihar (Table 5.1). A map is also prepared to show the distribution of these units (Fig. 51). The list reveals that industrialisation started in Bihar at the beginning of the present century. Till the end of the 19th Century the area was economically handicapped specially due to lack of transport facilities.[8] There was significant development of rail and road transport at the beginning of the 20th Century that helped the development of coal mining and other industries.[9] After 1900, raw materials like iron-ore, manganese, coal, limestone, copper, mica, bauxite etc. were variably in the use. Since these raw materials are weight loosing, and incur heavy transportation cost, the associated industries were at the sites of these raw materials. Finally, industries were set up on large and medium scales based on modern techniques. This modern trend, however, revolutionised the resource, region and the people as well.

Altogether six industrial complexes have evolved : Jamshedpur and Dalmianagar are the complexes of pre-independence period while Sindri, Ranchi, Barauni and Bokaro complexes are the outcome of the post-independence period or during the plan period. Therefore, Jamshedpur is the oldest complex whereas Bokaro is the youngest complex. The following section presents a systematic and concise result about the evaluation and growth of each complex to ascertain their growth trend. The growth trend is mainly based on production and employment data from the various years. Spatial extension and growth of population have also been considered. Three figures are to explain. Figure 53 shows the population trend. Figure 54 shows the production trend while Fig. 55 shows the employment trend.

JAMSHEDPUR COMPLEX

The Jamshedpur Complex is one of the oldest and the largest industrial complexes of the country. More than twenty-five industrial units have already been established one after another keeping pace with time since 1907. More than 1 million workers are engaged in various units clustered around the mother plant, TISCO (Table 5.2).

TABLE 5.2 : **Units in chronological order : Jamshedpur complex, 1980-81**

Name of the unit	Year of Est.	Installed capacity	Production in % of the capacity	Labour employed (persons)
1	2	3	4	5
The Tata Iron & Steel Co. (TISCO)	1907	2.2 mill. tons of pig iron	88.00	
		2.0 mill. tons of ingot and 1.5 mill. tons of saleable steel	Above 100.00	41,000
The Indian Cable Co.	1920	20 mill. yds. of cables.	68.00	37,000
Tinplate Co. of India.	1920	80,000 tons	100.00	5,400
M/s Jesog & Co.	1921	Not available.	—	600

1	2	3	4	5
The Indian Steel & Wire Products Co.	1921	70,000 tons	80.00	2,700
The Agrico.	1923	40 lakhs	100.00	1,500
The Indian Hume Pipe Co.	1926	N.A.	—	250
The Tata Foundry Co.	1927	4,500 tons. Rly. Sleepers	100.00	3,200
The Indian Oxygen and Acetylene Co. Ltd.	1935	4 mill. Cu. m. oxygen 4.7 lakh Cub. m. Acety-lene 2.1 lakh cu. m. nitrogen	100.00	300
Jamshedpur Eng. & Machine Manu-facturing Co. Ltd. (JEMCO)	1936	50 tons.	100.00	360
Tata Engineering & Locomotive Co. Ltd. (TELCO)	1945	4600 vehicles in a year.	100.00	33,000
The National Metallurgical Laboratory.	1950	To train engineers and sustain new technology.		
The Indian Tube Co.	1953	2 lakh tons tubes.	100.00	4,000
Tata Robin & Fraser Ltd.	1962	Not available.	—	500
Tata Yodagawa Ltd.	1968	20,000 tons rolls.	70.00	4,500
Tata Maintenance shop.	1968	Manufacturing a wide range of steel plant equip-ment, e.g. Coke oven machines, rolling stocks, cranes, etc.	100.00	3000
Tata Electric Furnace Shop.	1971	30,000 tons of alloy and spe-cial steel.	100.00	1700
M/s Usha Alloys Ltd.	1974	10,000 tons of alloys.	80.00	380

1	2	3	4	5
Electro Flux Refining Shop.	1974	7,000 steel billets.	90.00	1200
Tata Ring Rolling Mills.	1975	2 mill. rings annually.	100.00	600
Continuous Casting Plant.	1978	to cast various sizes of square billets.	100.00	500

Source : Arranged from Literature obtained from TISCO and other Cos., Jamshedpur.

PRODUCTION TREND OF TICO

The Tata Iron and Steel Co. was established in the year 1907 and the production of pig iron and ingot steel started in 1911 and 1913 respectively. At the initial phase 4,600 workers were employed. The Company had a rated capacity of 100,000 tonnes of ingot steel annually. The First World War stimulated production due to greater demand. The supply of all imported goods were held up and thus the company availed the opportunality by expanding its capacity twice within a short period of 7 years, and raised the capacity to 425,000 tonnes of saleable steel and 1,25,000 tonnes of ingot steel and nearly 8 lakh tonnes of pig iron in 1930. But between the thirtees, in spite of a vast home-market, the company was plagued with the stiff competition of imported English goods. But the Indian Government came forward with a tariff protection measure of Indian steel and the Company got a new lease of life. The period of Second World War again benefited the company at its maximum. During this period besides raising its production capacity of saleable steel to 670,000 tonnes, above 9 lakh tonnes of pig iron and 245,000 ingot, it produced many structurals like, wheels, tyres, axles, bullet proof armour plates and also dynamo grade electric steel sheets. In 1950 the company launched upon a massive modernisation and expansion programme to raise the capacity of production to two million tonnes of pig iron and saleable steel separately. The programme was completed in 1960 and the production of TISCO raised to several folds. The Company produced the maximum height of production during the year 1966-67. And, thereafter the production trend started to decline up to 1974-75. During 1976 another modernisation schemes were started but the completion scheme is yet to meet. During the year 1980-81 the company worked at its full capacity, still it has not come out from the basic troubles, like aging of furnaces and machines, power shortage and competition from other public sectors. Till 1968-69 TISCO remained the number one steel producer in India. But from 1969-70, however, the company has been replaced to the second largest producer of saleable steel. Further on, the rise of Bokaro steel plant has again threatened its position to the third, still its national importance is at the apex. A decadewise production of pig-iron, ingots and saleable steel is given to show the trends of production of the company.

TABLE 5.3 : **Decadewise production of TISCO**

Years	Figures in tonnes		
	Pig-iron	Ingot steel	Saleable steel
1920-21	2,32,368	77,900	1,25,000
1930-31	8,00,000	100,000	4,25,000
1940-41	9,11.000	245,000	6,70,000
1950-51	9,72,000	8,40,000	8,00,000
1960-61	13,79,000	16,43,000	12,63,000
1966 67	20,00,000	20,00,000	19,26,000
1970-71	16,64,000	17,16,000	13,75,000
1980-81	15,10,000	17,80,000	15,20,000

Source : Seventy-fifth Annual Report, 1981-82, The Tata Iron and Steel Co. Ltd., p. 26.

TISCO from its inception has attracted several other units to establish in its environs. Table 5.3 presents a chronological growth of the industrial units (Fig. 52). Among these units, the Telco is reputed for automobiles at national and international levels. The plant is massive and produces thousands of automobiles. Table 5.4 shows the growth trend in production of automobiles from Telco.

The Tinplate Co. of India, the only factory of its type in India, has been producing 152,000 tonnes of tinplate annually. It employs more than 5 thousand persons.

Besides, a number of other small and medium sized factories

are located in and around TISCO to act as ancillaries and produce varieties of steel products which are of great demand in the local markets.

TABLE 5.4 : **Telco's production through decade**

Years	Automobiles in number
1960-61	12,000
1970-71	27,000
1980-81	36,000
1981-82	46,000

Source : 'Telco' : Published from P.R.O., Telco, Jamshedpur April, 1982, pp. 1-11.

EMPLOYMENT TREND

The employment trend shows an upward trend from 4600 workers in 1910 to over 1 million in 1980-81. Table 5.5 indicates the employment trend of Jamshedpur Complex from 1950-51 to 1980-81.

TABLE 5.5 : **Employment trend of Jamshedpur**

(*Figures in persons*)

Years	TISCO	Telco	Others	Total
1950-51	19,000	—	5,000	24,000
1960-61	26,000	5,800	6,200	38,000
1970-71	32,756	22,000	19,244	74,000
1980-81	41,000	33,000	27,390	101,390

Source : Obtained from Tisco's P.R.O. in January 1982.

Spatial extention

The Jamshedpur Complex has also shown a spatial extention. In 1907 the total occupied land was only 4 sq. kms. which later on, expanded to 9 sq. kms. in 1911-12. In 1930 it acquired another chunk of land totalling to 22 sq. kms. The trend of expansion rose again to 40 sq. kms. in 1951 to 64.7 sq. kms. in

1961. This was the maximum expansion which continued up to 1974. After 1975, the complex continued its expansion trend by extending to Mango, Jugsalai and Adityapur suburbs called as the Greater Jamshedpur Complex.

Population growth

The decennial population variation may also be used as a parameter for testing the growth pattern of an industrial city. The growth of population of Jamshedpur at every stage bears direct relation to the expansion of the parent steel works as well as the establishment of other ancillery industries. This interrelationship of population and industries has been shown in Fig. 52. The decade of 1921-31 was the busiest period of industrial activities, since the TISCO expanded itself and five new units were established. As a result, 61.19 per cent of growth of population was recorded. The growth rate was very low in comparison to the growth rate of first decade of 1911-21 when it was recorded as 911.28 per cent (Table 5.6). The next decade of 1931-41 witnessed a population influx in Jamshedpur with an addition of 72,936 persons. This was the period of stabilization and maximum growth of TISCO and its associaries. The decade of 1941-51 was a period of population depression due to the second world war and also migration of people outside Jamshedpur on account of country's partition in 1947. During 1951-61 there was again a significant growth. The period was marked with the great leap forward for the Steel Company when its production was raised to 'Two Million Tonne target'. This was also the rise of Telco's. The decade 1961-71 showed the lowest growth rate in the history of Jamshedpur as shown in Table 5.6. This was due to the establishment of other new steel centres at Rourkela, Durgapur, Bhilai and Bokaro. Even the establishment of Ranchi Complex also affected its growth. The latest decade of 1980-81 shows slight improvement, firstly due to the addition of Adityapur and Mango regions and secondly, the rise of other services mostly commerce and transport.

Table 5.6 also reveals that Jamshedpur ranked fifth in the urban population hierarchy of Bihar in 1921. But within four decades it outnumbered other towns and was placed on the

TABLE 5.6 : **Decennial population variation of Jamshedpur**

Year	Population	Decade variation	Percentage of decade variation	Relative urban population hierarchy
1911	5672	—	—	—
1921	57360	+ 51688	+ 911.28	V
1931	92459	+ 35099	+ 61.19	—
1941	165395	+ 72936	+ 78.88	III
1951	218162	+ 52767	+ 31.90	—
1961	332138	+113976	+ 51.63	II
1971	355783	+ 23585	+ 17.06	II
1981 (Prov.)	438781	+ 81998	+ 28.46	III

Source : Arranged from : Jamshedpur Adityapur Complex—A Report published from L.S.G. Department, Government of Bihar, p. 17.

second, closely trailing behind Patna, the State Capital. This position was maintained up to 1971. But according to the 1981 provisional Census report, Ranchi has replaced Jamshedpur from second to third position.

DALMIANAGAR COMPLEX

Among the Pre-Independence Complexes, Dalmianagar comes to next only after Jamshedpur. This complex, however, started to grow with the first industrial unit of Sugar factory in 1933. After that a number of other industrial units, e.g., cement, paper, chemicals, asbestos cement, vanaspati and soap etc. were added subsequently one after another within a period of two decades (Table 5.7). These units mostly of medium-size are diversified in nature but are highly interlinked to one another, agglomerated within a limited space. Among the units the most important are sugar, cement and paper, which require special discussion.

The sugar factory at Dalmianagar was located with several other sugar factories in Bihar after the implementation of the Sugar Act in 1932. Its starting capacity was 1,000 tonnes of sugarcane per day but this was raised to 2,000 tonnes in 1940. The trend was more-less maintained up to 1962-63. But from 1964, the production trend sharply declined and in 1968 the factory was closed due to short supply of sugarcane, old machinery and paucity of capital, etc.

TABLE 5.7 : **Dalmianagar and its industrial units, 1980-81**

Name of units	Year of establishment	Production	Employment (persons)
M/s Rohtas Industries Ltd.			
The Sugar Factory	1933	2,000 tonnes per day (closed)	
Cement Factories (two units)	1937+ 1950	3,30,000 tonnes annually	3,000
Paper Factory	1938	46,000 tonnes	2,256
Chemical Factories	1939		
(a) Caustic Soda Plant		6000 tonnes annually	500
(b) Ferric Alum. Plant		12,000 tonnes	500
(c) Sulphuric Acid Plant		3,000 tonnes	250
Asbestos Cement Factory	1944	15,000 tonnes (closed)	
The Vulcanised Fiber Plant	1954	43 tonnes (closed)	
Pulp Paper Plant (Bagasse based)	1954	15,000 tonnes (closed)	
Paper Boards Plant	1954	30,000 tonnes	400
M/s Ashoka Cement Factory	1955	1,45,000 tonnes	900
Central Workshops	—	—	400
Soap Factory	1964	538	200

Source : Collected from P.R.O. Office, Dalmianagar.

The cement industry of Dalmianagar comprises of three units, two under R.I. Ltd. and third under M/s Ashoka Industry. The first unit was established in 1933 only after the sugar factories.

The initial capacity was 500 tonnes daily. In 1950 the second unit of the same capacity was installed. In 1955 the third unit was established altogether producing more than 4 lakh tonnes of cement per year.

The paper factory of Dalmianagar is among the largest paper producer of India. In 1965-66 the factory produced nearly 60,000 tonnes paper and 15,000 tonnes of other paper boards etc. surpassing all other Indian paper units. But recently, the factory is facing very hard days due to the shortage of raw materials like bamboos, sabaigrass etc. all the bamboos of Rohtas forest have been exhausted and Palamau forest is also not fully supporting it. Therefore, production has sharply declined to 35,000 tonnes during 1973-74. Lateron the company started transporting bamboos and sabai grass from Assam state and the production has slightly improved. The factory produced nearly 46,000 tonnes of paper during 1980-81 (Table 5.8).

The Heavy Chemical Factories were established in between 1939-42. Caustic Soda Plant, Sulphuric Acid Plant, Ferric Alum Plant, Potas Alum Plant are the main units under this industry. These chemicals are locally used in the paper, vanaspati and soap factories complex. At present 18 tonnes of caustic soda, 15 tonnes of chlorine and 3.8 tonnes of hydrocloric acid is produced per day. The sulphuric acid plant is the largest chemical unit which produces ferric alum, potas alum and ammon alum with 15 tonnes, 7 tonnes and 1 tonne per day respectively.

Among other units Asbestos Cement plant, Vulcanised Fiber Plant, Vanaspati Plant and Soap Plant are important. But now the former two have been closed due to scarcity of imported raw materials like asbestos and base paper. The Vanaspati unit is successfully running with a production capacity of 100 tonnes per day. Likewise, the soap factory based on the waste materials of Vanaspati factory produces 1.3 tonnes of 'Ashoka' washing bar soap daily.

TABLE 5.8 : **Production trend of Dalmianagar complex**

(*Figures in tonnes*)

Produces	1950-51	1960-61	1970-71	1980-81
Sugar	25,000	57,000	closed	closed
Paper	14,000	92,000	40,441	46,000
Cement	272,000	355,238	472,000	476,000
Vanaspati	6,000	9,800	23,000	27,000
Caustic soda	4,560	4,600	6,148	6,248
Ferric alum	—	2,398	4,878	4,878
Soap	—	—	538	840
Others	5,000	12,000	22,000	14,000

Source : R.I. Ltd. Office, Patna.

Table 5.8 reveals that the complex development was at its maximum during 1960-61. The declination started afterward since factories like sugar, asbestos, cement, vulcanised fiber and pulp paper were closed. The paper factory is also facing hardship in respect of raw materials.

Employment basis

During the 1940's the Dalmianagar Complex was formed with more than 6 units, all employing nearly 7,000 labourers. In 1950 the employment figure raised to 8,800 and in 1960, it further increased to 12,000. But in 1970 and 1980 the employment figures have came down confirming a declination trend (Table 5.9).

TABLE 5.9 : **Employment trend of Dalmianagar complex**

(figures in persons)

Factories	1950-51	1960-61	1970-71	1980-81
Sugar	1,500	2,000	closed	closed
Cement	2,600	3,100	3,600	3,900
Paper	1,800	2,300	1,900	2,256
Other units.	2,900	4,600	4,800	2,798

Source : R.I. Ltd. office, Patna.

Spatial expansion

Since 1960 the spatial extension has not shown any improvement. Initially, only 3 square kms. of area were under the R.I. Ltd. which expanded to 8.8 sq. kms. in 1960.

Population trend

Prior to 1930 Dehri was no more than a village in the Sasaram Sub-division. After the establishment of the sugar, cement, paper, chemicals etc. in quick succession the population figure suddenly rose to 8,281 and Dehri became a town in 1941.[10] In 1951 this increased to nearly 15,000.

Table 5.10 clearly indicates that the total population in 1941 trebled in a decade consequent upon the maximum growth of industrialisation. But in 1951-61 the growth trend has not been so rapid. The next decade of 1961-71 showed the slowest growth rate due to the closure of many units. In 1971-81 the

TABLE 5.10 : **Population growth of Dalmianagar complex**

Year	Population
1921	3,245
1931	N.A.
1941	8,231
1951	24,496
1961	36,092
1971	46,037
1981	90,407

Source : (i) District Gazetteers, Shahabad, p. 99.
(ii) Provisional Population Table, paper II, p.

growth reveals the increase in population only due to rise of commercial and other transportational services.

SINDRI COMPLEX

The Sindri Complex comes third in the temporal succession after Jamshedpur and Dalmianagar complexes. This complex is, however, the first to be established after independence in 1947 and production started from October, 1951. The complex comprises of many independent units, like, the Ammonia Sulphate Plant, the Sulphate Nitrate Plant (Double Salt), Urea Plant, a Ammonium Synthesis Plant and the Triple Superphosphate Plant. These are all vertically linked to one another making the Sindri Fertilizer Plant. Besides, several other units like Bihar State Super-phosphate Plant, M.S. Pyrites and Chemical Development Co. Ltd. and lastly, Coke Oven Plant, Gas Plant etc. make a most sophisticated industrial complex in the country (Table 5.11).

Production trend

The industrial landscale of Sindri is dominated by the fertilizer plant. The plant produces three kinds of fertilizer, e.g., ammonium sulphate, urea and ammonium sulphate nitrate (double salt). During 1952-53 nearly 2.2 lakh tonnes of ammonium sulphate was produced. The production was raised to 3.3 lakh tonnes in 1956-57. The factory was taken by F.C.I. (The Fertilizer Corporation of India) in 1961. At that time the plant was

TABLE 5.11 : **Sindri complex and its units : 1980-81**

Name of the units	Year of establishment	Production (Annual)	Employment (persons)
M/s Sindri Fertilizer and Chemicals Ltd.	1947		7,433
(a) Ammonium Sulphate Plant		3.5 lakh tonnes	
(b) Ammonium Sulphate Nitrate Plant (Double Salt)		1.2 lakh tonnes	
(c) Ammonium Synthesis Plant		N.A.	
(d) The Triple Super-Phosphate Plant		3.5 lakh tonnes	
(e) Coke Oven Plant		600 tonnes	
(f) Gas Plant		N.A.	
(g) Power Plant		80,000 K.W.	
(h) Urea Plant		24,000 tonnes	
M/s Bihar State Super-phosphate Factory (Sulphuric Acid)	1958	10,000 tonnes	500
Superphosphate		12,983 tonnes	
M/s Pyrites and Chemical Development Co. Ltd.	1974	15,000 tonnes	400
M/s Associated Cement Co. Ltd.	1955	3 lakh tonnes	1,000

Source : Collected from various sources of Publication.

producing 3.20 lakh tonnes of ammonium sulphate, 87,000 tonnes of double salt and nearly 20,000 tonnes of urea annually. Its capacity utilization was nearly 75 per cent. But after taking over the plant, a decline-trend started. The main cause of the declination in production was shortage of gypsum and aging of machineries. Therefore, a modernization and rationalisation scheme were taken in 1975 to overcome them. Even a shift from gypsum to Pyrites was approved. A Triple Superphosphate Plant, the biggest in the country was commissioned in 1975. This unit produced another 3.26 lakh tonnes of phosphate.

The superphosphate factory of Bihar is another unit which was established in 1958 with a capacity to produce about 25 tonnes of sulphuric acid and 50 tonnes of superphosphate per day. The factory has been extensively modified on the advice of the F.C.I. and since then the production has increased immensely. During 1980-81 the factory produced nearly 12,983 tonnes of superphosphate which was more than the target.

The Sindri Cement factories, under the group of A.C.C. is the major unit of the Sindri Industrial Complex which was established in 1955. Its establishment was based on the 'sludge', a waste product of the fertilizer factory as the main raw material. In the initial stage the production was about one lakh tonne which has increased to 3 lakh tonnes in 1971 and since then it has maintained its production target.

Employment trend

At the time of commissioning the production the total employment was 2,791. In 1961 this figure increased to 5,000 and further nearly 10,000 in 1971. This increase was due to expansion in the fertilizer unit and commissioning of other plants. The fertilizer factory was the main employer. The total employment figure was slightly lesser than 10,000 in 1981. This was only due to the larger pull of labourers in the Bokaro steel plant located at a distance of 50 kms. only.

Spatial expansion

Nearly 8 sq. kms. of land were originally occupied for the erection of the fertilizer plant. Lateron, another 4 sq. kms. of land were taken for the Bihar Superphosphate and cement factories and also for their residential township.

Population trend

Sindri is a town of recent origin and its development started in the year 1947 when the Government of India decided to set up a fertilizer plant in this area. Originally it was a rural area and in 1941 there was a population of 5,827. Since then the progress has been very substantial as shown in Table 5.12. The principal factor responsible for this high rate of growth of population was the employment opportunities. As the employment opportunity was saturated, the growth trend slightly slackened. The population has again increased in 1981 due to large scale migration of people from Jharia to Sindri on account of the landslides in the coal fields. Similarly, the modernization and expansion of the plants have also affected the growth of population positively.

TABLE 5.12 : **Population trend of Sindri complex 1941-1981**

Years	Population	Growth in persons	Growth in percentage
1941	5,827	—	—
1951	13,045	+ 7,218	+ 166.00
1961	41,315	+ 28,270	+ 300.00
1971	46,812	+ 5,497	+ 12.00
1981 (Prov.)	70,542	+ 23,730	+ 52.00

Source : Census reports.

RANCHI COMPLEX

The Ranchi Complex is the outcome of our plan period. It is the fourth in order of chronological evolution of the complexes in Bihar. The Heavy Engineering Corporation at Hatia is the main plant of the complex.

The growth of Ranchi complex starts with the growth of the H.E.C. from 1959. The H.E.C. is a unique plant. It is a three-in-one complex, comprising of the Heavy Machine Building Plant (HMBP), the Foundary Forge Plant (FFP) and the Heavy Machine Tools Plant (HMTP). Forging castings, machine building and machine tool, equipment manufacturing are all done through this great mono-mighty engineering organisation.

Production trend

The volume of production has been increasing continuously since 1963 the year of start. Table 5.13 shows the production trend of H.E.C. characterised by ups and downs. The 1976-77 year is the landmark in the production history of H.E.C. which has crossed all the previous.

TABLE 5.13 : **Production trend in the H.E.C. 1965-66 to 1981-82**

(*Production fig. is in lakh Rs.*)

Years	H.M.B P.	F F P.	H M.T P.	Total for H.E.C.
1965-66	285.48	48.23	12.00	346.00
1966-67	466.73	95.48	30.00	592.18
1967-68	556.92	179.60	37.00	786.00
1968-69	1000.00	272.00	43.00	1315.00
1969-70	—	Not Available	—	—
1970-71	—	—	—	—
1971-72	3400.00	1800.00	412.00	5612.00
1972-73	—	—	—	—
1974-75	5613.00	2400.00	617.00	8630.00
1976-77	7218.00	3136 00	889.00	11240 00
1978-79	5400.00	2300.00	800.00	8500.00
1979-80	—	—	—	5200.00
1980-81	—	—	—	6800.00
1981-82	—	—	—	1700.00

Source : Compiled by the author.

Spatial expansion

In 1957 the H.E.C. acquired about 6 sq. kms. of land for the construction of plant. Further it was extended and another 11.20 sq. kms. of land were included under the H.E C. Township in 1961-62. In 1967-68 another 5 sq. kms. of land were added embracing about 22 sq. kms. of land under the H.E.C. Other ancillaries are widely distributed in different parts of Ranchi town covering a diversified zone of about 200 sq. km. Thus this complex becomes one of the most extensive complexes in the country (Table 5.14).

Population trend

The establishment of H.E.C. at Ranchi spurted the growth of population. Although this growth is as drastic as any industrial centre but Ranchi has also remained one of the important commercial and administrative centres. Therefore, population grew by 61 per cent during 1951-61, 43 per cent during 1961-71 and 77 per cent during 1971-81 (Table 5.15). This complex acts as hub for many economic activities as well and is the centre of attraction for skilled and unskilled workers.

TABLE 5.14 : **Industrial units of Ranchi complex 1980-81**

Name of the unit	Year of establish-ment	Production	Employ-ment
The Heavy Engineering Corporation Ltd. (HEC)	1959		30000
(a) The Heavy Machine Building Plant (HMBP)		45000 tonnes machinery	
(b) The Foundry Forge Plant (FFP)		105000 tonnes of steel. Cartage 80000 tonnes of of rolled and finished steel.	
(c) The Heavy Machine Tools Plant.		10000 tonnes heavy machine tools	
Bharat Ball Bearing Co., Ratu.		1404000 nos. annually	662
M/s Usha Martine Black Ltd., Tatisilwai.		7200 M/T	600
Electric transformer and motors, Tatisilwai.		150000 K.V. annually.	400
High Tension Insulator Factory, Namkum.		24000 tonnes	520
M/s Chotanagpur Engineering Works Ltd., Ranchi.		N A.	200
The Lac Research Institute.		N.A.	N.A.
The Govt. Vaccine Institute.		N.A.	N.A.
The Ranchi Distillery.	1908	16000 L.P. Leters per month.	100
Central Designs and Research Institute, Dhurwa.		Training Centre.	500

Source : Arranged from various sources, Ranchi.

TABLE 5.15 : **Population trend of Ranchi complex**

Years	Population	Decade variation	Growth in percentage
1951	125045	—	—
1961	202478	+ 77433	+ 69.9%
1971	259409	+ 46937	+ 43.0%
1981	487485	+ 228007	+ 77.0%

Source : Based on Bihar District Gazetteers, Ranchi and provisional population totals.

BARAUNI COMPLEX

The Barauni Complex is the fifth large scale enterprise in the study area. It originate during the 3rd plan period. Its master unit, the Indian Oil Refinery was commissioned under public sector in July, 1964. North Bihar was fortunate to have such type of prestigious plant which uptil now remained agrarian with a few spotted industrial centres. Subsequently, in 1969 a thermal power with its three sub-units was also installed at Barauni. Again a fertilizer complex has also been established here in September, 1976. Moreover, the setting up of the Petrochemical complex, a cement factory, a nylon plant and a tractor manufacturing plant is under serious consideration.

Production trend

The Indian oil Refinery is the premier unit which was designed to refine 2 million tonnes of crude oil annually. Its capacity was further expanded to 3 million tonnes. But this capacity has hardly been fulfilled. It has been refining a little over 2.6 million tonnes per annum. This limitation of production is caused by the limited supply of crude petroleum from Assam. To come over this restriction of supply, Barauni was linked through the pipelines with Haldia Port near Calcutta for crude supply. In 1975, the Oil India took a scheme of Rs. 40 crores to expend the Naharkatia Barauni pipeline system to receive 2.25 million tonnes of crude oil per year for Barauni Refinery. The production of oil refinery was badly affected during 1980-81 due to interrupted supply of crude oil from Assam on account of the

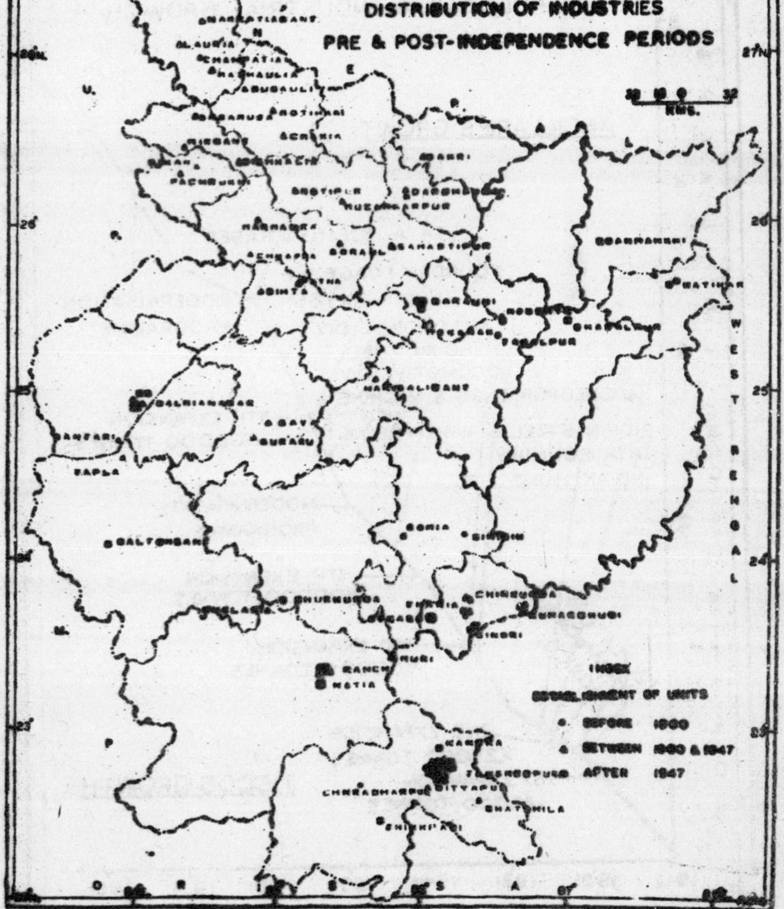

BIHAR
DISTRIBUTION OF INDUSTRIES
PRE & POST-INDEPENDENCE PERIODS
KMS.
WEST BENGAL
INDEX
ESTABLISHMENT OF UNITS
BEFORE 1900
BETWEEN 1900 & 1947
AFTER 1947

Fig. 51

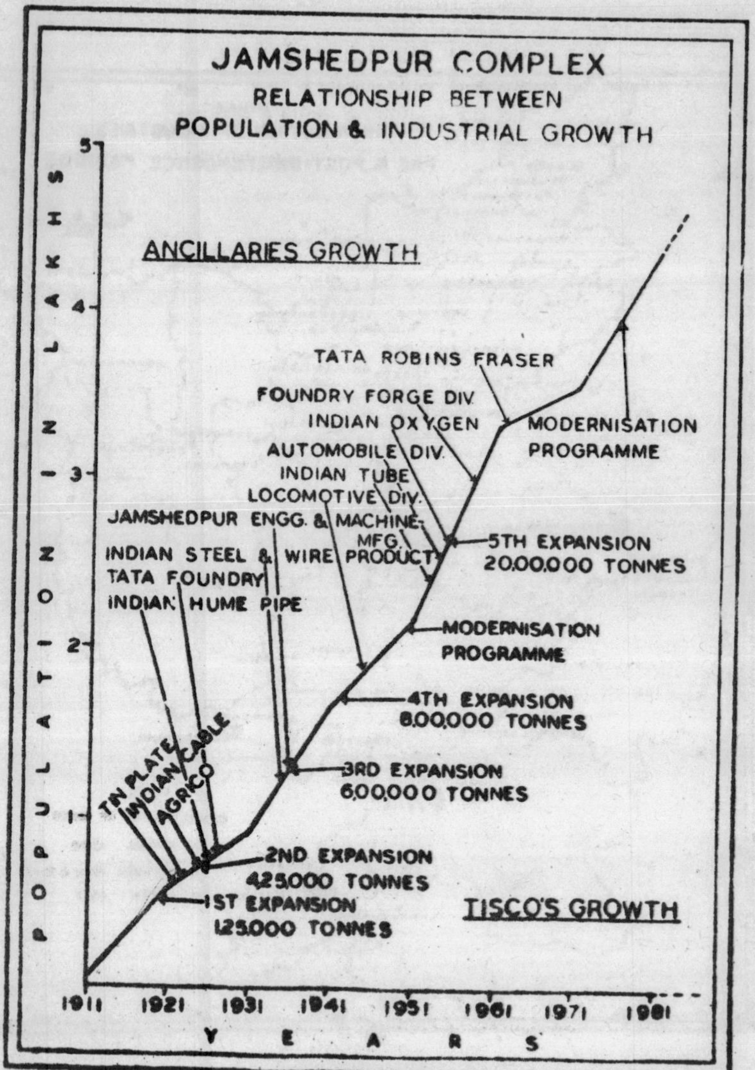
JAMSHEDPUR COMPLEX
RELATIONSHIP BETWEEN
POPULATION & INDUSTRIAL GROWTH
POPULATION IN LAKHS
ANCILLARIES GROWTH
TATA ROBINS FRASER
FOUNDRY FORGE DIV.
INDIAN OXYGEN
MODERNISATION PROGRAMME
AUTOMOBILE DIV.
INDIAN TUBE
LOCOMOTIVE DIV.
JAMSHEDPUR ENGG. & MACHINE MFG.
INDIAN STEEL & WIRE PRODUCT
TATA FOUNDRY
INDIAN HUME PIPE
5TH EXPANSION 20,00,000 TONNES
MODERNISATION PROGRAMME
4TH EXPANSION 8,00,000 TONNES
3RD EXPANSION 6,00,000 TONNES
TIN PLATE
INDIAN CABLE
AGRICO
2ND EXPANSION 425,000 TONNES
1ST EXPANSION 125,000 TONNES
TISCO'S GROWTH
1911 1921 1931 1941 1951 1961 1971 1981
YEARS

Fig. 52

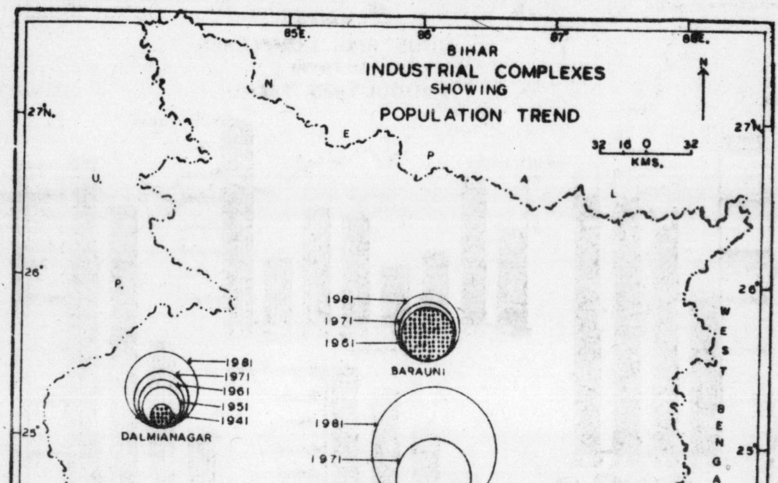
BIHAR
INDUSTRIAL COMPLEXES
SHOWING
POPULATION TREND
N
32 16 0 32
KMS.
85E.
86°
87°
88E.
27N.
26°
25°
24°
23°
N
E
P
A
L
U.
P.
M.
P.
WEST BENGAL
O R I S S A
1981
1971
1961
BARAUNI
1981
1971
1961
1951
1941
DALMIANAGAR
1981
1971
1961
BOKARO
1981
1971
1961
1951
1941
SINDRI
1981
1971
1961
1951
RANCHI
1981
1971
1961
1951
1941
1931
1921
1911
JAMSHEDPUR
500000 PERSONS
300000 "
100000 "
50000 "
20000 "
5000 "
POPULATION BEFORE ESTABLISHMENT OF INDUSTRIES

FIG. 53

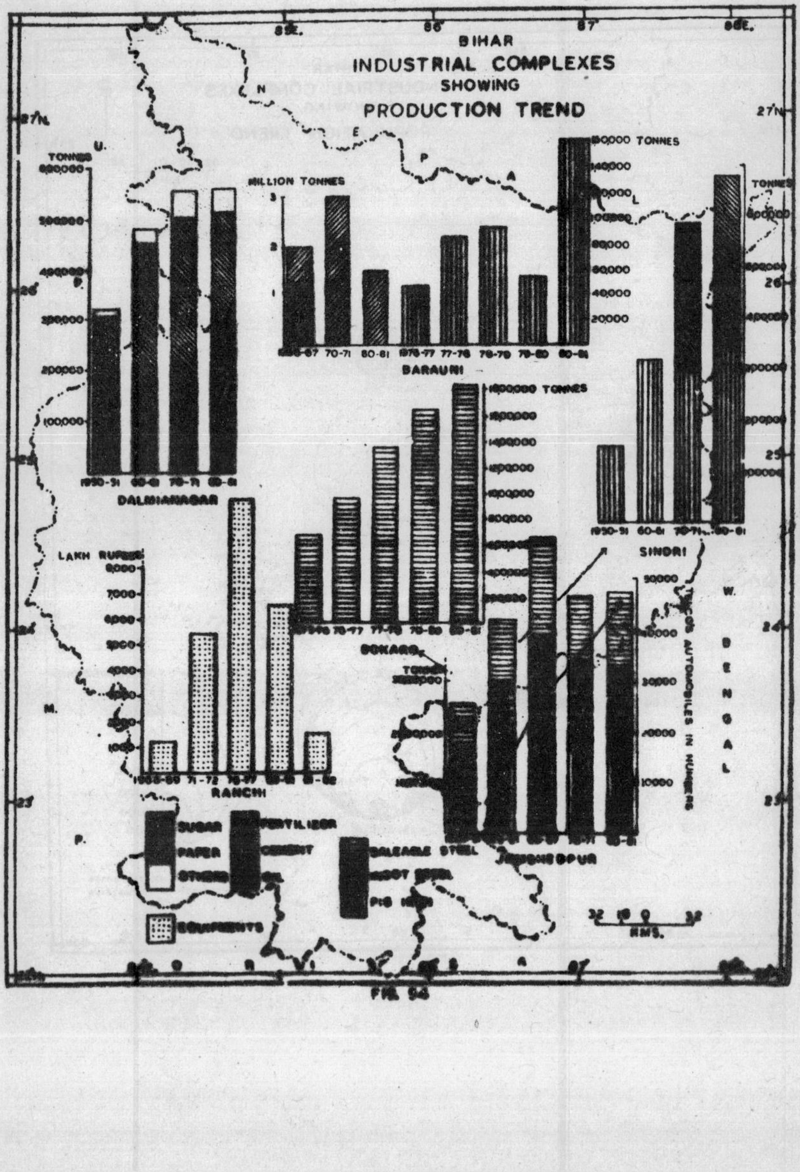
BIHAR
INDUSTRIAL COMPLEXES
SHOWING
PRODUCTION TREND
TONNES
DALMIANAGAR
MILLION TONNES
BARAUNI
SINDRI
BOKARO
LAKH RUPEES
RANCHI
JAMSHEDPUR
AUTOMOBILES IN NUMBERS
SUGAR
PAPER
FERTILIZER
CEMENT
EQUIPMENTS
W. BENGAL
KMS.

FIG. 94

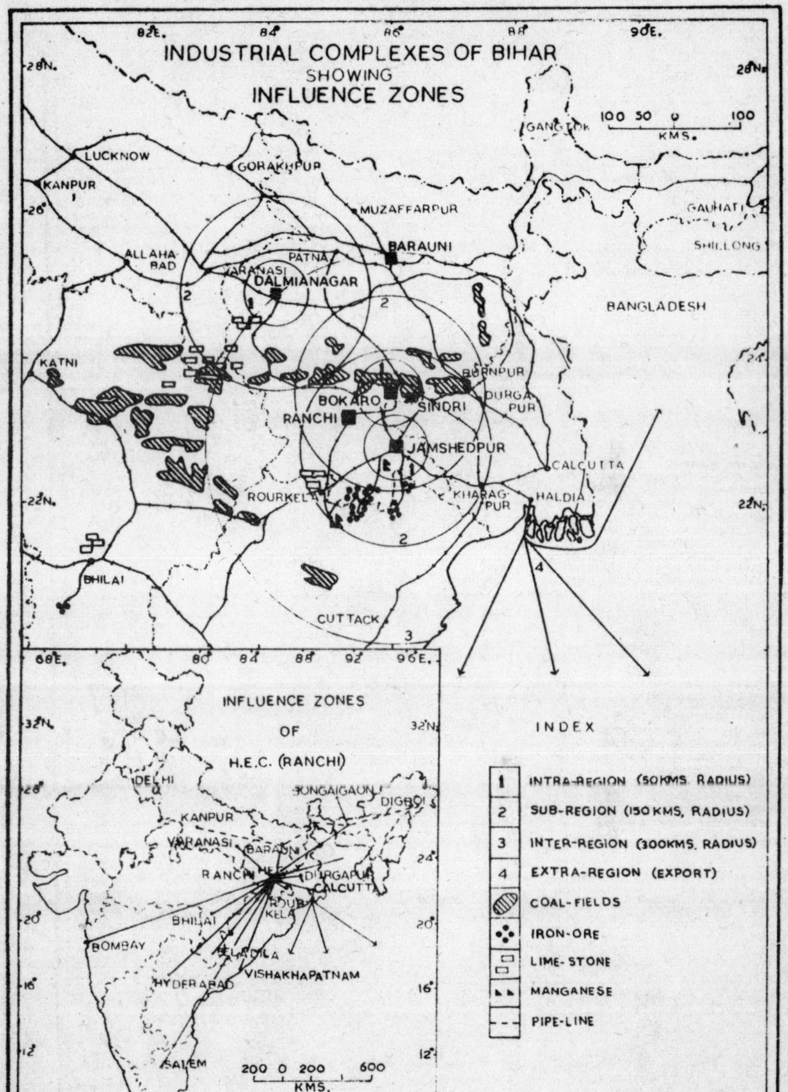

INDUSTRIAL COMPLEXES OF BIHAR
SHOWING
INFLUENCE ZONES
100 50 0 100
KMS.
LUCKNOW
KANPUR
GORAKHPUR
MUZAFFARPUR
GANGTOK
GAUHATI
SHILLONG
ALLAHABAD
VARANASI
PATNA
BARAUNI
DALMIANAGAR
BANGLADESH
KATNI
BURNPUR
BOKARO
SINDRI
DURGAPUR
RANCHI
JAMSHEDPUR
CALCUTTA
ROURKELA
KHARAGPUR
HALDIA
BHILAI
CUTTACK
INFLUENCE ZONES
OF
H.E.C. (RANCHI)
DELHI
BONGAIGAON
DIGBOI
KANPUR
VARANASI
BARAUNI
RANCHI
DURGAPUR
CALCUTTA
ROURKELA
BHILAI
BOMBAY
BELADILA
VISHAKHAPATNAM
HYDERABAD
SALEM
200 0 200 600
KMS.
INDEX
1 INTRA-REGION (50 KMS. RADIUS)
2 SUB-REGION (150 KMS. RADIUS)
3 INTER-REGION (300 KMS. RADIUS)
4 EXTRA-REGION (EXPORT)
COAL-FIELDS
IRON-ORE
LIME-STONE
MANGANESE
PIPE-LINE

FIG. 50

regional movement. Thereby the production was marred, affecting the functioning of other dependent units.

The fertilizer factory started production since 1976. It is designed to produce 330,000 tonnes of urea annually. Unfortunately, from its beginning it has not achieved its terget due to the short supply of napthe, the basic raw material and also due to power hurdles. The factory had produced only 43,401 tonnes of urea in 1976-77, 1.8 lakh tonnes in 1977-78 and 1.01 lakh tonnes in 1978-79. In 1979-80 it produced only 9,700 tonnes due to power shortage. To tide over this power shortage, the Board of Hindustan Fertilizer Corporation has ordered the installation of 16 M.W. captive power plant at Barauni for only fertilizer plant.[11] This project is yet to start. During 1980-81 most of the days the factory had to be closed on account of the non-supply of Naptha from the adjacent oil refinery. But this condition has been improved and therefore, the factory achieved a record production of 1,61,372 tonnes of urea in 1981-82.[12]

Employment trend

The Oil Refinery, the fertilizer and the thermal plant altogether provide an employment opportunity to nearly 5,000 persons. No influx of labour is found here as found at other newly steel and engineering plants.

Areal expansion

The Barauni Complex occupied 30 sq. km. of area in 1960-61. It has further managed to acquire another 3600 acres of land for the expansion of future industries like petro-chemical, cement and others.

Population trend

In 1961 Barauni was a town with a population of 46,000. This was credited only due to the opening of the Rajendra bridge across the Ganga river and since then Barauni become an important traffic point. Another factor which contributed to the growth of population was the establishment of Indian Oil refinery in 1964. But during 1961-71 the population growth was not considerable. This was due to the selection of Begusarai as district headquarters which attracted more people in comparison to

Barauni. The Indian Oil refinery provided a limited employment opportunities to the people in comparison to other industrial complexes in the state. During 1971-81 there was an increase in the growth of population caused by the establishment of fertilizer plant. The 1981 provincial Census has separated Barauni Oil Township from rest of Barauni. This township contains a population of 11,000 entirely related to the industrial activities of Barauni.

BOKARO COMPLEX

The Bokaro Complex is the recent addition to the industrial landscape of Bihar. It is the most ambitious of all the other steel plants in the country. It is a four-phased expansion plant of 10 million tonnes of steel production and is one of the largest in Asia. It is a hundred per cent indigenous plant, fashioned and manufactured by the Indian machinery and engineer-experts. A preliminary report about the Bokaro steel project was prepared in 1959 and a detailed Project Report in 1962. Later on, an agreement was signed in 1965 between the Government of India and the Soviet Union for financial and technical collaboration. The first foundation stone for the erection of the first furnace was laid down in 1968.

Bokaro has made a rapid progress within a decade. Apart from the first blast furnace commissioned on 3rd October, 1972, two converters in the steel melting shop have been started in 1974 along with a number of other units. The commissioning of the slabbing mill in 1974 was a positive step towards production of finished steel products. This slabbing mill is the only universal slabbing mill in the country and has an hourly capacity to slab 600 to 800 tonnes of ingot steel. Bokaro's hot strip (HSM) was commissioned in December 1975. This is the most modern in the world and has a capacity of rolling 4.75 million tonnes of ingot steel. In 1976 Bokaro's second blast furnace and the third coke oven battery were started. Bokaro's performance during the year 1977 was overall successful with an upward trend in production and construction works also. The third blast furnace of the plant has already started production and thus the first stage of 1.7 million tonnes target has been achieved. The construction work of the second phase had already been started from 1976 simultaneously with the first phase.

In the beginning of 1978 the first Cold Rolling Mill (CRM) first of its type in country and also in S.W. Asia, was inagurated. Consequently the fourth coke oven battery was started and has been completed in 1979. In July 1979 a slag granulation plant having a capacity of 1.35 million tonnes production of granulated slag per annum for cement manufacturing was completed at a cost of about Rs. 9.5 crores. In 1980 the fourth Blast furnace came into action. In March, 1981 the fifth coke oven battery was lighted up. This battery is one of the first three batteries required for the completion of 4 million tonnes stage of the plant. The second Cold Rolling Mill is expected to be commissioned by March, 1983. The Sail authority also approved the expansion of the BSL from 4 M/T to 4.75 M/T with an estimated cost of Rs. 141 crores. Even the feasibility of its expansion to 10 M/T is under active consideration. Thus, Bokaro Complex is a massive integrated steel plant in making.

Production trend

The production trend of Bokaro Steel Plant has been very encouraging. The target has been achieved more than 100 per cent. During the first financial year of 1973-74, the output of hot metal from the blast furnace was 92 per cent of the target and 81 per cent of the rated capacity. It has improved to 104 per cent of the target and 85 per cent of the rated capacity during 1974-75. The production of pig iron and ingot steel was 103 and 109 per cent respectively of the targets during 1974-75. In 1974-75 the plant has produced 2.4 lakh tonnes of pig iron. In 1975-76 about 7.5 lakh tonnes of ingot steel was produced. Production of 10,34,777 tonnes of ingot steel during the year 1977 was an improvement of 31 per cent over the 1976 performance. The plant achieved its 1.7 million tonnes of production target of ingot steel in 1979-80, and in 1980-81 it exceeded the target by 64 per cent of extra-production.

Employment trend

In 1971 there were 14,000 workers in plant which subsequently rose up to 17,000, 25,000 and 32,000 in 1975, 1977 and 1981 respectively.

Areal expansion

The Bokaro Steel City expands over an area of 167.25 sq. kms. Out of which nearly 40 sq. kms. of land are under the plant.

Population trend

For the first time in 1971 the Bokaro Steel City (BSC) was credited to town with a total population of 97,007. This population figure increased to 261,240 in 1981. This is impact of steel plant which brought a dynamic change in the city area and surroundings.

Analysing the growth trend and applying the model discussed earlier the following results are obtained :

From 1920 to 1967 Jamshedpur has shown

$$T^{+1}+S^{+1}+D^{+1}=G\ (+)$$

Means, all round progress leading to the upward trend. But after 1968 to 1980-81 it has

$$T^{+1}+S^{+0}+D+\,\text{–}=G$$

=No progress in spatial extension and some times growth in production, some time loss; again, growth in labour employment and growth of population, finally results a growth trend, not as apparent as in the first case.

(ii) In the case of Dalmianagar, from 1933 to 1960 the first model $T^{+1}+S^{+1}+D^{+1}=G\ (+)$ has applied. But after 1961 to 1981 it has been found that $T^{+1}+S^{+0}+D^{-}=G\ (-)$ means loss in all direction, production, employment and number of industrial units.

(iii) Sindri and Barauni have always shown

$$T^{+1}+S^{+1}+D^{+-}=G\ \pm$$

means no progress apparently.

(iv) Ranchi and Bokaro are very much fitting in the first model of all round growth trend, that is

$$T^{+1}+S^{+1}+D^{+1}=G\ (+).$$

MAGNITUDE OF COMPLEXES

Magnitude is a size or comparative importance of the Plants under the study. On the basis of following parameters a magnitude of a complex may be measured. They are capital investment, profitability, size (on the basis of labour employment or the areal expansion) and volume of infent-output.

In this study, however, data related to capital investment, profitability and volume of input-output were not available. It is very difficult to obtain data on these lines particularly of large plants. These are, therefore, rejected even if they can be of much value. To measure the order of magnitude employment data is used as it is easily available with the respective offices.

On the basis of labour employment it is clear that Jamshedpur Complex is by far the most important followed by Ranchi, Bokaro, Dalmianagar, Sindri and Barauni Complexes. This is quite evident from Table 5.16. Therefore, Jamshedpur is the first order of magnitude, while Ranchi and Bokaro fall in the Second order, since they employ almost the same length of workers. The same is the case with Sindri, Dalmianagar and Barauni which have been categorised as third order of magnitude because they employ less than 10 thousand workers (Fig. 55).

TABLE 5.16 : **Employment size and order of magnitude of industrial complexes, 1980-81**

Name of the complex	Employment	Order of Magnitude
Jamshedpur	101390	I
Ranchi	38781	II
Sindri	9788	III
Bokaro	32000	II
Dalmianagar	9654	III
Barauni	7500	III

Saurce : Lal, B B., Census of India, 1981, paper I and II, provisional population totals.

FACTORS AFFECTING THE GROWTH OF INDUSTRIAL COMPLEXES

The factors affecting the growth of industrial complexes are many. They are internal and external geographical factors among which, the raw material base, the power base, the availability of infrastructural facilities, developed regional market, growth of industrial linkages, economics of concentration, advanced technology and the Governmental decisions. They are discussed at length in the succeeding section.

Raw material base

Bihar is one of the richest mineral states of India. During the year 1980-81, Bihar continued to occupy the first place in the production of minerals. It accounts for 29.5 per cent of the total national value of minerals with Madhya Pradesh contributing 16.5 per cent, West Bengal 10.75 per cent, Bombay High 10.4 per cent and Gujarat 6.4 per cent.[13] Bihar, especially the Chotanagpur region is the mineral-store house, rich enough in possession of metallic minerals like iron-ore, manganese, tungten, copper and others as also mica and refractories. Moreover, the importance of these minerals is immense due to the close availability of best quality of coking coal. The geographical proximity of these minerals combined with transportation, market and labour facilities, has given the industries a wide base. The region, however, has proved itself one of the most suited locational sites in the world for the localization of heavy industries like iron and steel and other engineering industries. And, therefore, heavy industrial centres of Jamshedpur, Bokaro and Ranchi have been located in this belt of the regional climaxes of India.

The region is well defined into several mineral belts, e.g., iron-ore, coal, copper, mica, bauxite, limestone, etc. (Fig. 16). The iron-ore belt extends across Singhbhum, Bonai, Keonjhar and Mayurbhanj districts of Bihar and Orissa. The Iron Belt produces about 70 per cent of the best quality of haematitic ore. "The zone contains a reserve of 2,800 million tonnes (provides being 43% of India's reserve and accounts for 63% of all India output).[14] Similarly the manganese belt of Bihar and Orissa is closely located near the iron belt facilitating it more economical in transportation. So far as the coking coal is concerned, it is solely concentrated in the coal fields of Damodar Valley of Jharia and Raniganj of Bihar and West Bengal respectively. Of the total reserve of coking coal (about 3,200 million tonnes as the proved reserves and further about 2,000 million tonnes as indicated and inferred reserves) of the country 86 per cent is in Bihar and virtually the remainder in West Bengal.[15] It may be concluded, however, that the region is not only suitable for the location of iron and steel industry only, but it is equally suited for the establishment of heavy engineering, chemical, fertilizers, alloys and cement industries. After independence, the exploitation of these minerals has increased by many folds giving rise to the establishment of several, large, medium and light industries. Jamshedpur, Ranchi, Sindri, Bokaro, Dalmianagar, Barauni and several others have been marked by the important industrial undertakings.

Power base

Besides coal, Bihar has immense water to utilize it in the form of hydel power. A number of perennial rivers are here which have been utilized for the development of water power. The D.V.C. Schemes on the Damodar river is the main hydel power source for the industries of the region. The establishment of the D.V.C. in 1948 has augmented the pace of industrialisation. Other hydel projects on the Subarnarekha river have been developed to supply power to the H.E.C., Hatia, Ranchi. It is a fact that the huge power potential has not been utilized at par of its requirement.

The thermal power has remained one of the major considerations of industrial location in Bihar. A number of thermal power stations, like the Patratu, the Bokaro, the Jharia, the Barauni and the several others have acted as the base of the industrial development. Besides, almost all important industrial centres have set up their own captive power stations (Fig. 17). Therefore, availability of hydel and thermal power, has caused the large concentration of industrial centres.

Availability of infrastructure facilities

An industrial agglomeration is directly influenced by the availability of infrastructural facilities, like roads, railways, water supply, banking, health and educational services, etc. These are very essential for the establishment and development of industry. When these facilities are fully developed in industrialist tends to set up a new plant in order to minimise the cost of production. When one major industrial undertaking starts and as the infrastructure facilities develop, numerous other units are located in due course of time and thus a complex phenomenon growth.

The industrial complexes in Bihar explain the view very well. The TISCO at Jamshedpur was established in 1907 in a complete virgin rural environs. Gradually the infrastructure facilities were developed and more industrial units were set up. (Fig. 51). Similarly the Bokaro Steel City is a new industrial centre where infrastructure facilities are in the process of development and so several industrial units are still to develop around. The regional setting of all the industrial complexes have indicated that these complexes are well connected with roads and railways. Mostly, these complexes are located at the nodal points of the National Highways and Broad-Gauge rail-lines. Jamshedpur, Ranchi, Dalmianagar and Barauni are directly located on the main line of transportation route, where as Sindri and Bokaro are located on the diverted route. These industrial centres are again connected with their resource regions as well as the commercial regions in the country.

Developed regional markets

In fact, rich mineralogy of the State has governed the locational pull of these industries, but nevertheless, the market orientation is not less important. The market orientation of these complexes is to a great extent regional and inter-regional and to a limited extent extra-regional (Fig. 50). The supply of iron and iron products, agricultural tools, fertilizers, cement, paper, etc.; to the whole state from Jamshedpur, Sindri, Barauni and Dalmianagar is a regional consideration. Moreover, the equipment for the Bokaro Steel Plant supplied by the H.E.C. is also on the regional consideration, whereas the H.E.C. is supplying every type of machines and equipments to all industrial centres of the country, the Telco is sending its trucks and other vehicles to every corner of the country. Jamshedpur supplies varieties of iron and steel and other structurals to Calcutta and Bombay regions, Barauni supplies petroleum to Kanpur, Delhi and Haldia, all are done on the inter-regional or at national market level. Considering the international or extra-regional market, Indian Iron and Steel, automobiles and other engineering equipments are in good sale in the Middle East, South East Asian countries, African countries and also in the advanced countries like, U.S.S R., Yugoslavia, Turkey, Egypt and Cuba. Thus, the larger markets of sub-regional, inter-regional and extra-regional have highly influenced the growth of these industrial complexes of the state.

Growth of industrial linkages

The inter-dependence of plants has acted one of the most vital internal geographical factors for the growth of industrial complexes. Tisco at Jamshedpur, mainly produces pig iron and steel. These products are variably used in the other units which have been set up nearby. Telco, the Tata Foundaries Co., Agrico and several other units thrive on Tisco's output. In return, these units fulfil the various demands of the mother plant in the form of machines, vehicles, wise nut, bolt, etc. The establishment of the H.E.C. Ltd. at Hatia approximately in the midst of the main iron and steel producing centres, is again strongly held by this industrial linkage phenomenon. Likewise input-output relation is well marked among the existing units of the Rohtas Industries Ltd. at Dalmianagar. The paper factory was using bagasse of the sugar factory. Cement is used for cement, asbestos, pipes, sheets. Chemical factories supply chemicals to paper, vanaspati and soap factories. Vanaspati factories supply its dirt to soap manufacturing. Sindri's cement factory is entirely based on the sludge of the fertilizer plants. Barauni fertilizer functions on the supply of naptha from the oil refinery. Thus the linkage phenomena have to a great extent influenced the growth of industrial complexes in the region.

Economies of concentration

"When an industry or a major part of it concentrates itself within a relatively small area, important advantages often accrue to it as a result of what have been called economies of concentration".[16] These economies are the outcome of several units in terms of common expenditures like hospitals, universities, laboratories, parks, inner roads, railways, bridges and other common facilities. The Tata Industries group at Jamshedpur has got one National Metallurgical Laboratory, one hospital, colleges, parks and other social places for all. Similarly, the Rohtas Industries Ltd., has also got common amenities. Again different units produce the goods of different varieties and supply them to the common market making it hetrogeneous in nature for the consumers. So, the market becomes more economical to the consumers. For example, Jamshedpur has become the most important regional market for its iron and its products. Moreover, specialisation in particular goods also invites complex phenomena. "A number of the small scale engineering units in Chotanagpur are dependent on the large scale ones for their business. They take on job work and specialise in such fields as casting, machinery, plating, welding, lining and painting. They incur lower overhead costs. Because of their specialisation in particular lines...units manufacturing wire nails, industrial fasteness, ferrous metal and iron products etc., have sprouted up in Chotanagpur Division with a view to acquiring the economics of agglomeration".[17]

Advanced technology

One major factor which has contributed to the industrial concentrations is the technical progress recorded in the techniques of production.[18] From coal, several products like coke, chemical colours etc. are produced. Again coke is used in the making of steel, fertilizers etc. Similarly out of one petroleum, a host of materials are produced. The establishment of Sindri fertilizer plant has been done on coal. Likewise expansion of the fertilizer plant at Barauni was done on the basis of naphtha, a bye-product from the oil refinery. Naphtha is transformed into ammonia and nitrate fertilizers through the advance technological progress. Modern technique to utilize the waste product of iron and steel, that is 'slag' and 'sludge', a waste product of fertilizer factories, are being utilized as the basic raw material for the cement factories. For example Jhinkpani Cement factory is fully dependent upon the slag supply from Tisco. Similarly Sindri cement factory runs through the sludge of the fertilizer factories. Numerous other cement factories are proposed to be established in the proximities of larger plants, like Bokaro, Barauni etc.

Government's policy

The government's policy, specially in the democratic set up becomes very much operative for the growth of industries. The government facilitates not providing better infra-structures only, but also by giving several protective and concessional avenues for the proper growth. Whenever, a factory suffers from financial hardship or other managerial problems, the government comes forward for the rescue of the firms. After independence, the Indian government has taken several economic measures to accelerate the pace of industrialisation in the country. The 2nd Five-Year Plan was primarily industry oriented. Numerous heavy plants have been set up in the Chotanagpur region, out of a social welfare strategy of the government.

Therefore, the rich mineralogy, high power potentiality, facilities of roads and railways, extended regional, inter-regional and to a limited extent international market conditions, and huge labour availability are the external factors while the inter-dependability, economics of concentration, developed regional infra-structural facilities and several others are internal factors which have governed the complex growth of Jamshedpur, Ranchi, Sindri, Bokaro, Dalmianagar and Barauni industrial centres. Apart from these centres, several others such as Ramgarh, Patratu, Dhanbad, Bermo and Ghatsila are centres of industrial complexes in offing. Therefore, the future prospect of industrialisation in the state is very bright. It is, however, a fact that the industries are facing acute problems like, power shortage, transportational bottlenecks, financial troubles, older machines and instability in functions due to the political upsurgences. Without solving these problems, a better industrial prospect cannot be achieved.

REFERENCES

1. Roy Chaudhury, P.C. (1960), *Bihar District Gazetteers*, Champaran, p. 258.

2. Bradely, B. (1910), *Chotanagpur: A little known Province of the Empire*, London, p.2.

3. Pandey, P. (1970), op. cit., p. 53.

4. Majid, S.M. (1949), "The Industrial Geography of Bihar", Unpublised Ph.D. Thesis, Department of Geography, University of London, p. 41.

5. Pandey, P. (1970), op. cit., p. 126.

6. Choudhury, M.R. (1973), "Iron and Steel Industry in India", *Industrial Situation in India*, Vol. 11, p. 43.

7. Bose, P.N. (1904), "Notes on the Geology and Mineral Resources of Mayurbhanj", *G.S.I.*, Vol. 31, p. 167.

8. Mukherjee, M. (1970), op. cit., p. 101.

9. Karan, P.P. (1955), "A Historical Geography of Chotanagpur", *Indian Geographical Journal*, Vol. 30, p. 357.

10. Roy Chaudhury, P.C. (1966), *Bihar District Gazeetters*, Shahabad, p. 166.

11. *Bihar Information* (1930), Vol. 22, p. 42.

12. *The Indian Nation*, Patna, Vol. LII, No. 103, May 3, 1982, p. 3.

13. *The Searchlight*, Patna, 30th January, 1981, p. 5.

14. Thapan, D. (1966), "The Iron and Steel Belt of India" in R.L. Singh (ed.), *Applied Geography*, National Geographical Society of India, Varanasi p. 173.

15. Dayal, P. (1977), "The Energy Resources of India", Presidential Address, Section of Geology and Geography, *64th Indian Science Congress*, Bhubaneshwar, pp. 1-26.

16. Beacham, A. (1948), *Economics of Industrial Organization*, Sir I. Pitman & Sons, London, pp. 1-172.

17. Prasad, K.N. (1973), op. cit., p. 55.

18. Patni, R.L. (1968), "Criteria for Location of Industrial Plants in India : Changes and Problems", Paper presented at the *21st International Geographical Congress*, Symposium on the Industrialization in the Developing Countries, Patna, pp. 1-76.

6

LINKAGE, PATTERN AND FUNCTIONAL CHARACTERISTICS OF INDUSTRIAL COMPLEXES

THE PREVIOUS chapters have exclusively dealt with the external conditions responsible for the establishment and growth of industrial complexes in Bihar. The present chapter, however, attempts to highlight the internal conditions of the complexes. The internal conditions include linkage, pattern and the functional characteristics. These variables are related to one another and are very essential for the maintenance and continuation of the industry and its associated units. Therefore, it is quite relevant to analyse these conditions and this attempt is made towards this direction.

LINKAGE

In common parlance, 'linkage' is variously used. In industrial literature it means a phenomenon which occur among different industrial units primarily located at one place. Actually it is a functional link (internally) between one firm to another based on input-output model, common labour pool, capital link, technological link, etc. In geography it is commonly known as inter-relationship or interdependency of one parameter to another. In this mechanism the output of one unit becomes input for other, and thus, both the units are benefitted. Moreover, such linked or related industries often require types of labour skills and there is room, therefore, for a relatively high degree of labour mobility between firms.[1] The advantages accrued are known as 'economies of concentration', which is one of the most interesting part of the industrial economics.

Linkage is of various types. It functions among the intra-industrial and also in the inter-industrial complexes. In the intra-complexes, it is of four types as propounded by Jarrett,[2] Estall and Buchanan[3] and Kuchhal.[4] These are vertical, horizontal or lateral, diagonal and technological linkages. Fig. 56 presents the linkage type adopted from Jarrett.

Vertical linkage

It is a functional 'interlink' between separate firms each normally forming one stage in a series of operations.[5] It is also known as industry or sequence or process integration. It is the union or combination of the successive stages or processes of manufacture of the finished article--beginning from the raw materials, passing through manufacture to the finished product and distribution. The units combined together do not complete side by side but stand end to end, the one receiving the products of the other as its own raw materials, finally forming to one single establishment.[6] The iron and steel industry is one of the best examples, where iron-ore, coal, limestone and others—raw materials pass through several stages of manufacturing, ultimately into steel or further into other steel structurals, as shown in Fig. 56(A). This accomplishes economics of storage, selling, buying and transporting materials between the various processes. But it also suffers from the acute drawbacks, like, in case of dislocation of any of the intermediate processes the whole organisation may be thrown out of operation. Again, highly integrated industries tend to become inflexible and there by difficult to adapt to business oscillations.[7]

Horizontal or lateral linkage

Such type of linkage takes place when a number of different industrial units produce goods which are finally assembled as part's of a single larger product. Actually it is units integration in which units of similar character are engaged in the same sphere of activity and compete on the same plane. For example automobile is the outcome of several industrial units located side-by-side, as apparent in the Fig. 56(B). Such type of linkage is very common and provide benefits to external economics in buying, manufacturing, selling and research. These external economics, however, lack in the case of the vertical linkage. This type is adopted just to eliminate competition and to acquire monopoly in production and marketing.

Diagonal linkage

It occurs when different goods are manufactured by different units and these are used by other industries. It is also known as service-integration processes. Its contacts are thus with a number of different units and it does not establish a link as in the cases of vertically and horizontally oriented firms. Washers, nuts and bolts, for example, are widely used in manufactured products, while tools of different kinds find wide usage in industry. Fig. 56(C)

Technological linkage

It is a novel concept in which a single manufactured product is variously used as the raw materials for other industries. For example, steel is used in several other industrial products, like wire, tinplate, implements, wheel, etc. Likewise steel wire may be manufactured into nails, screws, chains, electrical fuses, coated wiring and cables, etc. Fig. 56(D) explains it.

But inter-industrial linkage is strongly held through the input-output model.

The industrial complexes of Bihar are characterised by these linkages. A table has been prepared to show the linkages existing in the complexes. The table is mainly concerned with the intra-complexes linkages only.

Table 6.1 reveals that Jamshedpur is the complex of complexes. Tisco, the premier plant is complex in itself (Fig. 57). More than twelve units are integrated vertically, horizontally, diagonally and also technologically. Telco, another sister complex is combined with several independent units located side by side to fetch finally the locomotives, trucks, buses, excavators, shunters, and several other heavy engineering equipments. All the units of Telco are horizontally integrated. Likewise, the Indian Tube Company is again a tube complex where varieties of tube plants are laterally developed. The similar is the case

TABLE 6.1 : Industrial Complex and Linkages

A. JAMSHEDPUR COMPLEX

Vertical	*Horizontal*		*Diagonal*	*Technological*
The Tata Iron & Steel Co (TISCO)				
(a) Six Coke Oven Batteries ↓	1. By Product Plants	(i) Coal Tar	(a) Four Power Houses	All are related to steel groups
(b) Six Blast Furnaces ↓		(ii) Ammonium Sulphate	(b) Oxygen Plant	
(c) Three Steel Melting Shops (S.M.S.) ↓		(iii) Crude Benzol	(c) Granulation Plant	
(d) Two Blooming Mills ↓		(iv) Pure Tolvene	(d) Other Refractories Plants	
(e) Seven Finishing Mills →		(v) Solvent Naphtha	(e) Cement Plant (Jhinkpani)	
(f) Several Structural Producing Plants (finished)		(vi) Still Bottom	(f) National Metallurgical Laboratory	
	2. Finishing Mills	(i) Sintering Plant	(g) Shops	
		(ii) Calcining Plant	(i) Pattern Shop	
		(iii) Skelp Mill	(ii) Structural Shops	
		(iv) Two Soaking Pits	(iii) Model Rooms	
		(v) Pig Casting Plants	(iv) Central Stores	
		(vi) Bar Forging Plant		
		(vii) B.N.R. Plant		
1. Sheet Bar Millet	3. Railway Structurals	(i) A Wheel Plant		
2. A Plate Mill		(ii) A Tyre Plant		
3. Sponge Iron Plant		(iii) An Axle Plant		

Vertical	*Horizontal*	*Diagonal*	*Technological*
The Tata Engineering Locomotive Co. Ltd. (TELCO)			
No Vertical Linkage	1. Steel Foundry for Locomotive Plants	(a) Power Plants	Related to Engineering
	2. Alloy Iron Foundry for Grey Malleable Iron Castings for Tata's Vehicles.	(b) Oxygen Plants	
	3. Several plants horizontally integrated for:	(c) Ancillary Plants	
	(i) Automobiles—trucks, buses, tipper truck, etc.	(d) Other engineering plants, for repairing work, etc.	
	(ii) Locomotives—electrical & diesel	(e) Other servicing centres	
	(iii) Excavators	(f) Sales department	
	(iv) Industrial Shunter, etc.	(g) Research labs.	

Vertical	*Horizontal*	*Diagonal*	*Technological*
The Indian Tube Co. Ltd.			
No Vertical Linkage	1. A Continuous Weld Tube Mill 2. A High Speed Continuous Weld Tube Mill	→ Tube for gas water, steam, structural and mechanical purposes.	All integrated into tube-works
	3. The Electric Resistance Weld Tube Mill	→ Tubes for boilers, bicycles, furniture and transformers	
	4. The Cold Rolling Mill	→ Cold rolled steel strip	
	5. The Seamless Tube Mill	→ Tubes for high pressure steam and hydraulic applications such as boiler and flue tubes, oil pipeline etc.	
	6. The Pole Plant	→ Tubular poles for transmission and lighting columns	

Fig. 56

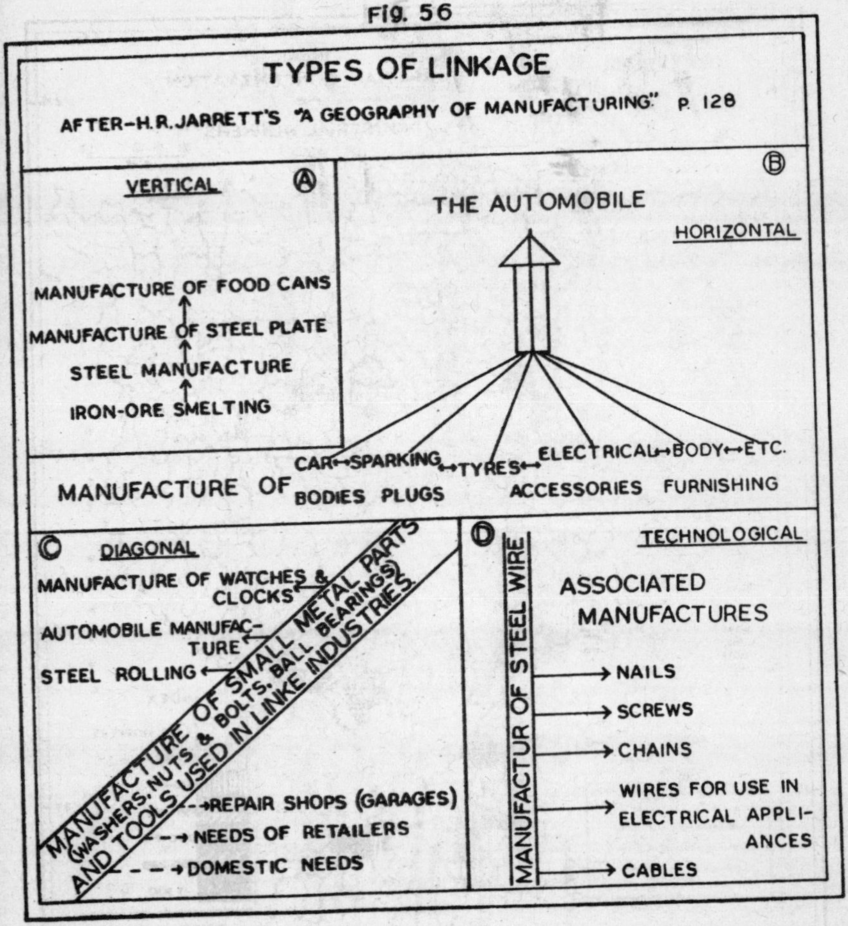
TYPES OF LINKAGE
AFTER-H.R.JARRETT'S "A GEOGRAPHY OF MANUFACTURING" P. 128
VERTICAL
A
MANUFACTURE OF FOOD CANS
MANUFACTURE OF STEEL PLATE
STEEL MANUFACTURE
IRON-ORE SMELTING
B
THE AUTOMOBILE
HORIZONTAL
MANUFACTURE OF
CAR BODIES
SPARKING PLUGS
TYRES
ELECTRICAL ACCESSORIES
BODY FURNISHING
ETC.
C
DIAGONAL
MANUFACTURE OF WATCHES & CLOCKS
AUTOMOBILE MANUFACTURE
STEEL ROLLING
MANUFACTURE OF SMALL METAL PARTS (WASHERS, NUTS & BOLTS, BALL BEARINGS) AND TOOLS USED IN LINKE INDUSTRIES
REPAIR SHOPS (GARAGES)
NEEDS OF RETAILERS
DOMESTIC NEEDS
D
TECHNOLOGICAL
MANUFACTUR OF STEEL WIRE
ASSOCIATED MANUFACTURES
NAILS
SCREWS
CHAINS
WIRES FOR USE IN ELECTRICAL APPLIANCES
CABLES

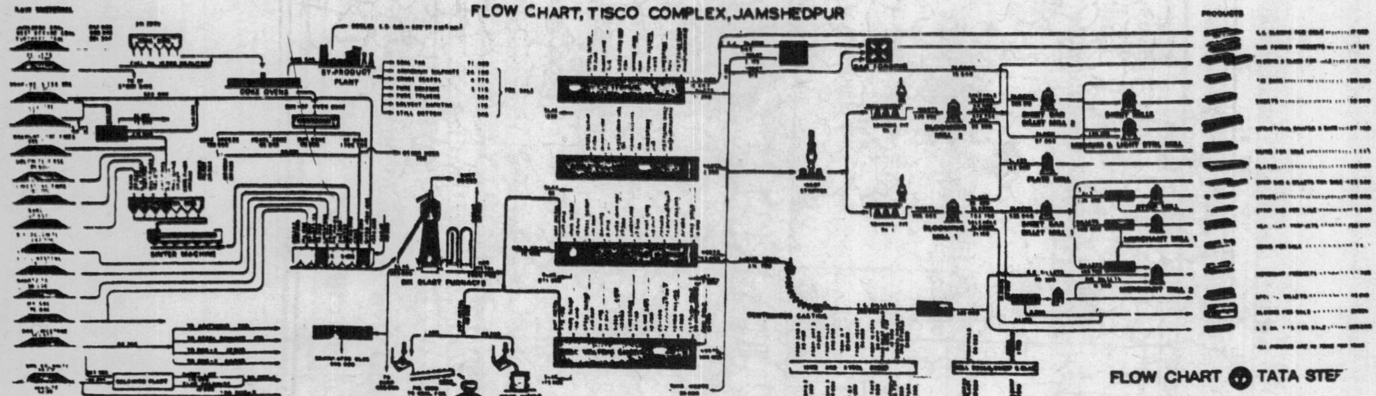
FLOW CHART, TISCO COMPLEX, JAMSHEDPUR
BY-PRODUCT PLANT
COKE OVENS
SINTER MACHINE
FLOW CHART TATA STEF

FIG. 57

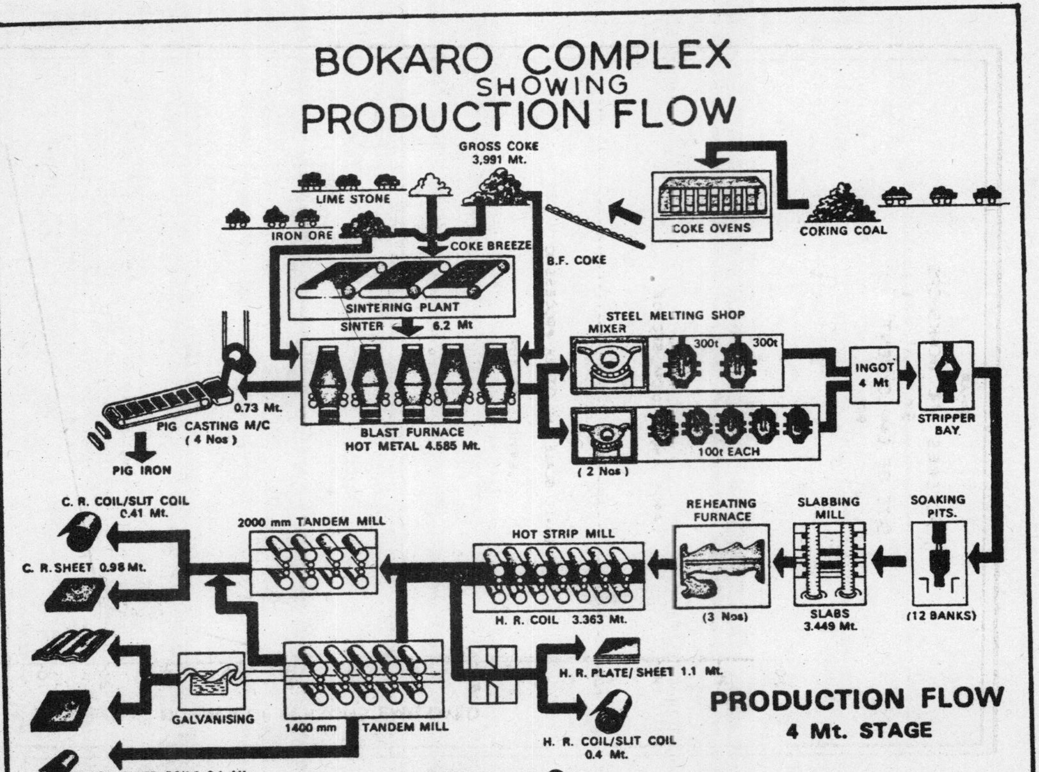
BOKARO COMPLEX
SHOWING
PRODUCTION FLOW
GROSS COKE
3,991 Mt.
LIME STONE
IRON ORE
COKE BREEZE
B.F. COKE
COKE OVENS
COKING COAL
SINTERING PLANT
SINTER 6.2 Mt
STEEL MELTING SHOP
MIXER
300t
300t
INGOT
4 Mt
STRIPPER
BAY
0.73 Mt.
PIG CASTING M/C
(4 Nos)
PIG IRON
BLAST FURNACE
HOT METAL 4.585 Mt.
100t EACH
(2 Nos)
C. R. COIL/SLIT COIL
0.41 Mt.
2000 mm TANDEM MILL
HOT STRIP MILL
REHEATING
FURNACE
SLABBING
MILL
SOAKING
PITS.
C. R. SHEET 0.98 Mt.
H. R. COIL 3.363 Mt.
(3 Nos)
SLABS
3.449 Mt.
(12 BANKS)
H. R. PLATE/ SHEET 1.1 Mt.
GALVANISING
1400 mm TANDEM MILL
H. R. COIL/SLIT COIL
0.4 Mt.
BLACK PLATE COILS 0.1 Mt.
PRODUCTION FLOW
4 Mt. STAGE
Fig. 58

TABLE 6.1 (*contd.*)

The Tata-Robins-Fraser Ltd. (*T.R.E.*)

No Vertical Linkage

1 Specialised machinery for bulk materials handling and producing plants.
- Wagon tipsters
- Stocking, **blending and** reclaiming **machines**
- Drag scrapers
- Belt conveyors ← **idlers**, mini-hoists

2. Mechanical and Electrical Vibrating Equipment Plants
- Grading screens
- Feeders
- Conveyors
- Shake-outs
- Bunker vibrators, etc

3. Mechanical Feeder Plants
- Apron and table feeders
- Washing trommels
- Blake mills
- Log washers
- Spiral concentrators
- Sent and slurry pumps
- Jaw crushers
- Hammer mills gravity breakers

4. Other enterprises in relation to TISCO act horizontally and diagonally and all belong to Tata-group or Steel-group, are therefore, technologically combined also.
5. Tin Plate Company of India
6. Indian Steel & Wire Products
7. Jamshedpur Engineering Co. Ltd. (JEMCO)
8. Agricultural Implements Company, Ltd (AGRICO)
9. The Indian Cable Co.
10. Indian Oxygen Ltd.
11. Tata Yodogawa Ltd.
12. Maintenance Shop
13. Ring Rolling Mills
14. Electro-Flux Refining Shop
15. Electric Furnance Shop

B. RANCHI COMPLEX

Vertical	*Horizontal*	*Diagonal*	*Technology*
The Heavy Engingering Corporation (*H.E.C.*)			
No Vertical Linkage	(a) Heavy Machine Building Plant (H.M.B.P.). (b) Foundry Forge Plant (F.F.P.) (c) Heavy Machine Tools Plant (H.M.T.P.)	2. Bharat Ball Bearing Co. Ratu 3. Usha Martine Black Ltd., Tatisilwai 4. High Tension Insulator Factory, Namkum 5. Chotanagpur Engineering Works Ltd. 6. Central Designs & Research Institute, Dhurwa	All are concerned with engineering

TABLE 6.1 (*contd.*)

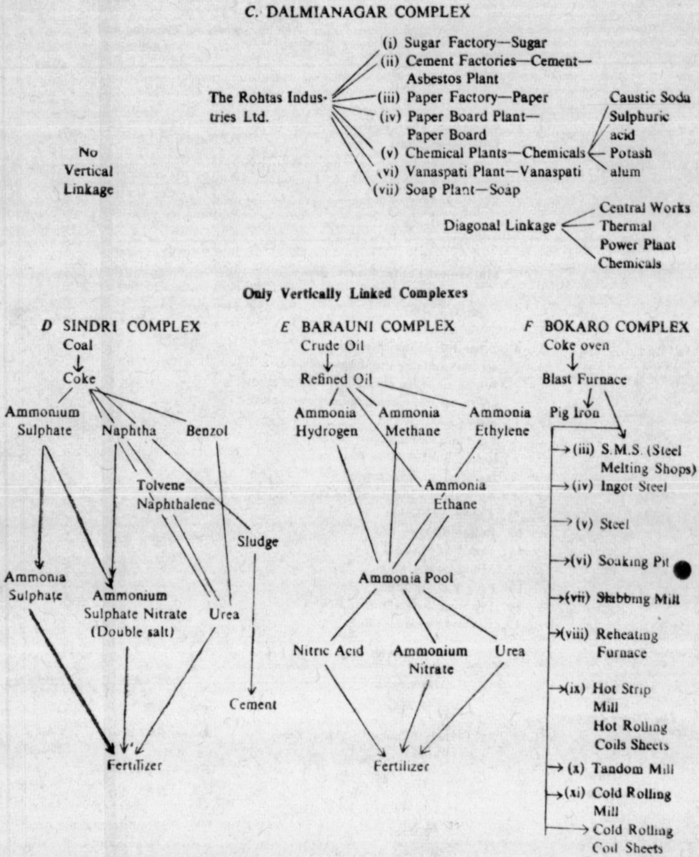

Sources: (i) Jamshedpur, the Steel City, January, 1, 1970, pp. 1-165
(ii) Tata Steel, Challenge and Response, Feb. 1981, pp. 1-35
(iii) H.E.C. News—Vol. 15, No. 3 & 4, Nov. 13, 1981, pp. 1-15
(iv) From Ore to Steel at Bokaro—An Information Digest, Bokaro, 1982, pp. 1-12
(v) And Several other Sources related to Sindri, Barauni and Dalmianagar Industries.

with Tata-Robins Fraser Ltd. which specialises in the manufacturing of machineries for handling bulk materials and processing. The Tinplate Company of India, Indian Steel and Wire Products, Jemco, Agrico, etc. are also horizontally combined whereas Indian Cable Co. Ltd., Indian Oxygen Ltd., Tata-Yodogawa Ltd., National Metallurgical Laboratory and several others perform service or diagonal linkage. All units of Jamshedpur complex specialise in steel and steel products and therefore, these are based on common roots or technological linkage. Thus, Jamshedpur is a fully developed complex where all four types of linkages are found.

The Ranchi complex is dominated by one complex, e.g., H.E.C. and its three units, HMBP, F.F.P. and HMTP. These complexes are horizontally interrelated. The vertical linkage is not found. Other ancillaries plants of Ranchi are diagonally linked.

The complexes of Sindri, Barauni and Bokaro are only vertically linked. Fig. 58 shows the linkage of Bokaro Steel Plant. Their horizontal expansion is still awaited. Dalmianagar presents neither vertical nor horizontal nor diagonal and not even technological linkage. Actually it is a varied nature of agglomerated industries closely inter-related to one another. Since all the industrial products, e.g., sugar, paper, cement, vanaspati, soap, chemicals are branded under the Rohtas Industries Ltd., therefore, all the units may be put under horizontally linkage as shown in Table 6.1.

Thus, Jamshedpur is the only complex which is fully developed while other complexes are partially developed as complexes. The future expansion still awaits their development as a full complex.

The inter-complex linkage is well developed between Ranchi (H.E.C.) and Bokaro complexes. The H.E.C. has played a significant role in setting up Bokaro Steel Plant by supplying sophisticated equipment to every iron and steel making facilities starting from material handling, coke oven and blast furnace to steel melting shop and rolling mills. It has supplied over 1,70,000 tonnes of equipment and technological structures.[8] Bokaro's second stage expansion programme, almost 85 per cent of all required equipments are being supplied by the H.E.C.

Bokaro in return supplies all required hot and cold rolling coils, sheets and other steel products for the construction of equipment and other machinery goods. Other complexes are poorly related to each other on the line of input-output matrices.

PATTERN

Pattern relates to the spatial arrangement of population. In the case of external diffusion, generally it gives compact or scattered pattern. But when it is taken to analyse the internal structure of an industrial concern, it presents intensive or extensive pattern. Here it is proposed to know the external and internal phenomena of industrial complexes and on the basis of this discussion, heavily industrialised, industrialised and agglomerated complexes may be identified. A complex which occupies a limited geographical space for its location and is combined with all types of linkages, e.g., vertical, horizontal, diagonal and technological, such type of complex is treated as heavily industrialised with a compact pattern. In contrast when a complex extends over a larger space and is partially linked, it means the complex is new, less industrialised and presents a scattered pattern for future expansion.

The industrial complex of Bihar is tested on this scale. Table 6.2 shows the number of units arranged on linkage basis. Spatial expansion is also provided in kms. leading to a pattern and finally a comparative industrialisation level has been included. This table clearly indicates that the Jamshedpur complex is the oldest and fully developed. It is highly industrialised complex with intensive and extensive forms and presents a compact pattern. Sindri and Dalmianagar are older complexes and present compact pattern. But these complexes are partially developed. Sindri displays only vertical integration while Dalmianagar horizontal. Sindri is a industrialised complex while Dalmianagar is agglomerated centre with various industries.

The newer complexes like Ranchi, Barauni and Bokaro present scattered pattern and are only partially linked complexes. It indicates that these complexes are passing through the phases of industrialisation. They have not achieved their full length of growth as found in Jamshedpur complex. Therefore,

TABLE 6.2 : **Industrial complex and their characteristics**

Name of the Complex	Year of establishment	Old or New	Units on the basis of linkage					Internal pattern intensive or extensive	Spatial expansion (in kms)	External pattern compact or scattered	Industrialisation pattern
			Vertical	Horizontal	Diagonal	Technological	Total				
Jamshedpur Complex	1907	Old	8	7	10	25	25	Intensive+ Extensive	64	Compact	Highly industrialised.
Ranchi Complex	1958	New	—	3	7	10	10	I+E	200	Scattered	Industrialised
Sindri Complex	1947	Old	7	—	1	8	8	Intensive	15	Compact	Do
Bokaro Complex	1968	New	8	—	1	9	9	Do	40	Scattered	Do
Dalmianagar Complex	1933	Old	—	8	2	10	10	Extensive	12	Compact	Agglomerated
Barauni Complex	1964	New	4	—	1	5	5	Intensive	25	Scattered	Less Industrialised

Source : Compiled by the author.

horizontal and diagonal growth are still awaited. The Ranchi complex, where vertical integration is not available it has to expand its industries more horizontally and diagonally. The Bokaro complex where vertical integration is still in progress, when horizontally and diagonally added would be the heavily industrialised complex. Barauni where pace of industrialisation is comparatively slower presents a less industrialised complex. But the future prospect is very much expected since a petro-chemical complex, a cement factory, and other small scale industries have already been proposed to be located in the near future.

FUNCTIONAL CHARACTERISTICS

Function is a qualitative activity of a firm which depends upon both the external and internal conditions of that firm. If a firm is mineral-based, its form will be heavy, extensive and intensive; and function will be varied, complicated, and of metallurgical character. If it is agricultural-based, its form will be medium or light, intensive or extensive, and also of varied functional characteristics. Function is also dependent upon size, form and aging of the plants. If the plant is large scaled, older with compact pattern and strong in linkages, it will show a stable functioning of diversified products. If the plant is large scaled but newer with scattered pattern and partially linked, it will show unstable functioning of specialised products. These ideas are tested in the case of industrial complexes in Bihar.

While dealing with the growth of industrial complexes it was stated that the older complexes like Jamshedpur, Sindri and Dalmianagar present a stable growth with stability in functional capacity, whereas the newer complexes like, Ranchi, Bokaro and Barauni present a unstable growth pattern with instability in functional efficiency. It was also stated that older complexes reveal compact pattern with diversified products whereas the newer complexes, scattered pattern with specialised products.

On the production side, the industrial complexes of Bihar present varied nature of function. For example, the Jamshedpur complex specialises in metallurgical goods, while Ranchi in heavy engineering. The Sindri complex produces fertilizer and cement, Bokaro specialises in steel. The Dalmianagar and Barauni complexes are diverted in character specialising in sugar, paper, cement, chemicals, vanaspati, soap and oil refinery, fertilizer and chemicals respectively.[9] This variability is due to the vast and varied resource bases, covering from metallic, non-metallic minerals to forest and agriculture. The Jamshedpur and Bokaro complexes are mainly based on metallic minerals and produce metallic goods, e.g. iron and steel and other related structurals. The Sindri, Dalmianagar and Barauni complexes are dependent upon the non-metallic minerals like coal, limestone, petroleum and other forest and agricultural items. The Ranchi complex, however, is based on the secondary products of metallurgical goods and specialises in heavy engineering and other machinery and equipment construction.

The second functional characteristics of these complexes is the adoption of advanced technical processes passing through a series of transforming stages and finally to a finished stage. This happens in two ways. In the first instance, a series of raw materials pass through a sequence of stages and ultimately produce one item, while in other case, one raw material passes through several stages and produce several items. This can be explained with citing examples. In the first case, one tonne of steel is the outcome of 1.7 tonnes of coal, 1.5 tonnes of iron-ore, 0.5 tonnes of limestone, 0.2 tonnes of manganese, 0.11 tonnes of dolomite, quartzite and other minerals. All these raw materials have to pass through coke oven, blast furnace, steel melting shop, blooming mills, and other various stages of manufacturing. Likewise, in other case, crude petroleum while passing through the processes of refining produces several items like refined oil, paraffin, naphtha, gases, gas oil etc. So also happens in the case of fertilizer production. Thus, technological processes are the main functional quality.

The third functional characteristic of the complexes is the linkage phenomena, where one product of plant becomes the input for the other plant and thus economics of production is achieved. Moreover, even waste product is converted into other useful materials. The huge compilation of slag from steel plants is reused in the making of cement. Likewise, sludge, a waste product of fertilizer plant is also used as a raw material for the manufacturing of cement. Bagasse, the waste of sugar plant is used as a source of fuel and also a raw material for the paper pulp plant. Oil refinery releases cooking gas, oxygen gas and other gases which are again used in various ways.

The industrial complexes of Bihar are characterised by this type of function. For example, Tisco's slag is used by the cement factory of Jhinkpani. The sludge of Sindri fertilizer is used locally in the cement factory. Similarly, vanaspati factory's dirt is utilized by the soap factory of Dalmianagar. Again, the paper pulp plant of R.I. Ltd. of Dalmianagar was based on the bagasse of the sugar factory. The sugar factory, however, closed now and paper pulp plant has also stopped functioning. The Bokaro Steel Plant is going to establish two cement factories, one near the steel plant and another at Bhavanathpur in Palamu district. These factories will use slag of their steel plant as their raw material. Similarly another cement factory is in offing at Barauni just to utilize sludge of fertilizer factory. Therefore, the use of waste materials is the unique functional characteristic of the complexes of Bihar.

The fourth characteristic relates to the management control and the general outlook. The complexes of Bihar are under the control of both the public and the private sectors. The Jamshedpur and the Dalmianagar complexes are running under the private management where maximum utilization of materials and profit maximisation are the main consideration. Naturally, these complexes shift from one product to another according to the demand and high cost of products. After 1970, Tisco started production of steel structurals just to avoid the competition in pig iron and steel from other newly erected steel plants in public sector. Similarly, Telco shifted to produce more commercial automobiles and excavators from the production of locomotives. Similarly, R.I. Ltd. at Dalmianagar maintained its production tempo only in cement, paper and vanaspati, because these commodities are highly required in the markets and through which maximum profits gained by the management. But such tendency does not exist in the public sector. They are run o n the principle of welfare scheme where eradication of poverty and raising the standard of living of people are the general outlook. But unfortunately such plants suffer due to red-tapism, curruption and unionism which ultimately affect the capacity utilization and smooth functioning.

Table 5.2 reveals that public sector plants seldom achieve hundred per cent of their installed capacity. These plants perform a prototype style of functioning. The private management is always attentive to these points and fall of production is seriously taken. Bokaro, Ranchi, Sindri and Barauni complexes are under the public control where all kinds of managerial defects persist and, thus, their functional efficiency is often marred by these shortcomings.

CLASSIFICATION OF COMPLEXES

An Industrial complex may be divided on the basis of function, pattern and linkage. Functionally a complex may be classified into two parts : (a) mono-complex and (b) multi-complex. The mono-complex specialises in one type of activity, for example, oil refinery complex, fertilizer complex, iron and steel complex, etc. The multi complex combines several complexes into one geographical unit, for example, Jamshedpur complex and Ranchi complex. Thus, Tisco, The Indian Tube Company at Jamshedpur, Bokaro Steel Plant, Sindri Fertilizer and Chemicals and Barauni's Oil Refinery and Fertilizer, all are examples of mono-type of complex. But the Jamshadpur complex comprises of several complexes and the Ranchi complex consists of several mono-mighty engineering complexes, like HMBP, F.F.P., and HMTP. The Sindri complex, the Barauni complex and the Dalmianagar complex are examples of multi-complexes.

On the basis of linkage, an industrial complex is classified into two broader groups; (a) vertical complex and (b) horizontal complex. A vertical complex is a complex in which industrial units are vertically integrated to produce one type or several types of products. An iron and steel plant is the best example of vertical complex. In a horizontal complex several units act independently but their end product is the one or the same.

Such integrated enterprise is called horizontal complex. The automobile, the watch factory, the shoe factory, etc. are the examples of horizontal complex. Tisco, Bokaro Steel Plant, Sindri Fertilizer, Barauni oil refinery and fertilizer plant are the examples of the vertical complex while the H.E.C. the Telco and the Rohtas Industries Ltd. at Dalmianagar are the examples of horizontal complex.

On the basis of pattern, two types of complexes are identified. They are : (a) inner complex and (b) outer complex. Every complex displays these characteristics, one the main complex and other the dependent complex. In Jamshedpur complex Tisco is the main complex which is also treated as the inner complex, where as other complexes like Telco, the Indian Tube Co., T.R.F. etc. are the dependent or the outer complexes. Similarly in Ranchi complex the H.E.C. is the inner complex and other units are the parts of outer complex. In Bokaro there is only one complex, that is inner complex. Dalmianagar has no inner complex but all are linked to outer complex. In Barauni complex the Indian Oil Refinery is the inner complex while the fertilizer is the outer complex. In case of Sindri, the fertilizer and the chemicals Ltd. are the inner complex and the cement and Bihar phosphate units are in the outer complex.

Thus the following conclusions are obtained from the above analysis and discussion. Firstly, among the industrial complexes of Bihar intra-complex linkages have well developed. Jamshedpur is the only complex where all four types of linkages are developed. Other complexes are partially linked mostly vertical or horizontal. Secondly, inter-complex linkage is not well developed except between H.E.C. and Bokaro. This is simply because of their varied natures of production technology. Thirdly, these complexes are characterised by both compact and disperse type of pattern. The older complexes have compact pattern and are highly industrialised, whereas the newer complexes are scattered and less industrialised. Here industrialization is yet to come in full swing. And, lastly, these complexes present a various type of functions. For example, the Jamshedpur—a multi complex specialises in metallurgical goods while Ranchi a mono-mighty complex specialises in heavy engineering. The Sindri complex produces fertilizers and cement, while

Bokaro a mono-type complex produces steel and steel structurals. The Dalmianagar and the Barauni complexes are diverse in character specialising in sugar, paper, cement, vanaspati, chemicals and oil refinery and fertilizer respectively.

REFERENCES

1. Estall, R.C. & Buchanan, R.O. (1968), *Industrial Activity and Economic Geography*, London, p. 94.
2. Jarrett, H.R. (1977), op. cit., p. 129.
3. Estall, R.C. and Buchanan, R.O. (1968), op. cit., p. 95.
4. S.C. Kuchhal (1969), *The Industrial Economy of India*, Allahabad, p. 408.
5. Estall, R.C. and Buchanan, R.O. (1968), op. cit., p. 94.
6. S.E. Kuchhal (1969), op. cit., p. 409.
7. *ibid.*, p. 410.
8. *H.E.C. News* (1981), Vol. 15, No. 3-4, Nov. 15, 1981, p. 6.
9. Singh, R.P. (1980), "The Industrial Complex of Bihar", *Geographical Review of India*, Vol. 42, p. 229.

7

SOCIAL RELEVANCE, PROBLEMS AND PLANNING OF INDUSTRIAL COMPLEXES

THE PREVIOUS chapters have basically dealt with geographical and economic aspects of the industrial complexes. In this chapter a brief account of social relevance of industrial complexes is presented. It is because of the fact that industrial studies should not be necessarily conceived with spatial pattern, production and employment trend, but also from the angle of social goal. A pertinent question, therefore, arises that what are the social implications of such type of study ? The question, however, is well expected because every project of advanced study must incorporate the social implications. Any economic measure is mooted to achieve a target, and the target is primarily related to the social system of a region. The achievement of expected target means that the economic measures have been rightly taken, timely implemented and correctly handled. The failure and the partial achievement means some problems which have gagged the growth. These problems may be physical, economic and social. It is essential to discuss these problems because one after understanding the nature of problems, plans can be suggested for liquidating them. Planning, therefore, becomes the most venerable aspect of the study. Consequently social relevance, problems and planning are the sequences of one aspect and hence an attempt is made to study this aspect in relation to industrial complex.

SOCIAL RELEVANCE

This study relates to a regional analysis approach through industria isation. Industrialisation is vital part of the National Economic Measure which aims to remove regional imbalances and to uplift the socio-economic status. These three variables are set in a frame to achieve the goal of socio-economic equity by removing poverty and raising the standard of living. The setting of these variables leads to a construction of diagrammetic model.

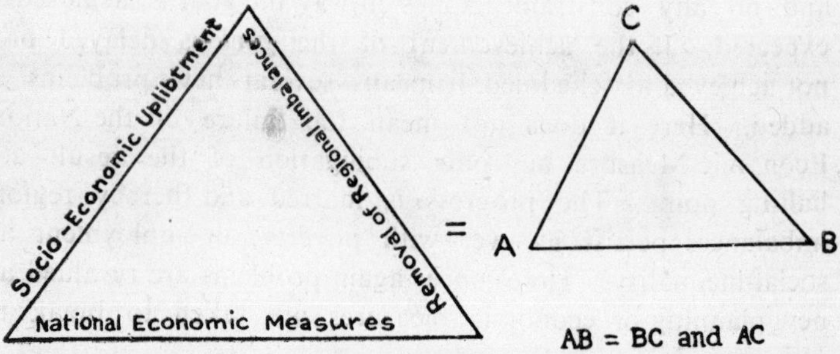

AB = BC and AC

= A to B ± (Varying)

The base may be large and small, but the apex is fix, forming an isosceles triangle. Forming apex or locating apex is not as important as reaching the apex or achieving the goal. As the base AB moves upward, the BC shortens down accordingly and the distance between AB and AC becomes shorter. This scheme is taken phasewise (Time-factor), ultimately AB goes up very high, obliterating BC and the triangle changes into a single line forming it and former axis. Thererefore, AC and BC are equal as illustrated below :

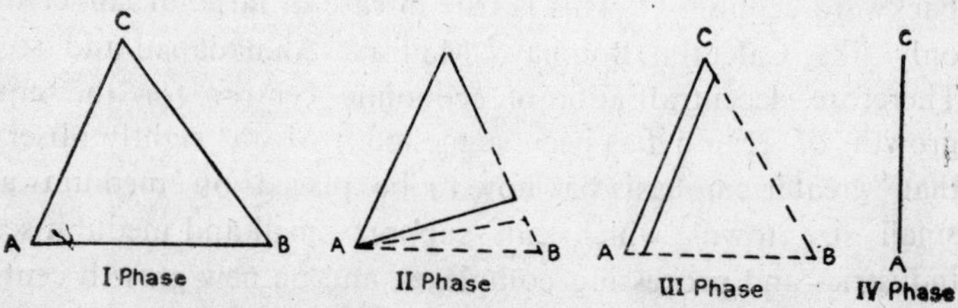

The first phase is a position from where economic planning starts. In the second phase economic planning proceeds upward, till regional imbalances are gradually removed. In the third phase regional imbalances are completly removed and the target of national planning is achieved through social and economic upliftment as is apparent from the final stage.

The achievement of goal depends upon several other conditions present in the region. If all the conditions are perfect and no any constraint comes in way the goal is achieved as expected. If the achievement of the goal is delayed or is not achieved as scheduled, it means several new problems are added. Here it does not mean the failure of the National Economic Measure but only subjugation of the result at a halting point. The progress is marred and thereby regional imbalances persist as ever with poverty, unemployment and social-inequality. Here once again problems are revalued and new planning or economic measures are taken to break the vicious circle.

Like most of the underdeveloping countries, India has also taken industrialisation as a parameter of the National Economic Measure through which she wants to achieve economic efficiency and social equity. This pace of industrialisation has been augmented after independence by expanding the production capacity of the old units and further establishing newer larger plants. These plants have acted as the regional growth centre or focie and have influenced the intra, inter or even extra regions (Fig. 50). But sometime this trend has been looked upon as a contrary force. The establishment of larger plant on the regional vertices accentuates the economic activities at a few pockets, like "Oases in the deserts of primitive economy",[1] or 'cathedrals in the desert'[2] or 'regional industrial complexes'[3] in backward economy. This is true in case of large urban centres only like Calcutta, Bombay, Madras, Ahmadabad and so on Therefore, decentralisation of economic centres for the equal growth of region has been suggested. Misra[4] rightly observes that "greater emphasis has now to be placed on medium and small size towns which can support small and medium scale industries and processing complexes and on new growth centres for industries which are tied to mineral and other resources located away from the existing urban centres specially in backward areas". Bose[5] suggests that "the decentralisation of industries is a worthy objective but in the absence of basic overhead facilities like cheap power, and transport, there cannot be really any decentralisation". Further he argues that 'in a region, there should be both concentration of industries and decentralisation of industries. The concentration should not be round a few dominant cities but in the whole region. Decentralisation should not mean the multiplication of nodal points which are not functionally related to each other, but diversification of the economy on a sound economic basis ensuring as far as possible, an optimum distribution of population in settlements of varying sizes—from hamlets to million plus cities.[6] It is a fact that only creation of nodal points in economic isolation will not solve the problem. They must be linked together to further diffuse to smaller centres. The comparatively large centres act as stimulating centre and small centre as supporting centre based on the principle of centripetal and centrifugal forces. Thus through this process an economic mobilisation takes place in the whole region. It is sometimes argued that the poor economy as ours is not suited to the establishment of large capital intensive industrial complex rathers the spread of small scale industries in order to provide jobs.

The large scale industrial centres are the centres of mother plants which give birth to thousands of small and medium scale industries. The Jamshedpur complex, for example, today is not only the premier steel producer of the country but it has become a source of several other medium and small scale industries in the state. The similar is the case with the H.E.C. (Ranchi) and Bokaro Complexes. Actually these are the torch-points from where lights of economic activities are thrown in every direction in the country. These centres have not only mobilised the resource potentialities of the region but have also provided jobs for lakhs of people. The Telco produces nearly 45000 trucks, buses and other commercial vehicles annually and these are plying on the regional, national and even international roads engaging thousands and thousands of people directly and indirectly. The closure of Telco on the name of large scale plant would be a irrecoverable loss on the national plane and this loss would not be compensated by establishing hundreds of other small scale industries.

It is further important to point out that industrialisation cannot be augmented without establishing and encouraging large scale industries. It is, however, a fact that to accumulate lakhs of people at an industrial centre does not mean the growth of urbanisation through industrialisation. It would be just a gathering point of people where different sorts of social problems are created. People are engaged in several kinds of malpractices exploiting one another and thus a large gap between rich and poor becomes evident. Contrast to this view is that a planned industrial centre is characterised by a social system where every variable of urbanization is in a positive form providing a better living condition. Industrial complexes of Bihar are the centres of positive urbanisation created out of industrialisation. Jamshedpur is the modern and well planned urban centre of the country where living condition of people is ideal. Other new industrial centres like Ranchi, Bokaro, Durgapur, Rourkela, Bhilai have also been developed on the pattern of Jamshedpur.

The establishment of large plant in the backward region is also supposed to be the most effective measure through which problem like 'regional unbalances' may be oozed out. This has been really proved in the case of South Bihar. A few decades back, prior to the establishment of large plants like Tisco, Telco, H.E.C., Sindri Fertilizers, Bokaro and several other industrial units, the region was no better known as the 'jungle region' with a few traditional activities related to the forest resource. But now, the region has been completely changed. Use of modern technology in the field of industry in association with several advanced countries, like, British, German, Russian and soon has brought modernity in the social system of the region. Now the region is humming with several primary, secondary, tertiary and quaternary activities and has trodden a path of prosperity. It is, however, a fact that it has not proved itself a panacea to solve all the problems of the region. An example is often cited that such type of plants of massive magnitude have little impact on the economy of state, because the per capita income has remained the lowest even after the functionning of these complexes.[7] Bihar is characterised by poverty stricken society, fast growing population, agrarian base, lack of capital and lack of intra-structures—social as well as economic. They have restricted the effect of industrialisation in Bihar and have been comparatively more efficient in neighbouring states. In West Bengal is located the largest port, industrial-financial-commercial-consumer conglomerate-Calcutta, which draws upon all the advantages of industrialisation of Bihar.[8] Still it has given a new orientation. Changes in traditional values and social out look, have been slow but steady and have paved new path of prosperity. These are long range measures, naturally, their effects are slow and gradual.

Industrial centres in Bihar are planned, accommodative and probably without any urban chaos. They are also entirely different from industrial centres of Calcutta, Bombay, Madras, Kanpur. These big cities are under the pressure of appalling conditions where human value has greatly reduced. A major percentage of population lives in industrial slums without any established system of life. Congestions, squalors and inhygeinic conditions prevail here. People living in these slums are neither urban nor rural but a bad mixing of the two.[9] Fortunately, industrial condition in Bihar has not reached to that point of urban-retardness. The industrial complexes of Bihar have developed from a rural background where hygeinic conditions still continue. These complexes have developed their own township with all modern facilities and amenities of urban society. They are neat and open with substantial buildings, broad roads, a number of green parks, water bodies, and other natural sites. Schools, colleges and even Universities are provided with better facilities. Hospital and several health centres are available for treatment of labour when they are in need of medical urgency. The location of industrial complex along the river has not only provided fresh water to the factories and townships but scenic beauties as well. Moreover, rivers have led the ways for roads and railways which follow the valley pattern particularly in the Chotanagpur Plateau Region.[10]

PROBLEMS

Bihar has not achieved her progress as expected even after the establishment and growth of several industrial giants. The main problems which have trickled down the benefits out of industrialization are many.

The first problem which held the progress is the acute poverty of the region. Bihar started her progressive march to modern industrialisation from the beginning of the present century. Since then a stride of industrialisation has been achieved on account of vast natural resources found in Bihar. In spite of this industrial progress, the economic disparities continue to grow making Bihar one of the most backward states of the country. The per capita income is the lowest in Bihar and is called 'a rich land inhabited by the poor'. In reality, the acute poverty has been the main obstacle behind the economic betterment, which has restricted the consumer-market and prevented the industrial efficiency. In the absence of strong consumer market at intra or sub-regional level, the industrial products are sent to other rich inter or extra regional markets. All the advantages of industrialisation have been taken way from here. Bihar has predominantly agricultural economy with about 71 per cent of her total population engaged in it. Eighty Seven per cent of her total population lives in the rural areas with minimum purchasing capacity. All these conditions have acted as constraints in not allowing advantages of industrialisation to the general masses. No doubt, the recent industrialisation has created employment opportunities in the state, but the people of Bihar are less industrious, home sick and shy. The result is that the better benefits are derived by bordering districts of neighbouring state. Industrialisation has also fostered favourable conditions for the growth to small and medium scale industries but the poor people did not show any seriousness to avail the opportunity due to lack of capital. Even the capitalists and feudals of the society remained shy to invest their money on the growth of small scale industries. The absence of middle class income group in the state was the main hurdle which failed to utilize the opportunities. The enterpreneurs outside the state have tried to establish the medium and small scale industries here. But due to high tariff, high rates of electricity interruptions in power supply, poor consumer markets, shortage of raw materials and governments apathy have compelled them either to close down the factory or shift to other state. Thus, the spread effect of the giant complexes have been ill-received producing discouraging result. The absence of medium and small scale rural industries has intensified the pressure on land with growing number of population. This has resulted into a wide gulf between haves and have-nots on social and economic planes and has further accentuated the regional disparities at a point of disaster. "Perhaps there is no part of India where this disparity is greater than in Bihar".[11] Recently, a trend of flow of agricultural labourer from agriculturally over-crowded rural areas to the industrial cities has noticed. This migration is caused by a great difference between rural and urban wages and the respective standard of living and has adversely affected the rural and the urban economy. The rural region is becoming dormant, deficient and depopulated on account of young-emigrants. This has further deteriorated the agricultural production and aggravated food shortages. The urban area also experiences the same result. The standard of living in urban area is constantly affected by the influx of new people as they are anxious to get jobs at almost any price, prepare to lodge in the most insanitary hovels and unaccustomed to any form of modern social organization.[12]

The second most serious problem is the tremendous growth of population. The population explosion in this state has eaten up all the benefits created during the Five Year Plans. This has further precepitated the apalling conditions resulting into unemployment, food shortage, high prices etc. The baffling problem arising out of this has frustrated all the economic and social upliftment programme to a halt. Until and unless this problem is solved no better prospect can be expected either on the regional or the national level.

The shortage of power is the most serious problem which has affected the working and growth of industries adversely. Before independence thermal was the only source of power for the industries. But after independence the Damodar Valley Corporation used to supply hydel power to the industrial centres. The supply from D.V.C. since then has gradually reduced to a very unsatisfactory level. Several other thermal and hydel projects have been established to meet the rising power demand. After 1970 no new plant has been established. This has thus widened the gap of supply and demand at a very inconvenient point. The thermal and hydel plants are also getting old with several technical problems. This has led to the breakdown and non-functioning of many public thermal plants. Two and three units of the Patratu Thermal Power Complex are always non-functioning due to technical disturbances. This power supply interruption frequently observed has marred the industrial production badly. The industrial centres not owning their own captive power plants have to suffer a lot. During 1979-80 and 80-81, the H.E.C. has incurred a loss of Rs. 34.7 crores and Rs. 51.13 crores respectively. This is attributed to inadequate and interrupted power supply.[13] Most of the small scale industries have closed their shutters down due to this power shortage. If this shortage continues the industrialisation and other economic development programmes may suffer.

The poor quality of coal with high content of ash has reduced the operational efficiency of the sophisticated machine and thereby affected their productivity and durability. The good quality of coal is limited in space and quantity. The Jharia coal field is the only good coking coal supplier and her reserve is very limited. If the present rate of consumption continues the Jharia Coal will hardly last for next fifty years only.[14] In such condition without good quality coal further heavy industrial set up would be restricted. Therefore, it is essential to develop techniques for the efficient utilization of poor quality of coal because their reserve is ample here.

The political instability, high prices of commodities, rampant corruption in public life and less enterpreneurship are other problems which are maladies of the present industrialisation.

A few more problems are also important to be highlighted. Such problems are of technical in nature. Structurally, an industry collects various raw materials and then it changes them into useful forms. This transformation from raw materials to finished goods emits waste products. These waste products are again reused as a raw material to produce by-product. But generally emissories of dust and smoke and discharge of other impurities into the atmosphere bring hazardous pollution. The wastes are excreted in the form of dirty water polluting streams and rivers. Such phenomenon is documented by Karan in one of his studies on environmental pollution.[15]

All the industrial complexes in Bihar are located along the river. The industries not only receive water from the river but also discharge 'dirts' in the river. For example, the Subarnarekha, the Damodar, the Son and the Ganga rivers are being polluted by the industrial plants along their sides. The Son water from Dehri to down-stream is completely polluted providing inhygeinic conditions for men and animal. The similar is the case with the Ganga river. The Indian Oil Refinery at Barauni emits all its dirts to this Ganga damaging its piousness. But fortunately these rivers are full of spate during the rainy seasons and thus flush out all the dirts in the ocean.

The protection of the river from the pollution is the foremost duty of a planner. If this pollution continues to grow it would have the worst effect of industrialisation.

PLANNING

It is seen that poverty is the main problem of the state. How to get rid of this basic problem has remained the only question to be solved since the independence ? Several plans, projects and programmes have been launched by the government to reduce and relieve poverty. But due to rapid growth of population, the problem of poverty continued as ever. A planning to assail the poverty is still an imperative measure. For the eradication of poverty, two kinds of suggestions are in view, e.g., first, to improve agriculture and secondly, to adopt industrialisation. Therefore, agriculture and industry, both are the essential parameters to be considered. Agriculture is the mainstay of economy upon which nearly 87 per cent of population depends directly and indirectly and more than 50 per cent of the state's income is derived from it. Industry, on the other hand, provides employment opportunities, augments resource mobilisation, brings technological knowhow, hammers on the 'traditionality', the root of poverty and finally raises the standard of living of the general people. Unfortunately, it has remained one of a serious flaws in the implementation of plans that at a time one parameter, either agriculture or industry was taken as the part of other. This gave an unbalanced treatment. While dealing with one, other was neglected. When one aspect was under consideration, the problems associated with other aspect in the same period became so serious in magnitude that all the advantages achieved were minimised. Again when another aspect was taken, the first one was completely ignored which resulted another separate problems. In this way numerous problems were added and impact of plans has been limited, failing to arrest the problem of poverty. For example, the First Five Year Plan was mainly concerned with agriculture. Industry was completely ignored. Agriculture improved no doubt but it remained lopsided in the absence of industrial growth. During the Second Five-Year Plan period, industry was taken on priority and this time agriculture was ignored. Industrial breakthrough was appreciably reckoned with but failure on the agricultural front minimised all with virtually no achievement on the social part. In spite of several industrial strides, the per capita income remained more or less the same. During the Third Five Year Plan a mixed approach of agriculture and industry was launched. To create opportunities for employment, to ease the regional imbalances through economic decentralisation from regional climaxes to the depressed regions and to provide maximum facilities to develop the infra-structures were the positive measures. Unfortunately in the beginning, the land plan was impeded by Chinese attack diverting expenditure on defence. Again a brief war with Pakistan combined with natural calamities like droughts and floods, the plan was a total failure. The situation was further accentuated with the enormous rise of population. Food shortage and stagnation of industrial production were the chief characteristics before launching the Fourth Five Year Plan. The Fourth and the Fifth Plans have remained without any remarkable achievements. Political instability, low productivity, corruption and economic uncertainty all have precipitated a condition of confusion. No apparent plans are noticeable. Even the Sixth Five Year Plan is only on patch-work style with political propaganda.

But in reality, a little progressive measure is evident to combat the morass of poverty.

It is evident that the eradication of poverty is a colossal task which requires arduous planning. Agriculture and industry are very much essential on which the Indian Society is based. A plan, therefore, should be must which includes both agriculture and industry. If steel-plate and cups are manufactured, rice and tea must also be produced enough to eat and drink in the steel plate and cup. It means both agriculture and industry are essential to develop. A foreign writer has described that "the honour and dignity of increasing the production value of land should be established and maintained, she should keep one foot on land and the other on industry, nationally and individually. Without a prosperous agriculture there could be no sustained prosperity". Therefore, it is suggested that agriculture and industry both should be taken together to combat with the problem of poverty.

The development of agriculture and industry in isolation will not be helpful. They should be mutually interdependent. Industrial development cannot be dissociated with the progress in the agricultural sector. The development of processing and manufacturing depends upon food and raw materials derived from agriculture particularly in a developing country like India where the economy is largely agro-based.[16] There is also scope for scientific processing of agricultural produce so as to minimise losses and produce quality products.

Agricultural development is an essential pre-condition for over all economic growth of an agricultural state like Bihar. It can be implemented in two ways, as envisaged by Banerjee.[17] Firstly, expansion of farm areas and secondly, adoption of more intensive methods of cultivation thereby improving the farm output.

Table 2.5 reveals that at present about 48 per cent of the total land is under plough which is comparatively higher than the country as a whole. Nearly 13 per cent of the total land is culturable waste land. This 13 per cent of culturable waste land or nearly 3513000 hectares[18] of land can be easily brought under the plough with little effort. This will enhance the agricultural output in quantity.

It is a fact that during the Five Year Plans agricultural infrastructure have been developed in which irrigational facilities, fertilizer availability, better seeds, agricultural credits and technological uses have been adopted. These measures have transformed the traditional subsistence agriculture to the commercial plane and also for the use of urban and industrial centres. But they have also brought some technological, economic and sociological gaps in the present social set up aggravating the situation more adversely. Now it is suggested that the adoption of these measures should be carefully dealt with. The rational distribution of these infra-structure will ease the problem.

Water is the main problem which deserves special consideration. In the case of Bihar it gets as a natural hurdle. When it is excess, it becomes a havoc of floods destroying the crops and when it is short it becomes a problem of drought destroying the cereals. Bihar is a chronic state which suffers from both floods and drought. Unless and until this problem is solved self-sufficiency in cereal production would be an utopian talk. Therefore, to tide over to this tardy problem is essential. The diversion and preservation of excess water during the rainy season through artificial tanks and reservoirs will be useful. This reserve water should be utilized during the drought period. Geographically and geologically, Bihar is aptly suited to this scheme. This scheme should be implemented on priority basis. Besides, crops should be insured against draught and flood havocs. Farmers should be provided with essential farm incentive in time like, better seeds, fertilizers, irrigational implements and agricultural credits. Farming should be improved and made attractive to educationist and technicians. Moreover, rural development is essential not only because our major percentage of population lives in villages but also because of the development in rural economy. Agriculture and allied activities like animal husbandry, dairying, forestry, fishery, etc. and cottage and small scale industries have to be taken on priority as they provide considerable scope for labour absorption and income generation. Therefore, their availability is an essential requirement for self-sustained and automatic process of economic growth.

Industry is also a part of much broader process of economic development which involves resource mobilisation through developed infrastructure and finally brings changes in the pattern of economic and social life of the people.[19] It creates employment opportunities for the skilled and unskilled labour and thus bears the burden of growing population. Again it bridges the gulf of regional disparities by establishing a link between developed and underdeveloped regions. Moreover, it creates an atmosphere of economic development in which agro-based, mineral-based and other forms of industries flourish. Therefore, a pertinent question arises that how an industrial economy would be self-sustaining and growth generating. Bihar has enough industrial growth where small, medium and large scale industries have developed. Besides, there are six industrial complexes. But it has been realised that despite this industrial growth, its impact on the general people is meagre. Therefore, another suggestion would be how to make these industries more efficient.

For this purpose an industrial planning is suggested. Linkage in the industrial system would be an appropriate answer for these industries. It becomes imperative and can be explained through a model.

Linkage Hierarchy in Industrial System

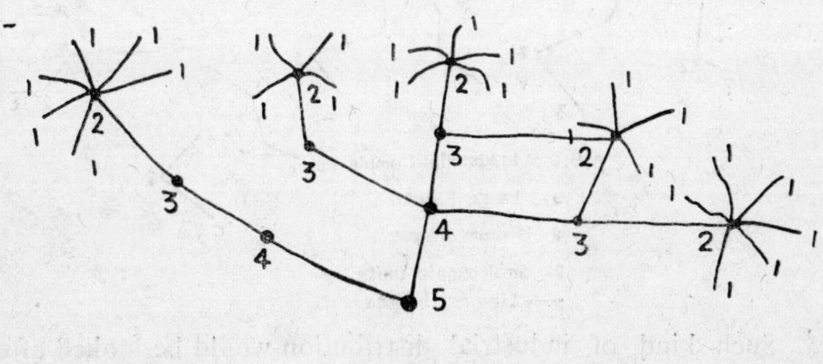

1. Village Level — Cottage industries or village industries mostly associated with agriculture.
2. Block Level — Engineering or repair work on small scale or cottage or khadi etc.

3. District Level — Large scale or medium scale industrial set up where small scale act as associaries.
4. Regional Level — Large scale processing industries based on capital intensive creating industrial atmosphere.
5. National Level — Large scale on the regional or national vertex.

This hierarchy in industrial system is essential to have spread effect from regional level to village level through district and block levels. In such a system no unit either located at the village or town will run in isolation but acts as a part of system. Similarly creation of industrial complex on the basis of technological and areal linkages will facilitate the regional mobility on the national level, minimising the regional disparities.

Linkages of industrial complexes on regional or national levels

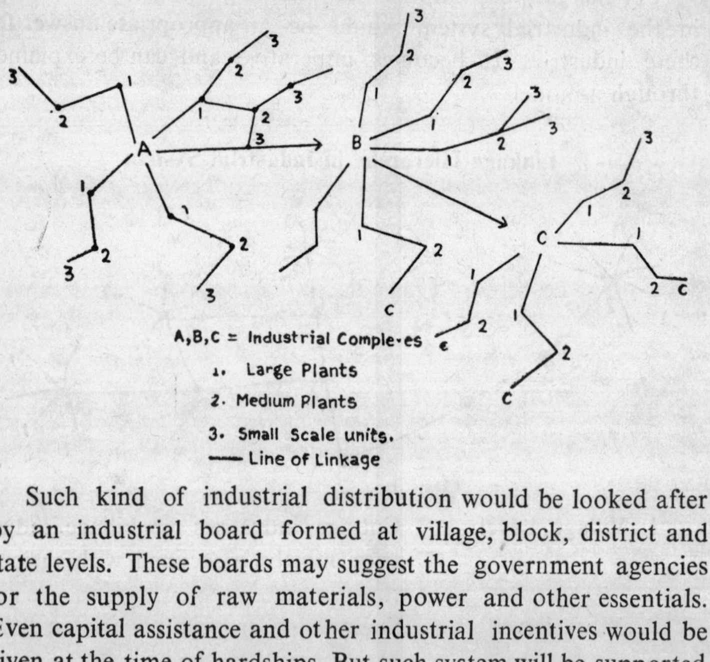

Such kind of industrial distribution would be looked after by an industrial board formed at village, block, district and state levels. These boards may suggest the government agencies for the supply of raw materials, power and other essentials. Even capital assistance and other industrial incentives would be given at the time of hardships. But such system will be supported by the hierarchy of commercial centres for the consumption of these industrial products. It has been seen that Bihar lacks, like Calcutta or Bombay, to sell its industrial products. In the absence of such markets, industrial products are sent to the markets outside the state. Therefore, creation of commercial centres on the higher magnitude is very much essential. Jamshedpur is becoming a commercial centre of steel and steel products. But other industrial centres, like Ranchi, and Bokaro are not developing such tendency to become regional markets. They have to sell their products through Calcutta port and markets.

The third suggestive measure is related to power supply. It has been realised that power shortage is one of major impediments in the growth of industrial economy. This power shortage is due to ill-functioning of the old thermal and hydel power plants. Bihar is fortunate to have ample amount of coal and water resources. To cope with the rising trend of industrialisation, increase in power generation is very much essential. For this newer plants in both thermal and hydel are required. Unless and until power is generated no further industrialisation can be proposed.

Palamu, Santhal Parganas, Nawada, Aurangabad, Nalanda, Gaya, Saharsa, Madhubani and Hajipur are industrially backward districts. These districts should be given priority for the new industrial set up. The Bihar Government has already taken a decision and the feasibility report is ready to set up an aluminium complex based on the bauxite reserves in Palamu district, at an estimated cost of Rs. 100 crores.[20] Besides, a coal-based fertilizer plant at Giddi in Hazaribagh district, a pyrite based fertilizer complex at Amjhore each at a cost of Rs. 40 crores, several cement plants and other industrial units have to be set up in different parts of comparatively lesser industrialised districts of Bihar.

Pollution by industrial activities, although not so serious in Bihar can be corrected in two ways. First, the industrial wastes can be reutilised and secondly, the industrial 'dirt' can be mechanised through various physical and chemical processes and re-utilize in the factories instead of releasing it in the rivers.

The influx of migrating people from rural industrial centres can be checked by developing counter magnetic towns in the countryside with necessary infrastructure and provisions of essential services. This way reduce pressure on big industrial cities and may indirectly ease the congestion and other inhygeinic conditions of those cities.

Recently for better economy integrated approach has been proposed. This approach incorporates different sectors like agriculture, industry, rural and urban and also implies inter-relationship between socio-economic factor and physical landscape. Integration is not only between different sectors but also between different area levels and towns and villages within a hierarchy of functions.[21] This integration approach has been accepted as the measure to face the rising trend of inequality on the regional and social levels.

REFERENCES

1. Prasad, K.N. (1963) op. cit., p. 55.

2. Maseley, M.J. (1974), op. cit., p. 5.

3. Hamilton, F.E.I. (1967), op. cit., p. 406.

4. Misra, R.P. (1971), op. cit., p. 11.

5. Bose, A. (1974), *Studies in Indian Urbanization*, 1901-71, Tata McGraw Hill Publishing Co. Ltd., New Delhi, p. 205.

6. *ibid.*

7. Misra, R.P. (1971), op. cit., p. 10.

8. Bose, S.R. (1971), *Economy of Bihar*, K.L. Firms Public Calcutta, p. 34.

9. Ganguli, B.N. (1973), *Population and Development*, New Delhi, pp. 54-55.

10. Karan, P.P. (1964), op. cit., p. 347.

11. Sharma, T.R. (1946), op. cit., p. 288.

12. Mukherjee, R.K. (1945), *The Indian Working Class*, Hind Kitab Publication, Bombay, p. 4.

13. *The Indian Nation*, Patna, Saturday, Feb. 27, 1982, p. 4.

14. Dayal, P. (1977), op. cit., p. 6.

15. Karan, P.P. (1980), "Perception of Environmental Pollution in Chotanagpur Industrial Area, India", in L.R. Singh (ed.), *New Perspectives in Geography*, Indian University Press, Allahabad, pp. 177-181.

16. Chaudhuri, M.R. (1970), op. cit., p. 2.

17. Banerjee, B. (1969), "The Infrastructure of Indian Agriculture in B. Banerjee (ed.), *Essays on Agricultural Geography*, University of Calcutta, p. 258.

18. Bihar Statistical Handbook, 1978, *Directorate of Statistics and Evaluation*, Govt. of Bihar, p. 33.

19. Chaudhuri, M.R. (1970), op. cit., p. 2.

20. *The Searchlight*, Patna, Tuesday, December 2, 1975, p. 1.

21. Rao, V.L.S.P. (1976), *Development Strategy*, For An Agricultural Reglon. University of Mysore Press, Mysore, p. 5.

8

SUMMARY AND CONCLUSION

INDUSTRIAL Geography has been regarded as one of the most dynamic branches of economic geography as it is primarily related to the study of industry and industrial problems. The problem may be regional, national or international and may also be related to developed or developing countries in terms of technological uses. The content of this branch has not remained only the theoretical bases of locational aspects as adopted by the economists but also with spatial pattern and its relevance to the socio-economic needs of the society. Therefore, the importance of such study has become more relevant to enquire into the problems of regional disparities, unemployment and poverty. Industrial geographers have particularly emphasized over empirical inquiries based on analytical approaches and have sought for generalisations. Such type of study not only help in the formulations of theories and laws but also become pragmatic in approach. Therefore, the importance of industrial geography lies in theoretical development of geography as well as in solving the problems of national development.

Industrial complex, where a set of specific industries is closely related, is a significant aspect of industrial geography. It is a recent approach and the aspect is still in its initial stage of inquiry and theory formulation. Its study approach is distinct from the industry in isolation. The clustering of industries at a particular location is spatially and economically efficient as it shares identical resources or markets or have strong inter-industry linkages. Even the unrelated activities enjoy indirect benefits when located together. These benefits are due to the availability of infra-structural facilities, better transport, more capital, abundant labour and the use of a common technology. Once a system of corporated character is established and whole economic processes are set in motion, more and more economies and other advantages grow in folds. Even at the penultimate stage of the industrial development, when all the geographical considerations on which the first location was attracted, vanish, the factories run in motion on the principle of 'geographical inertia'. In contrast, the individual firms have to bear all the troubles and also not to be in a position to avail the advantages of economies of concentration. It is a fact that this system of industrial clustering also suffers from certain disadvantages, e.g., unhealthy competitions between various firms, strong and militant unions, affecting works and wages sometimes leading to strikes, overcrowding features, traffic congestions, urban taxes and pollution hazards, etc. In spite of these, the regional efficiency and regional inter-dependency has been the craze of the atomistic economy of the twentieth century, rapidly giving way to the economy of giant industrial combines.

The term industrial complex has been variously defined by many economists. Perroux and Boudeville have defined the industrial complex equal to growth pole or growth centre. A growth centre, as Boudeville defined as a set of expanding industries located in an urban area and inducing further development of economic activity throughout its zone of influence. Perroux also advocated that every pole or foci is a centre of economic attraction and repulsion and in this process the whole region is brought under the economic upliftment. Similarly, Friedmann by his 'general theory of polarised development' has attempted to explain systematic inter-relations between development and space. Myrdal has also supported their views through his 'core periphery' model. But these ideas have been criticised. Lasuen found no specific process of inter-relationship between a growth pole or centre and the region. Their input-output model is static and unsuitable for a conceptual framework. Hermensen has advocated that every centre or a nodal point of a region would not be a growth pole. Those centres, which have propulsive industries, large scale firms, technically advanced, innovating and dominating and which exert a strong influence on their environment and are capable of generating sustained growth over a prolonged period of time have been treated as growth pole. Richardson has noted that an industrial complex develops in or around the growth pole itself and supports industries dispersed over the zone of influence. Hansen has also admitted propulsive industries as essential for a growth centre and mentioned three basic characteristics of a propulsive industry : that (a) it must be relatively large, (b) it must be a relatively fast growing sector and (c) the quality and intensity of its inter-relations with other sectors should be important so that a large number of induced effects would be transmitted. Balassa defined an industrial complex as a centre of numerous industries belonging to a group of activities subjected to production, marketing and other inter-relationships. Allen and Maclennan supported Balassa's view and advocated an industrial complex as 'an auto-sufficient system' capable of inserting itself in the general development of the area in which it has been located. For this the region should be economically advanced and able to sustain the spread effects of the industrial complex. Klassen also defined an industrial complex as a 'clustering of industries' or 'industrial bundles'; which has been characterised by a dynamic and complicated processes of functions. Finally, Isard has defined industrial complex as a set of activities occurring at a given location and belonging to a group of activities which are subject to important production, marketing or other inter-relations. This definition has been adopted as a base of discussion since it fulfills the basic characteristics of an industrial complex.

It has already been discussed that an industrial complex contains the basic elements, inter-relatedness of economic activities and the geographical proximity of location. Inter-relatedness or linkage is related to one unit to another in terms of direct interfirm transactions, joint demand for the products or services of other industrial units and joint use of common resources and facilities, like labour and other social infrastructures. The inter-relatedness is only possible when the firms are closely located within a limited geographical area.

Industrial complex in the manufacturing processes presents

the most complicated phenomena. It is a technical operations passing through a series of phases. Isard has identified several types of complexes mostly based on activity or activities in the manufacturing processes. The first type is of large establishment of basic industries. Here several raw materials have to pass through several successive stages in the processing of an end product. Iron and steel, cement and engineering industries have been explained as examples. The second type comprises of industries in which one raw material bifurcates into several by-products and finally these by-products lead to the manufacture of one product. Fertilizer has been cited as example of this group. The latest method for preparing synthetic paper out of oil has added the importance of petro-chemical complexes. The modern industrial pattern tends to maximum utilisation of raw materials. Even the waste products are reused into more useful forms and it also protects land and people from the anger of pollution hazards and unnecessary dumps of waste materials.

It has been seen that industrial complexes have developed in the regions, (1) where coal and more recently, hydro-electric power or petroleum are available, (2) where raw materials like iron-ore, limestone, manganese and others are produced in bulk, (3) in or near large centres of population where there is an abundant labour supply and a good market of consumers, (4) at good trading locations such as port cities, (5) advance technology which incorporates uses and re-uses of products and by-products and (6) government's welfare policies to develop depressed areas by establishing such type of capital and labour intensive plants.

Most of the studies have been done by economists of France, Germany, U.K. and U.S.A. The most prominent among them are Weber, Hoover, Losch, Greenhut, Isard and others. Among the geographers Smith is significant. Industrial geography has changed substantially during the last thirty years from an almost exclusive pre-occupation with production to an emphasis on consumption and behavioural approach. The location of such plants mostly depends on subjective knowledge and understanding of the manufacturer. The great propounder of behavioural school is Pred. Likewise, the Russian writers have tried to establish the inter-dependency criteria of several production systems into the production-combination, that is, 'Territorial Production Complex'. Thus the study has dealt with three different subsections, say, economic approach, geographers or regional planners approach and socialistic approach. Through the economists approach a critical appreciation of Isard's, Klassen's and recent economists views have been evaluated. Similarly geographers approach have been thoroughly discussed. Isard is the most significant contributors on industrial complex. Similarly Klaassen's attraction approach has also been elaborated. Geographers approach on industrial complex is very limited. Very recently, geographers like Britton, Steed, Karaska, Richter, Luttrell and Choudhuri have contributed to different aspects of industrial complex. Most of the studies have emphasized on industrial linkage, one of the important aspects of a complex.

Indian approach to industrial geography has been classified into three groups. The first group included foreign contributors on Indian industrial aspect. The second group included Indian writers. The third group included industrial geographers of Bihar and their contributions. Finally, Indian approaches to industrial complexes have been critically evaluated. It has been seen that most of approaches dealt with locational aspect either related to an individual industry like iron and steel, cotton textile, aluminium, cement, fertilizer or to a particular region or a particular industrial town. The industrial complex aspect of Bihar has not been studied so far. This study has attempted to fill up this gap.

The primary purpose of this research was to study the industrial complexes in Bihar from the initial growth to present period and to discriminate between older and newer complexes on the basis of growth, pattern and functional characteristics. The main objectives were : (a) to delimit industrial complexes quantitatively, (b) to describe their regional characteristics, (c) to present a chronological study of the growth of industries, (d) to analyze the factors affecting the growth of industrial complexes, (e) to highlight the internal structure of complexes emphasising linkage, pattern and functional characteristics and (f) to present problems and planning of industrial complexes.

The state of Bihar has been selected as a case study. The plains of Bihar with fertile soils and abundant water resources are suitable for agriculture. But inadequate irrigational facilities and frequent floods have affected the agricultural production. The southern portion, a mineral-rich plateau region, contains a number of heavy industries. Nevertheless, due to the insignificant growth of ancillary industries in the small sector and non-purchasing capacity of the people for industrial produce, these heavy industries have not made an appreciable impact on the economy. Thus, both the vital sectors—agriculture and industry have been less rewarding and Bihar has remained one of the poorest states in the country. Physiographically, Bihar has been divided into two parts—plains and plateaus of the north and the south respectively. The northern portion is a part of the Gangetic plain which is geologically recent. The plains gently roll towards the south-east direction. The river Ganga and its numerous tributaries flow through this region. The southern portion is a plateau region and has remained one of the most richest metallic and non-metallic mineral-belts of the country. The region is known as the Chotanagpur Highland Region which is highly dissected and undulating. The Damodar and the Subarnarekha rivers with their several other tributaries flow through this part and provide ample water to industrial centres as well as facilitate generation of hydel power. Nearly 87 per cent of the total population lives in villages and directly and indirectly depends upon agriculture. Occupational pattern has been dominated by agricultural pursuits. Of the total workers engaged in agriculture, nearly 40 per cent have been categorised as agricultural labourers. Nearly 48 per cent of land is under cultivation, 18 per cent under forest, 14 per cent as a fallow land and the rest is under different uses and is unsuitable for cultivation. Rice, wheat, maize, gram, etc. have been the important cereals and are prominently grown in the plain region. Among the cash crops, sugarcane, jute and tobacco are important. These crops have acted as the base of several agro-industries like sugar, jute and cigarette and these industries have developed in the northern plains. The southern portion is agriculturally less significant. Here mineral's extraction and other secondary and tertiary activities are more important. Bihar has been one of the largest mineral producing states of India. During 1978-79 Bihar produced 29 per cent of the total value of mineral production in the country. It ranked first among all the Indian states in the production of copper-ore, pyrites, kyanite, quartzite, apatite, phosphate, mica, coal, china-clay, the bauxite, fire-clay, etc. It has also been one of the principal iron-ore manganese, limestone and atomic minerals producing states of the country. Other important minerals found in the state are asbestos, chromite, dolomite, felspar, silica and steatite. The Chotanagpur plateau, the richest mineral belt in India, has accounted for all reserves and productions of minerals of the state. The northern plain region completely devoid of important minerals, except Sodium and Saltpetre. The state has immense thermal and hydel power potentials. The installed capacity of power has been increased from nearly 60 m.w. in 1950-51 to 530 m.w. in 1977-78. The Damodar Valley Corporation and the Patratu thermal power stations except several other thermal and hydel power stations have been the major power supplying stations of the state. But this power supply has been found inadequate in meeting the growing demands of industrialisation. The pattern of power consumption has also been uneven as the bulk of power has been consumed by the Chotanagpur plateau region. Roads and railways are inadequate and unevenly distributed. Only one-fourth of the total road length in Bihar is surfaced and only five per cent of the total village is connected with all weather roads. The northern and southern regions are linked at Mokameh and Patna on the river Ganga by rail and road bridge. Several important National Highways pass through the state which have significantly influenced the pace of industrialisation. Likewise several important railway lines traverse through different parts of the state which have also provided facilities to develop secondary and tertiary activities. A large part of plateau region has not been still connected with railway lines. Hazaribagh and Ranchi have not been properly connected with railway lines although they are important industrial centres. On the basis of total working force engaged in industry and per capita value added by manufacturings, industrially, Bihar has been found one of the most backward states of the country.

According to the census report of 1971, industry had engaged only 5.1 per cent of the total working force as against the all-India average of 9.5 per cent. Moreover, per capita value added by manufacturing in Bihar at Rs. 29 is far less than Rs. 51 as against the country's average. But on the basis of rich mineral and power potentials and also due to the establishment of several high capital-intensive industrial complexes, the industrial condition of Bihar has been assessed as very promising in comparison to other Indian states. Several heavy, medium and small industries have been developed but on account of poor agrarian economy and fast growing population their impact had been restricted. The industrial development of the state has remained lop-sided on three points : first, whatever industrial development has taken place is largely confined to a few pockets in the Chotanagpur region. Secondly, the industrial structure is dominated by highly capital-intensive heavy industries with a meagre spread-effects. The growth of ancillary industries in the medium and small scale sectors has been extremely tardy. Thirdly, there has been predominance of engineering and mineral-based industries which have accounted for more than two-thirds of the total number of factories and three-fourths of the factory employment in the state. Agro-based and forest-based industries have been less developed as expected. Since her huge resources of metallic and non-metallic minerals are available, the industrial prospect of the state has been assessed to be very bright. With a population of 698 lakhs Bihar has been one of the most populous states in the country. The population has been found to be unevenly distributed. Generally, the plains have been the most populous regions accounting for three-fourths of the total population of the state. The plateau region has been found to be sparsely populated. This region has been found to be more urbanized than the plain region due to the growth of secondary and tertiary activities. It has also been found that about 82 per cent of the working force is engaged in agriculture, 2.6 per cent in manufacturing, 2.5 in household industry, 3.2 in trade and commerce and the rest in services etc. The districts of north Bihar have shown higher percentage engaged in agriculture while Dhanbad, Singhbhum and Ranchi districts have mostly non-agricultural workers primarily engaged in mining, manufacturing and other services.

Data used for the above problems are secondary in nature. They have been obtained from various sources. The census reports of 1971 and 1981 (provisional) have remained the main source. District Gazetteers, different Statistical Handbooks and Bihar Through Figures have been used for relevant data. Data related to production, labour employment and other industrial information have been obtained from various offices of the industrial concerns. Besides, Industrial Directory of Bihar has also been used for industrial data. These data have been statistically and cartographically analyzed to arrive at logical and meaningful conclusions.

Six industrial complexes have been identified : Jamshedpur, Ranchi, Sindri, Bokaro, Dalmianagar and Barauni. Ramgarh-Patratu, Dhanbad-Mumardhubi, Adityapur, Nawhatta-Rohtas have been found industrial complexes in offing.

These complexes have been identified and delimited on the basis of industrial workers engaged in industries in 1971. Industrial workers engaged in other than household industries have been taken into account. Anchalwise distribution map of workers was prepared, showing high concentration. This result was tested scientifically using location quotient formula.

Both of them were compared and anchals of high concentration of industrial workers were demarcated. Further, large and medium scale industrial units clustered together were marked. Again the centres of highly agglomerated industrial units were compared with the highly concentrated anchals on the basis of industrial workers. It has been found that two maps correctly matched with each other. The agglomerated industrial centres were found to be located in the highly concentrated anchals. These highly industrial centres were again set on the essential condition for an industrial complex. A set of industries at a given location, spatial proximity and linkages were considered as essential parameters for an industrial complex based on Isard's definition and six industrial complexes have been demarcated. The methods used have proved to be scientific and significant because the distribution of industrial workers and industrial units have been correctly represented. It has been found that regions of high concentration of industries may not be the regions of all industrial complexes. Linkage has been considered very important criterion for the delimitation of an industrial complex but this has not been used due to non-availability of data. Still the results obtained have been found satisfactory.

The following results have been obtained about the regional characteristics of the industrial complexes. Jamshedpur, Ranchi, Sindri and Bokaro complexes have been established in the mineral-belts of the Chotanagpur plateau region. Dalmianagar and Barauni complexes have been found to be located in the plain regions of Bihar. The locational trend of these complexes has been found to be raw materials oriented. The Barauni complex, however, has a different locational trend where national strategic point has become more dominant. Except Sindri and Bokaro, other four complexes have developed on the nodal points. Sindri and Bokaro complexes have developed on the linked routes. On the basis of surface configuration these complexes have been found to be located on the high plateau region (above 2000 feet), medium level (between 500 and 1000 feet) and plain region. The surface character has very much guided the nature and size of the complexes. The Ranchi complex has developed on the stable surface of plateau region. The Jamshedpur the Bokaro and the Sindri complexes are located in the valleys to avail the water and other facilities. The Dalmianagar and the Barauni complexes have been found in the plain region since they are medium and light-weighted plants. One common feature associated with all the complexes is their location along the banks of the river. Ranchi and Jamshedpur are located along the Subarnarekha river, Sindri and Bokaro on the Damodar river, Dalmianagar on the Son and Barauni on the Ganga river. These rivers have not only provided water facilities to the factories and townships but have become the means of excursion. Jamshedpur has been found an iron-ore oriented complex, Sindri as coal oriented, Dalmianagar as limestone and forest products oriented, Barauni as oil oriented, Bokaro as transport oriented where as Ranchi as the steel and engineering oriented. Moreover, Jamshedpur, Ranchi, Sindri and Bokaro complexes have developed in the tribal belt where intra-regional spread effects have remained less whereas

Dalmianagar and Barauni complexes have developed in the non-tribal belt having possibly more spread effects. On the basis of raw material, labour and market-flows, it has been possible to demarcate the zones of influence of each complex. Jamshedpur, Ranchi and Bokaro complexes have four types of zones of influence, e.g. intra-regional, sub-regional, inter-regional and extra-regional. Sindri and Dalmianagar have only intra-regional and sub-regional zones where as Barauni has inter-regional. This demarcation has been based on general consideration and not on reliable data. The results could have been quite different if other sources of data might have been used to demarcate the zones of influence.

The growth characteristics of each complex have revealed several significant. The real industrialisation started after 1901 consequent upon rail and road development and mineral exploration. The establishment of Tisco in 1907 gave the base for the modern industrialisation. Since then the pace of industrialisation has been phenomenal. Prior to independence Jamshedpur and Dalmianagar complexes had flourished under the private management. After independence the Sindri complex came into existence. The Ranchi, Barauni and Bokaro complexes were added subsequently during the second, third and fourth five-year plans respectively. These complexes have been established in the public sector in order to utilize the resources and also to meet regional deficiency. The growth trend of Jamshedpur till 1970 has been marked upward and thereafter a stable trend has been noticed. In the case of Dalmianagar an upward trend has been noticed till sixtees but after 1966-67, a downward trend has been observed. The similar is the case with Sindri where the growth trend has already been gagged by old machineries and shortage of capital. The Ranchi complex has always been in the grip of power-shortage with an unstable growth trend. The Barauni complex has still been in its initial phase of development and has not fully developed its infra-structure. Also the short supply of crude oil has marred its full production. The Bokaro complex has shown an upward growth trend from its very start because of the availability of adequate raw materials and power supply. On the basis of employment the Jamshedpur complex has been classified as first order of magnitude; Ranchi and Bokaro as second order; while Dalmianagar, Barauni and Sindri as third order. Due to lack of adequate data magnitude could not be ascertained on the basis of production, profits and investment.

The significant results obtained from the analysis of linkage, pattern and functional characteristics are the following. First, among the industrial complexes of Bihar intra-complex linkages are well developed. Jamshedpur is the only complex where all four types of linkages are developed. Other complexes are partially linked mostly vertical or horizontal. Secondly, inter-complex linkage is not well developed except between H.E.C. and Bokaro. Thirdly, these complexes are characterised by both compact and dispersed type of pattern. The older complexes, e.g., Jamshedpur, Sindri and Dalmianagar have compact pattern and are highly industrialised, whereas the newer complexes, e.g. Ranchi, Barauni and Bokaro are scattered and less industrialised. Lastly, these complexes present various types of functions. For example, Jamshedpur—a multi-complex specialises in metallurgical goods while Ranchi a mono-mighty complex in heavy engineering. The Sindri complex produces fertilizers and cement, while Bokaro a mono-type complex produces steel and steel structurals. The Dalmianagar and the Barauni complexes are diverse in nature specialising the sugar, paper, cement, vanaspati, chemicals, oil refinery and fertilizer respectively.

It has been observed that due to the acute poverty the advantages created by these industrial complexes have not reached to the general people. The spread effects of these complexes have remained less responsive in the absence of strong local and regional markets. It has also been observed that the implementation and its results have always been lop-sided. Agriculture and industry have been considered alternatively at the cost of other. The fast growing population has subdued all the benefits of the plannings. Thus, eradication of poverty by developing agriculture and industry simultaneously has been suggested on the priority basis. Industrial development in a few areas has augmented a trend of urban migration. This trend is considered as dangerous because it has affected agriculture and industry adversely. For this, an integrated rural and urban planning already launched by the state government has been appreciated. The pollution hazards created by industrialisation has also been considered as alarming. For this reutilization of the industrial wastes through different chemical processes has been suggested. It has also been argued that these industrial complexes have augmented the pace of urbanization and have also awakened the social consciousness among the tribal people who live around the complexes. These complexes have provided employment opportunities, resource mobilisation and establishment of numerous small and medium scale of industries in the region. For the removal of poverty and other related problems industrialisation has been suggested as a corrective measure. For this a plan of industrial hierarchy starting from village to block, block to district, district to regional and regional to national level has been suggested. This industrial hierarchy has to match with the cottage industry, small scale, medium scale, large scale and massive integrated industries. These industries have to be inter-linked. Besides, different industrial boards have to be created to look after these industries. Such type of plan would be an appropriate answer to these problems.

The following conclusions have been derived from this study : (1) the methods used to delimit industrial complex have proved to be scientific; (2) Jamshedpur, Ranchi, Sindri and Bokaro complexes have found to be located in the Chotanagpur mineral zone while Dalmianagar and Barauni complexes in the non-mineral zone of Bihar plain; (3) Jamshedpur, Ranchi and Bokaro complexes have established intra-regional, sub-regional inter-regional and extra-regional zones of influence. They have become complexes of national and international repute. Barauni complex has developed inter-regional zone of influence while Dalmianagar and Sindri have intra and sub-regional influence. On this basis it is concluded that Jamshedpur, Ranchi and Bokaro are three facets of one national integration of economic polarisation whereas, Sindri, Dalmianagar and Barauni are the supporting wings of major goal of economic achievement; (4) the older complexes have witnessed rapid growth in production, employment, areal expansion and urban population in the beginning and stability or downward trend recently. The newer complexes have been characterised by unstable growth trend; (5) the older complexes have shown compact pattern with several industrial units congregated together and are highly industrialised, leaving a little scope for future industrial expansion whereas the newer complexes are scattered over large space and less industrialised, leaving enough scope for further expansion; (6) the older complexes specialise in productions which are important at local, regional and national demand levels whereas the newer complexes in the products demanded at national and international levels; (7) Jamshedpur is the only complex where all four types of linkages are developed and other complexes are partially linked mostly vertical or horizontal. It means therefore, that Jamshedpur is the only fully developed complex and others are still in the process of complex development; (8) Jamshedpur has developed as complex of complexes. Ranchi, Sindri, Dalmianagar and Barauni have developed as multi-complexes whereas Bokaro has been a monotype complex and (9) it has been proposed to develop decentralised industrial complexes at village, block, district, regional and national levels along with strong interlinkages to reduce poverty and regional disparities, and to achieve effiquity in socio-economic level.

This study has significantly contributed to the field of Industrial Geography. It has added one more study on some aspects of industrial complex. It has already been indicated earlier that geographical studies on industrial complex are few in the world. Such studies are rare particularly on the problems of complex development in developing countries like India. The scientific generalisations made on older and newer complexes have provided several new ideas in understanding the growth pattern and functional characteristics. In this way, it is believed that this empirical study has helped in generalisations about the regional industrial system of eastern India.

Further research needs to be carried in five directions. First, there is a need to use more number variables to delimit industrial complex. This study has used only two variables for the delimitation of industrial complex. They are member of employed workers and member of industrial units. It is suggested that the future researchers may include variables like salaries and wages, value added by manufacturing, power consumption, investment, profits and industrial output. The delimitation can be made more accurate and precise if the above mentioned variables are analysed scientifically with the help of statistical techniques like index of concentration, index of standardization, location coefficient, labour coefficient and capital coefficient.

Secondly, delimitation of the zone of influence of industrial complex seems to be important research frontier which has been untouched uptill now. This aspect is important since it throws light on the strength of association between the centre and periphery and how much an industrial complex is influenced by its surrounding regions and vice-versa. The zone of influence may be delimited on the basis of raw materials supply, labour supply and consumer centres. Several statistical techniques like gravity model, entropy and net work analysis can be used to arrive at scientific results.

Thirdly, the study of linkage has been regarded as a significant theme in industrial complex analysis because it brings production efficiency and economic betterment. Linkage may be defined as a condition or relationship which develops during the economic processes between various units. The unit may be related to a geographic space, e.g., region or an economic unit like industrial unit etc. An industrial unit of the large plant is integrated on the linkage condition and this integration may be vertical, horizontal, diagonal and technological. These linkages may be based on interdependency, input-output, labour, market and other bases. Once a linkage is established it may incur economics in production and efficiency in space and dimension. Thus it may lead to the formation of industrial complex. This aspect has yet been quite neglected by Indian geographers and has thus remained a dynamic research topic requiring scientific analysis. Important statistical techniques like linear programming and input-output model may be applied using systems approach.

Fourthly, territorial production complex aspect of a region seems an important research frontier which requires scientific analysis. The utilization of all resources physical, economic and social through cycles of production may give rise to territorial production complexes. The modern concept of economic development, however, encourages the formation of such type of complexes on the basis of spatial interaction particularly in the developing countries. It minimises costs on production and maximises the economic effect. It would be a new approach to apply this concept in the Indian context. Various spatial interaction models like gravity entropy, linear programming and network analysis can be used.

Fifthly, the role of industrial complex on regional development may become a fruitful research topic as it is basically a study in its regional context. The resource mobilisation, creation of employment opportunities and achievement of socio-economic goals are the main purposes considered at regional level. An industrial complex may provide facilities to establish several medium and small-sized industries around its nucleus plant. It may also create several opportunities for other secondary and tertiary services and thus lead to regional development. Therefore, research related to this aspect demands thorough analysis and understanding so that proper planning can be made for regional development. Variables like employment, per capita income, literacy and urbanization may be used for this purpose.

APPENDIX

List of Anchals—Districtwise, Bihar 1971

Name of anchals	Total workers	Workers other than household industries	L.Q.
1	2	3	4
	PATNA DISTRICT		
Patna	129599	13886	4.4
Phulwari	37911	1035	1.1
Punpun	21897	190	0.4
Dhanarua	29386	94	0.1
Masaurhi	31019	722	1.0
Dinapur-cum-Khagaul	47130	2981	2.6
Naubatpur	31258	188	0.2
Paliganj	36387	300	0.3
Bikram	41603	322	0.4
Bihta	35057	841	1.0
Maner	28672	367	0.3
Barh	40670	962	1.0
Harnaut	29158	264	0.4
Fatwa	46799	1261	1.4
Bakhtiarpur	24677	239	0.4
Pandarakh	28314	127	0.2
Mokaman	43599	2128	2.1
Sarmera	17586	44	0.1
Bihar	55270	4256	3.2
Giriak	19715	44	0.1
Rajgir	34163	478	0.4
Islampur	30622	324	0.4
Ekangarsarai	83013	185	0.2
Hilsa	38714	213	0.2
Chandi	46398	101	0.1
Noorsarai	24111	231	0.4

1	2	3	4
Rahui	24334	656	1.1
Asthawan	38000	347	0.4
	GAYA DISTRICT		
Gaya Town	69469	5689	3.4
Bodh Gaya	29085	113	0.2
Sherghati	29888	462	0.6
Amas	22443	219	0.4
Imamganj	29081	237	0.3
Dumaria	15066	121	0.3
Gurua	21675	113	0.2
Paraiya	26908	511	0.8
Konch	29658	220	0.3
Tikari	36845	179	0.2
Belaganj	27687	178	0.3
Khizersarai	25908	289	0.5
Atri	39661	128	0.1
Manpur	18447	518	1.2
Wazirganj	41343	354	0.4
Fatehpur	33704	150	0.2
Mohanpur	24580	121	0.2
Barachatti	23381	72	0.1
Aurangabad	27831	602	0.9
Deo	20609	181	0.4
Kutumba	26660	293	0.5
Nabinagar	36453	282	0.3
Barun	22313	302	0.6
Obra	29151	419	0.6
Daudnagar	26391	628	1.0
Haspura	19900	77	0.2
Goh	29078	602	0.9
Rafiganj	36318	575	0.6
Madanpur	27007	252	0.4
Jahanabad	27723	655	1.0
Makhdumpur	35892	435	0.5
Kurtha	40827	379	0.4
Karpi	33474	190	0.2
Arwal	43481	255	0.2
Kako	23032	293	0.5
Ghosi	40470	177	0.2
Nawadah	40182	741	0.9
Akbarpur	27526	256	0.4
Narhat	19983	155	0.3

1	2	3	4
Hisua	29870	499	0.7
Warisaliganj	32056	496	0.6
Pakari Barawan	27594	99	0.1
Kawa Kole	24739	208	0.3
Gobindpur	26333	254	0.4
Rajauli	19858	351	0.7
Sirdala	28442	177	0.3
SHAHABAD DISTRICT			
Arrah	46573	2462	2.2
Udwant Nagar	20246	121	0.2
Jagdishpur	41981	412	0.4
Behea	18485	394	0.9
Shahpur	25834	153	0.2
Barhara	26682	232	0.4
Koilwar	21911	363	0.7
Sandesh	23292	130	0.2
Sahar	33531	156	0.2
Charpokhari	18273	79	0.2
Piro	34687	171	0.2
Tarari	27863	87	0.1
Sasaram	43976	1945	1.8
Rohtash	16391	2271	8.5
Nawhatta	14306	3807	11.0
Chenari	51719	45	0.03
Sheosagar	75214	191	0.1
Kargahar	130409	90	0.02
Dindra	120216	205	0.1
Dawath	84421	159	0.1
Bikramganj	100419	233	0.1
Karkat	105045	418	0.2
Nasirganj	95371	386	0.2
Dehri	162706	9740	2.2
Nokha	96474	176	0.1
Bhabua	116565	283	0.1
Bhagwanpur	76704	418	0.2
Adhaura	21755	9	0.01
Chainpur	76067	251	0.1
Chand	55665	12	0.01
Durgawati	59583	112	0.1
Ramgarh	106441	80	0.03
Mohania	87734	136	0.1
Kudra	63483	276	0.2
Buxar	128882	1145	0.4

1	2	3	4
Itashi	76063	283	0.2
Rajpur	120951	163	0.1
Simari	107610	206	0.2
Brahampur	105785	202	0.1
Dumraon	130740	1040	0.3
Nawanagar	95063	189	0.1
	SARAN DISTRICT		
Chapra	44739	1674	1.6
Revelganj	15065	362	1.0
Jalalpur	30937	622	0.8
Manjhi	30252	918	1.3
Ekma	25820	523	0.8
Banianpur	42218	855	0.8
Mashrakh	35557	497	0.6
Taraiya	31670	616	0.8
Marhaura	29582	1672	2.3
Amnaur	23903	427	0.7
Parsa	26998	419	0.6
Dariapur	29243	579	0.8
Sonpur	27473	612	0.9
Dighwara	14119	557	1.6
Garuha	28447	340	0.5
Siwan	31233	1943	2.6
Hussainganj	28171	1197	1.8
Andar	22031	393	0.7
Darauli	22104	233	0.4
Guthani	15207	457	1.2
Mairwa	30540	1014	1.4
Barharia	32524	555	0.7
Pachrukhi	27874	985	1.5
Goriakhothi	29251	426	0.6
Basantpur	26681	456	0.7
Bhagwanpur Hat	24116	324	0.6
Mahrajganj	23877	431	0.7
Daramdha	22905	356	0.6
Siswan	18434	290	0.7
Raghunathpur	23149	307	0.6
Gopalganj	32719	777	1.0
Manjha	83834	366	0.4
Uchkagon	33594	1348	1.7
Hathua	32521	599	0.8
Bhorey	22182	119	0.2

1	2	3	4
Bijaipur	18919	56	0.1
Katiya	30902	188	0.3
Kuchaikota	40771	926	0.9
Barauli	43060	729	0.7
Baikunthpur	36584	369	0.4
CHAMPARAN DISTRICT			
Motihari	45604	1819	1.7
Chakia	29474	924	1.3
Kalyanpur	42110	657	0.6
Kesaria	31243	276	0.4
Areraj	44542	351	0.3
Pahapur	24588	135	0.2
Harsidhi	33964	126	0.4
Turkaulia	48229	396	0.3
Sugauli	29697	635	0.9
Ramgarhwa	27994	242	0.4
Raxaul	27843	620	1.0
Adapur	26332	160	0.3
Narkatia	22153	73	0.1
Ghorasahan	37118	288	0.3
Dhaka	36178	238	0.3
Chiraiya	31751	220	0.3
Pataki	22616	81	0.1
Pakridayal	25339	224	0.4
Madhuban	32064	147	0.2
Mahai	19968	256	0.5
Bettiah	22033	1671	3.1
Nautan	29910	95	0.1
Bairia	30561	137	0.2
Jhakrahan	25448	46	0.1
Jogapatti	32573	106	0.1
Bagaha	53964	587	0.5
Madhubani	25972	91	0.1
Shidhaw	46484	908	0.8
Ram Nagar	36331	1035	1.2
Gaunaha	31168	148	0.2
Mainatanr	25862	74	0.1
Narkatiaganj	53013	1657	1.3
Lauriya	33405	992	1.2
Sikta	31540	251	0.4
Chanpatia	38752	944	1.0
Majhaulia	44861	1079	0.1

MUZAFFARPUR DISTRICT

1	2	3	4
Musahari	70227	4831	2.8
Kurhani	47689	902	0.8
Kanti	49986	702	0.6
Saraiya	38476	345	0.4
Parao	45297	374	0.3
Sahebganj	30692	208	0.3
Baruraj	47865	746	0.8
Minapur	42963	389	0.4
Bachaha	29340	137	0.2
Aurai	38516	158	0.2
Katra	31544	212	0.3
Gaighatti	33486	103	0.1
Dholi	29547	476	0.7
Sakra	32997	290	0.4
Hajipur	39343	1366	1.4
Lalganj	46538	703	0.6
Vaishali	32095	143	0.2
Goraul	40716	561	0.6
Mahua	38049	363	0.4
Patepur	37077	251	0.3
Jandaha	32508	189	0.2
Mahanar	21008	393	0.8
Sahdol	22906	239	0.4
Bidupur	52449	367	0.6
Raghopur	25857	85	0.1
Dumra	46005	976	0.9
Runisaidpur	46691	178	0.2
Be Leund	48456	190	0.2
Sheohar	28658	118	0.2
Piprarhi	26347	123	0.1
Bairgania	18564	628	1.4
Majorganj	25189	208	0.3
Riga	28723	773	1.1
Bathnaha	35343	148	0.2
Sonbarsa	31438	94	0.1
Parihar	39812	107	0.1
Surjand	29953	135	0.2
Bajpatti	25673	74	0.1
Pupri	32085	302	0.6
Nanpur	35797	216	0.3

1	2	3	4
DARBHANGA DISTRICT			
Darbhanga	64523	4633	3.0
Bahadurpur	30134	395	0.5
Hayaghat	39631	464	0.5
Singhwara	33399	330	0.4
Jale	36678	462	0.5
Keotiranway	31041	603	0.8
Mangachhi	49799	432	0.4
Benipur	47256	364	0.3
Ghanshyampur	43634	142	0.1
Biraul	37309	236	0.3
Bahari	36535	206	0.3
Samastipur	40951	1951	2.0
Ujiarpur	34390	350	0.4
Sarairanjan	30781	318	0.4
Tejpur Nonra	27236	142	0.2
Pusa	28262	559	0.8
Kalyanpur	42501	1702	1.7
Warisnagar	48816	765	0.7
Resra	48511	507	0.4
Singhia	24634	73	0.1
Kusheshwar Asthan	33844	97	0.1
Hasanpur	49788	660	0.5
Bithutpur	39196	219	0.2
Dalsinghsarai	41601	1087	1.1
Mohiuddinagar	20365	322	0.7
Patori	26935	197	0.3
Madhubani	38412	1230	1.4
Bisbi	40082	424	0.4
Berapatti	46348	363	0.3
Madhuapur	18428	80	0.2
Harlakhi	23259	147	0.3
Basopatti	21036	89	0.2
Tainapur	26901	466	0.7
Khagauli	35667	188	0.2
Babubarhi	27412	68	0.1
Ladania	21805	43	0.1
Lauraha	28471	102	0.1
Laurahi	32994	88	0.1
Phulparas	57199	131	0.1
Madhopur	51943	246	0.2
Jhanjharpur	20102	137	0.3

1	2	3	4
Andhra Tharhi	22830	68	0.1
Rajnagar	32925	410	0.5
Pandaul	35376	988	1.1

MONGHYR DISTRICT

Munger	173931	6045	1.4
Jamalpur	146636	8457	2.4
Tarapur	83811	818	0.4
Sangrampur	71060	196	0.1
Kharagpur	119116	1567	0.5
Dharhara	62836	1317	0.9
Surajgarha	136757	1112	0.3
Lakhisarai	140492	708	0.2
Sheikhpura	106983	735	0.7
Ariari	68362	156	0.1
Basbigha	100766	556	0.2
Baraihia	96547	263	0.1
Jamui	85368	412	0.2
Khaira	96225	97	0.04
Sikandra	126830	322	0.1
Halsi	84247	95	0.05
Lakshmipur	111676	896	0.3
Jhajha	110846	3010	1.3
Chakai	95386	98	0.04
Sono	86103	377	0.2
Begusarai I	182171	2911	0.7
Begusarai II	81701	144	0.1
Barauni	157262	2304	0.6
Teghra	77287	685	0.2
Bachhwara	92869	1019	0.5
Bhagwanpur	91811	568	0.3
Cheria Dariapur	75794	111	0.1
Khudabanpur	67922	165	0.1
Bakhri	130305	384	0.1
Balia	107593	410	0.2
Sahebpur Kanal	82714	324	0.2
Khagaria	137534	634	0.2
Alauli	114222	193	0.1
Chauthan	91063	139	0.1
Beldapur	78296	124	0.1
Gogri	98755	395	0.2
Parbatta	121282	212	0.1

1	2	3	4
BHAGALPUR DISTRICT			
Jagdishpur	69582	7096	4.2
Nathnagar	17682	731	1.7
Shahkund	28803	124	0.2
Sultanganj	30949	824	1.1
Bihpur	36008	311	0.4
Naugachhia	33573	709	0.9
Gopalpur	34319	142	0.2
Colgong	43539	738	0.7
Pirpainti	41264	399	0.4
Sonhaula	25422	63	0.1
Sakaour	30649	658	0.9
Banka	31082	185	0.2
Katoria	25876	72	0.1
Chanan	20525	180	0.4
Belhar	28629	135	0.2
Samkhuganj	30520	181	0.2
Amanpur	33982	267	0.4
Rajaun	28572	114	0.2
Dhuraiya	30253	67	0.1
Barhat	20739	90	0.2
Bansi	27605	259	0.4
SAHARSA DISTRICT			
Kahara	49299	749	0.6
Simri Bakhtiarpur	37802	107	0.1
Mahisi	26834	51	0.1
Nauhatta	20855	83	0.2
Sour Bazar	44138	109	0.1
Sonbarsa	37337	168	0.2
Salkhua	33286	111	0.1
Supaul	43129	415	0.4
Marauna	19489	31	0.1
Kishanpur	33148	71	0.1
Nirmali	24746	202	0.3
Basantpur	24440	254	0.4
Raghopur	41503	346	0.3
Chhatapur	38429	63	0.1
Tribeniganj	45731	93	0.1
Pipra	26663	142	0.2
Madhepura	43472	409	0.4

1	2	3	4
Singheshwar	43096	294	0.3
Kumarkhand	36290	65	0.1
Muraliganj	44495	391	0.4
Kishanganj	54706	410	0.6
Chausa	31197	244	0.3
Alamnagar	29713	47	0.1
PURNEA DISTRICT			
Purnea East	59603	1319	0.9
Kaityanandnagar	44487	211	0.2
Dhamdatia	44596	153	0.1
Bhawanipur	22988	113	0.2
Rupauli	33633	124	0.2
Barhara	33514	105	0.1
Banmankhi	53077	400	0.3
Kasba	33305	573	0.7
Baisa	19646	79	0.2
Amour	32423	233	0.3
Baisi	32822	265	0.3
Katihar	53733	4859	3.8
Pranpur	28951	99	0.1
Manihari	27896	166	0.2
Barari	47722	483	0.4
Falka	31609	177	0.2
Korha	33455	126	0.2
Kadwa	39649	379	0.4
Balrampur	16690	51	0.1
Barsoi	35346	155	0.2
Azamnagar	37317	221	0.2
Amdabad	19378	65	0.1
Araria	46821	604	0.5
Raniganj	53219	301	0.2
Bhargama	33330	54	0.1
Narpatganj	49278	206	0.2
Forbesganj	54248	2008	1.5
Kursakatta	18225	72	0.2
Sikti	19523	83	0.2
Palasi	25975	89	0.1
Jokihat	34236	117	0.1
Kishanganj	24970	1455	2.4
Kochadhamin	33069	292	0.4
Bahadurganj	32291	113	0.1

1	2	3	4
Terhagachh	17086	97	0.2
Dighal Bank	21634	57	0.1
Thakurganj	34821	403	0.5
Pothia	29306	83	0.1
SANTHAL PARGANA DISTRICT			
Dumka	32446	1392	1.8
Ranishwar	21308	117	0.2
Masalia	24943	53	0.1
Jama	28840	55	0.1
Jarmundi	30757	297	0.4
Saraiyahat	24731	350	0.4
Ramgarh	32637	45	0.1
Gopikandar	10903	21	0.1
Kathikund	15996	97	0.3
Shikaripara	31292	113	0.1
Jamtara	37656	2020	2.2
Narayanpur	24401	120	0.2
Nala	35114	547	0.6
Kundahit	27095	102	0.2
Deogarh	37306	1831	2.0
Madhupur	32706	1603	2.0
Mohanpur	23330	336	0.6
Sarwan	21220	267	0.5
Palojori	22815	225	0.4
Sarath	22999	56	0.1
Karon	18710	192	0.4
Godda	36970	376	0.1
Poreyahat	33600	116	0.1
Patherwa	30060	101	0.1
Mahagama	23130	151	0.3
Meharma	36308	166	0.2
Boarijor	21810	58	0.1
Sundar Pahari	13720	21	0.1
Rajmahal	42104	948	0.9
Barharwa	21371	188	0.4
Pathna	14722	274	0.8
Barhait	22092	92	0.2
Boria	30542	241	0.3
Sahibganj	17795	720	1.7
Paljhari	14070	599	1.8
Pakur	26938	1777	2.5

1	2	3	4
Maheshpur	34637	130	0.2
Pakhria	21388	49	0.1
Amrapar	10934	54	0.2
Latipar	18811	67	0.1
Airanpur	13051	194	0.6
PALAMU DISTRICT			
Daltonganj	21969	1196	2.3
Chainpur	26447	299	0.5
Bishrampur	33325	187	0.2
Hussainabad	34780	1390	2.3
Hariharganj	11820	185	0.6
Chhatrapur	22908	67	0.1
Patan	24506	59	0.1
Manatu	16029	58	0.1
Panki	20720	69	0.1
Lesliganj	16810	225	0.6
Latehar	18113	171	0.4
Guon	5120	32	0.3
Mahudanr	11395	43	0.2
Barwadih	12297	136	0.5
Manika	13962	25	0.1
Balumath	23703	73	0.1
Chandwa	12426	176	0.6
Garhwa	24138	395	0.7
Ranke	21055	78	0.2
Bhandaria	9090	38	0.2
Dhurki	11001	6	0.02
Untari	22958	140	0.3
Bhawanathpur	22269	110	0.2
Majhiaon	22706	115	0.2
Meral	22447	54	0.1
HAZARIBAGH DISTRICT			
Hazaribagh	28032	1361	2.0
Churchu	18216	96	0.2
Barkagaon	15893	92	0.2
Keredari	13099	33	0.1
Tandwa	12519	18	0.1
Katkamoandi	19839	146	0.3
Ichak	16109	61	0.2
Barhi	18646	154	0.3

1	2	3	4
Jai Nagar	14737	312	0.9
Kodarma	30387	1350	1.8
Markocho	13175	91	0.3
Barkatha	16466	43	0.1
Bagodar	33582	251	0.3
Bishungarh	26258	172	0.3
Gumia	29175	1901	2.7
Paterbar	20859	261	0.5
Jaridih	12371	366	1.2
Kasmar	12436	45	0.1
Gola	22377	70	0.1
Ramgarh	31829	1317	0.7
Mandu	28225	1431	2.1
Patratu	34379	2284	2.8
Chatra	24127	219	0.4
Simaria	19735	41	0.1
Pratappur	17580	81	0.2
Hunterganj	21504	77	0.1
Chauparan	22616	354	0.6
Itkhori	21621	33	0.1
Giridih	36756	1899	2.1
Pirtanr	16116	66	0.2
Dumri	26318	233	0.4
Nawadih	23360	270	0.5
Bermo	31976	1188	1.5
Birni	16854	10	0.02
Dhanwar	24695	193	0.3
Gawan	15619	324	0.9
Satgawan	9758	65	0.3
Tisri	12930	65	0.2
Deori	19326	35	0.1
Jamue	28537	112	0.2
Bengabed	18527	111	0.2
Gande	20873	87	0.2
	RANCHI DISTRICT		
Kanke	81186	8494	4.3
Namkum	50228	16145	13.3
Ratu	22557	2955	5.4
Bero	25378	144	0.2
Lepunge	10872	160	0.1
Bhandra	7438	6	0.03

1	2	3	4
Lohardaga	13998	518	1.5
Senra	16144	171	0.4
Kisko	11950	177	0.6
Kuru	15561	95	0.3
Chanho	13524	64	0.2
Mandar	15162	102	0.3
Burmu	22169	1342	2.5
Ormanjhi	15166	476	1.3
Angra	22146	231	0.4
Silli	23854	806	1.4
Khunti	23166	399	0.7
Murhu	19946	92	0.2
Rania	8123	4	0.02
Torpa	16317	581	0.1
Karra	19116	49	0.1
Bundu	16157	216	0.6
Sonahatu	23213	57	0.1
Tamar I	29169	55	0.1
Tamar II Erki	22103	14	0.02
Simdega	24312	178	0.3
Thethai Tanger	17197	66	0.2
Bolba	6288	11	0.1
Kurdeg	22506	88	0.2
Kolebora	12288	36	0.1
Bano	16388	29	0.1
Jaldega	17510	599	1.4
Gumla	28651	357	0.3
Palkoti	19506	40	0.1
Raidih	12918	33	0.1
Chainpur	9576	27	0.1
Dumri	13114	14	0.04
Bishunpur	9716	45	0.2
Ghaghra	19471	13	0.02
Sisai	17858	37	0.1
Verno	11595	15	0.1
Basia	15075	41	0.1
Kamdara	14629	19	0.1
DHANBAD DISTRICT			
Dhanbad-cum-Kenduadih-cum-Jagta	80180	3402	1.8
Jharia-cum-Jorapokhar cum-Sindri	90509	13009	6.0

1	2	3	4
Gobindpur	30713	936	1.3
Tundi	21113	91	0.2
Nisra-cum-Chirkunda	63918	11341	7.4
Baliapur	14864	740	2.1
Baghmara-cum-Katras	63585	2579	1.7
Chandankiyari	31544	403	0.5
Chas	77879	11364	6.1
Topchanchi	20358	377	0.8
SINGHBHUM DISTRICT			
Chaibasa	77759	1401	0.7
Tant Nagar	30549	60	0.1
Manjhari	42981	51	0.5
Kumardhubi	51241	44	0.03
Majhgaon	44213	11	0.01
Jagannathpur	61654	204	0.1
Jhinkpani	32655	1741	1.3
Tundu	39981	261	0.3
Noamundi	67938	775	0.5
Manoharpur	79481	1649	0.9
Goilkara	52353	342	0.3
Sonua	70911	1028	0.6
Bangaon	39182	110	0.1
Chakradharpur	119149	2613	0.9
Khuntpani	48517	126	0.1
Saraikela	76117	1200	0.7
Gobindpur	79997	260	0.1
Khersawan	50109	363	0.3
Kushai	40567	44	0.05
Chandil	57480	701	0.5
Ichagarh	63720	61	0.04
Nimdih	62494	103	0.1
Adityapur	63380	5150	3.4
Golmuri	474955	74480	6.5
Potka	116786	569	0.2
Patamda	87536	62	0.02
Ghatsila	67899	778	0.5
Dhalbhum garh	48471	191	0.2
Chakulia	76946	543	0.3
Bahragora	98969	99	0.04
Dumaria	36705	34	0.04
Musabani	56094	401	0.3

SELECTED BIBLIOGRAPHY

Ahmad, E. (1965) : *Bihar : A Physical, Economic and Regional Geography*, Ranchi University, Ranchi.

Alexander, J.W. (1958) : Location of manufacturing : Methods of measurement, *Annals of the Association of American Geographers*, Vol. 48, pp. 20-26.

Alexander, J.W. and Lindberg, J.B. (1961) : Measurements of manufacturing : Coefficients of correlation, *Journal of Regional Science*, Vol. 1, pp. 71-81.

Alexander, J.W. (1977) : *Economic Geography*, Prentice-Hall of India, New Delhi.

Alexandersson, G. (1956) : *The Industrial Structure of American Cities*, University of Nebraska Press, Lincoln, Nebraska.

Alexandersson, G. (1967) : *Geography of Manufacturing*, Prentice Hall, Englewood Cliffs, New Jersey.

Allen, K. and MacLennan, M.C. (1970) : *Regional Problems and Policies in Italy and France*, Allen and Unwin, London.

Alonso, W. (1967) : A reformulation of classical location Theory and its relation to rent theory, *Papers and Proceedings of the Regional Science Association*, Vol. 19, pp. 23-44.

Azam, S.S. (1968) : "Industrial Landscape of the Lower Son Valley in Bihar", Unpublished Ph.D. Thesis, Ranchi University, Ranchi.

Azam, S.S. (1970) : Pattern of industrial development at Dalmianagar, *Geographical Outlook*, Vol. VII, pp. 148-154.

Azam, S.S. (1975) : Cement industry in Bihar, *Geographical Outlook*, Vol. 10, pp. 59-70.

Balassa, B. (1969) : *The Theory of Economic Integration*, Pitman and Sons, London.

Baldwin, G.B. (1959) : *Industrial Growth in South India*, Glencal Free Press, Glenoe.

Banerjee, B. (Ed) (1969) : *Essays on Agricultural Geography*,

University of Calcutta, Calcutta.

Bandman, M.K. (1975) : Scheme and composition of optimization models of forming spatial production complexes in A.R. Kuklinski (ed.) *Regional Development and Planning : International Perspectives gizthoff.*

Banerjee, B. (1969) : The infrastructure of Indian agriculture, in B. Banerjee (Ed.), *Essays on Agricultural Geography*, University of Calcutta.

Baranson, J. (1967) : *Manufacturing Problems in India*, Syracuse University Press, Syracuse.

Basu, J. (1972) : "Development of the Integrated Iron and Steel Industry of India : A Geo-Economic Analysis of Present Position and Prospects", Unpublished Ph.D. Thesis, Calcutta University, Calcutta.

Beacham, A. (1948) : *Economics of Industrial Organization*, Pitman and Sons Ltd., London.

Bernard, P. (1970) : *Growth Poles and Growth Centres in Regional Development*, Vol. III, Report No. 74.14 UNRISD, Geneva, p. 64.

Bondeville, J.R. (1961) : A survey of recent techniques for regional economic analysis, in W. Isard and J.M. Cumberland (Eds.), *Regional Economic Planning : Techniques of Analysis for Less Developed Areas*, Organization for European Economic Co-operation, Paris, pp. 383-84.

Bondeville, J.R. (1966) : *Problems of Regional Economic Planning*, Edinburgh University Press, Edinburgh.

Bose, A. (1974) : *Studies in India's Urbanization, 1901-71*, Tata McGraw-Hill Publishing Co. Ltd., New Delhi.

Bose, P.N. (1904) : Notes on the geology and mineral resources of Mayurbhanj, *Geological Survey of India*, Vol. 31, p. 167.

Bose, S.R. (1971) : *Economy of Bihar*, K.L. Firma Publication, Calcutta.

Bradely, B. (1910) : *Chotanagpur; A Little Known Province of the Empire*, London.

Britton, J.N.H. (1969) : A geographical approach to the study of industrial linkages, *Canadian Geographer*, Vol. 13, pp. 185-98.

Brush, J.E. (1952) : The iron and steel industry of India, *Geographical Review*, Vol. 42, pp. 37-56.

Buchanan, R. O. (1959) : Some reflections on agricultural Geography, *Geography*, Vol. 44.

Casetti, E. (1966) : Optimal location of steel mills serving in quebec and southern ontario steel market, *Canadian Geographer*, Vol. 10, pp.27-34.

Chaudhuri, M.R. (1964) : *Iron and Steel Industry in India*, Oxford Book Co., Calcutta.

Chaudhuri, M.R. (1965) : Industrial estates in West Bengal, *Geographical Review of India*, Vol. 27 (11).

Chaudhuri, M.R. (1967) : Kulti-Burnpur, Case study of the growth and problems of an industrial complex, *Geographical Review of India*, Vol. 29, pp. 18-35.

Chaudhuri, M.R. (1969) : Problems of dispersal of industries in West Bengal, *The Deccan Geographer*, Vol. 7, pp.

Chaudhuri, M.R. (1969) : Growth pattern and problems of Durgapur industrial complex, *Proceedings of Indian Science Congress*, Session 56, Part III.

Chaudhuri, M.R. (1970) : *Indian Industries : Development and Location*, Fourth Edition, Oxford & IBH Publishing Co., Calcutta.

Chaudhuri, M.R. (1971) : *The Industrial Landscape of West Bengal*, Oxford and IBH Publishing Co., Calcutta.

Chaudhuri, M.R. (1972) : Industrial activities in the greater Calcutta industrial complex, *Industrial Situation in India*, Vol. 1, No. 1, pp. 21-26.

Chaudhuri, M.R. (1973) Haldia : A major port, industrial complex and city in making, *Industrial Situation in India*, No 2, pp. 48-53.

Chaudhuri, M.R. (1973) : Iron and steel industry in India, *Industrial Situation in India*, Vol.11, pp. 43-44.

Chaudhuri, M.R. (1979) : Industrial complexes : A trend report, in M. Raza, *et al.* (eds.), *A Survey of Research in Geography (1969-72)*, New Delhi, ICSSR pp. 80-82

Chorley, R.J. and Haggett, P. (eds.) (1967) : *Models in Geography*, Methuen, London.

Clark, C. (1945) : The economic functions of a city in relation to its size, *Econometrica*, Vol.13, pp. 97-113.

Clark, C. (1967) : *Population Growth and Land Use*, Macmillan Press, London.

Cooke, R.U. and Johnson, J.H. (Eds.) (1969) : *Trends in Geography : An Introductory Survey*, Pergamen Press, London.

Counto, A.F. (1973) : Opportunities for industrial growth of Bihar, *Commerce*, Vol.127, pp. 31-39.

Counto, A.F. (1974) : Programme of industrial state and areas, *Bihar Information*, Jan. 26. Vol.22, pp. 25-27.

Cox, K.R. (1972) : *Man : Location and Behaviour*, Wiley International, New York.

Das, B.L, (1973) : Findings of 1971 census in Bihar, *Commerce* Vol. 127, No. 3263, November 17, pp. 45-50.

Das, K.N. (1969) : *Physiography of Bihar*, Essays in Geography, Department of Geography, Bhagalpur University, Bhagalpur, pp. 87-94.

Das, H.P. (1978) : "Transport and Economy", Unpublished paper, Summer School in Geography, Gauhati University, Gauhati.

Dayal, P. (1953) : *Bihar in Maps*, Kusum Prakashan, Patna.

Dayal, P. (1958) : Location and development of aluminium industries in India, *National Geographical Journal of India*, Vol. 4, pp. 67-68.

Dayal, P. (1964) : Aspects of industrial location in India, *Transactions of the Indian Council of Geographers*, Vol. 1, pp. 1-9.

Dayal, P. (1968) : Sugar industry in India, *Abstracts of Papers of 21st International Geographical Union Congress*, New Delhi, p. 187.

Dayal, P. (1968) : The Bihar plain : A regional study, *Transactions of the Indian Council of Geographers*, Vol. 5, pp. 1-30.

Dayal, P. (1969) : Regional planning and industrial location in India, in K.N. Das (Ed.), *Essays in Geography*, Bhagalpur University, Bhagalpur, pp. 66-77.

Dayal, P. (1972) : Agricultural and industrial potentialities, in A.K. Dutta (Ed), *India : Resources, Potentialities and Planning*, Hunt Publishing Co., Dubuque, pp. 36-56.

Dayal, P. (1974) : "Bihar", *Encyclopaedia Britannica*, Chicago, pp. 984-88.

Dayal, P. (1975) : Characteristics of the major industrial belts of India, in A.K. Dutt and A.G. Hoble (eds.), *Rural-Urban Change in India*, University and Regional Council for

International Education, Pittsburgh, pp. 166-68.

Dayal, P. (1977) : The Energy resources of India", Presidential address, section of geology and geography, *64th Indian Science Congress*, Bhubaneshwar.

De Geer, Steen (1927) : The American manufacturing belt, *Geografiska Annaler*, Vol. 4, pp. 233-59.

Dhar, H. (1976) : Bihar lags behind despite resources, *The Economic Times*, Wednesday, Sept. 22, p. xiv.

Dicker, P. and Lloyd, P.E. (1972) : *Location in Space : A Theoretical Approach to Economic Geography*, New York.

Diwarkar, R.R. (ed.) (1978) : *Bihar Through the Ages*, Calcutta.

Dixit, K.R. (1963) : Growth and distribution of Indian paper industry, *National Geographical Journal of India*, Vol. 9, pp. 218-35.

Dutta, A.K. (1960) : "Jamshedpur and its Umland : A Study in Urban Geography", Unpublished Ph.D. Thesis, Patna University, Patna.

Estall, R.C. (1966) : *New England : A study in Industrial Adjustment*, Pitman and Sons, London.

Estall, R.C. and Buchanan, R.O. (1968) : *Industrial Activity and Economic Geography*, Hutchinson University Library, London.

Friedmann, J.R. (1966) : *Regional Development Policy : A Case Study of Venezuela*, MIT Press, Cambridge, Mass.

Florence, P.S. (1948) : *Investment, Location and Size of Plant*, Cambridge University Press, Cambridge.

Ganguli, B.N. (1949) : Iron and steel industry in Bengal-Bihar industrial belt, *Calcutta Geographical Review*, Vol. 11.

Ganguli, B.N. (1973) : *Population and Development*, New Delhi.

Ghose, A. (1965) : *Efficiency in Location and Inter-Regional Flows : The Indian Cement Industry During the Five Year Plans 1950-59*, North-Holland Publishing Co., Amsterdam.

Ghose, A. and Chakravorty, A. (1971) : Location of an industrial complex, *Indian Journal of Regional Science*, Vol. 3, No. 2, pp. 1-13.

Gilbert, A. (1974) : Industrial location theory : Its relevance to an industrialising nation, in B.S. Hoyle (Ed.). *Spatial*

Aspects of Development, John Wiley, London, pp. 271-89.

Gokhman, V.M. (1981) : The significance of growth poles in regional development, *Soviet Geography*, Vol. 22, pp. 255-71.

Goswami, S.B. (1956) : The regional setting of Dalmianagar, *Geographical Outlook*, Vol. 1, pp. 29-35.

Gupta, N.S. and Singh, A. (1978) : *Industrial Economy of India*, New Delhi.

Greenhut, M.L. (1956) : *Plant Location in Theory and in Practice*, University of North Carolina Press, Chapel Hill.

Greenhut, M.L. (1959) : Space and Economic Theory, *Papers and Proceedings of the Regional Science Association*, Vol. 5, pp. 267-280.

Greenhut, M.L. (1960) : Size of market Vs. Transport costs in industrial location survey and theory, *Journal of Industrial Economics*, Vol. 8, pp. 172-184.

Greenhut, M.L. (1967) : Inter-regional programming and the demand factor of location, *Journal of Regional Science*, Vol. 7, pp. 151-160.

Hagerstrand, T. (1967) : *Innovation Diffusion as Spatial Process*, Translated by A. Pred, Chicago University Press, Chicago.

Hamilton, F.E.I. (1967) : Models of Industrial Location, in R.J. Chorley and P. Haggett (Eds.), *Models in Geography*, Methuen, London.

Hansen, W.L. and Tilbout, C.M. (1963) : An Inter-Sectoral flows analysis of the california economy, *Review of Economics and Statistics*, Vol. 45, pp. 409-18.

Hansen, N.M. (1968) : *French Regional Planning*, University Press, Edinburgh.

Hansen, N.M. (1972) : *Growth Centres in Regional Economic Development*, The Free Press, New York.

Harris, C.D. (1954) : The market as a factor in the localization of industry in the United States, *Annals of the Association of American Geographers*, Vol. 44, pp. 315-48.

Hartshorne, R. (1936) : A new map of manufacturies belt of North America, *Economic Geography*, Vol. 12, pp. 45-53.

Hermansen, T. (1972) : Development poles and development, centres in national and regional development : Elements of a theoretical framework, in A.R. Kuklinski (Ed.), *Growth Poles and Growth Centres in. Regional Planning*, Monton, Paris and the Hague, pp. 29-30.

Hirchman, A.Q. (1958) : *The Strategy of Economic Development*, Yale University Press, New Haven and London.

Hoover, E.M. (1936) : The measurement of industrial localization, *Review of Economics and Statistics*, Vol. 18, pp. 162-71.

Hoover, E.M. (1937) : *Location Theory and the Shoe and Leather Industries*, Harvard University Press, Cambridge, Mass.

Hoover, E.M. (1948) : *The Location of Economic Activity*, McGraw Hill, New York.

Hoyle, B.S. (ed.) (1974) : *Spatial Aspects of Development*, John Wiley, London.

Indrapal, (1963) : Prospective site for a fertilizer factory in Uttar Pradesh, *Indian Geographical Journal*, Vol. 8 (1, 2).

Isard, W. (1956) : *Location and Space Economy*, MIT Press, Cambridge, Mass.

Isard, W. and Schoolar E.W. (1959) : Industrial complex analysis, agglomeration economics and regional development, *Journal of Regional Science*, Vol. 1, pp. 19-33.

Isard, W. and Schooler, E.W. and Vietorioz, T. (1959) : *Industrial Complex Analysis and Regional Development : A Case Study of Refinery*—Petrochemical-Synthetic Fiber Complexes and Puerto Rico, MIT Press, Cambridge, Mass.

Isard, W. (1960) : *Methods of Regional Analysis : An Introduction to Regional Science*, MIT Press, Cambridge, Mass.

Isard, W. and Cumberland, J.H. (Eds.) (1961) : *Regional Economic Planning : Techniques of Analysis for Less Developed Areas*, Organization for European Economic Co-operation, Paris.

Jarrett, H.R. (1977) : *A Geography of Manufacturing*, Macdonald and Evans, Norwich, Plymouth.

Johnson, W.A. (1966) : *The Steel Industry of India*, MIT Press, Cambridge.

Jones, C.F. (1938) : Areal distribution of manufacturing in the United States, *Economic Geography*, Vol. 14, pp. 217-22.

Joshi, K.L. (1978) : Geography of India : Resources and Regional Development, NCERT, New Delhi.

Karan, P.P. (1953) : Economic regions of Chotanagpur, *Economic Geography*, Vol. 29, pp. 216-50.

Karan, P.P. (1955) : A historical geography of Chotanagpur, *Indian Geographical Journal*, Vol. 30, pp. 355-62.

Karan, P.P. (1957) : Locational pattern of new centres of the Indian iron and steel industry, *Journal of Geography*, Vol. 56, pp. 366-74.

Karan, P.P. (1958) : The Bihar mica belt of India, *The National Geographical Journal of India*, Vol. 4, pp. 16-34.

Karan, P.P. (1958) : The areal distribution of manufacturing in India, *Journal of Geography*, Vol. 57, pp. 294-300.

Karan, P.P. and Jenkins, W.M. (1959) : Geography of manufacturing in India, *Economic Geography*, Vol. 35, pp. 267-71.

Karan, P.P. (1964) : Changes in Indian industrial location, *Annals of the Association of American Geographers*, Vol. 54, pp. 336-54.

Karan, P.P. (1981) : Perception of environmental pollution in Chotanagpur industrial area, India, in L.R. Singh (Ed.) *New Perspectives in Geography*, Indian University Press, Allahabad, pp. 177-81.

Karaska, G.J. (1966) : Interindustry relations in the Philadelphia economy, *The East Lakes Geographer*, Vol. 2, pp. 80-96.

Karaska, G.J. (1968) : Variations of input-output coefficients for different levels of aggregation, *Journal of Regional Science*, Vol. 8, pp. 215-27.

Karaska, G.J. (1969) : Manufacturing linkages in the Philadelphia economy : Some evidence of external agglomeration forces, *Geographical Analysis*, Vol. 1, pp. 354-69.

Karaska, G.J. and Bramhall, D.F. (eds.) (1969) : Locational analysis for manufacturing, MIT Press, Cambridge, Mass.

Karimi, S.M. (1963) : "A Short Note on Bhilai", *The National Geographical Journal of India*, Vol. 9, pp. 104-11.

Karimi, S.M. and Thakur, J.N. (1975) : Location of sugar industry in Bihar, *Indian Geographical Studies, Research Bulletin* No. 5, pp. 1-11.

Kay, S.J. (1952) : India's cotton textile industry, *Journal of the Royal Society of Arts*, Vol. 100, pp. 848-59.

Keeble, D.E. (1969) : Local industrial linkage and manufacturing growth in outer London, *Town planning Review*, Vol. 40, pp. 163-88.

Keeble, D.E. (1972) : Industrial movement and regional development in the United Kingdom, *Town Planning Review*, Vol. 43, pp. 3-25.

Kidwai, A.R. (1980) : Bihar : constraints gagging growth, *The Economic Times*, Bombay, Monday, June 9, P. I.

Kirk, W. (1956) : The cotton and jute industries of India : A study in concentration and dispersal, *Scottish Geographical Magazine*, Vol. 72, pp. 38-52.

Klaassen, L.H. (1967) : *Methods of selecting industries for Depressed Areas*, OECD, Paris.

Kolosorskiy, N.N. (1961). The territorial production combination in society economic geography, *Journal of regional science*, Vol. 3, pp. 1-25.

Kuchhal, S.C. (1969) : *Industrial Economy in India*, Chaitanya Publication House, Allahabad.

Kuklinski, A.R. (Ed.) (1972) : *Growth Poles and Growth Centres in Regional Planning*, Monton, Paris and the Hague.

Kuriyan, G. (1956) : Industrial development in India since independence, *Indian Geographical Journal*, Vol. 33, pp. 71-78.

Kuriyan, G. (1962) : An analysis of the spatial distribution of industry in India, *Indian Geographical Journal*, Vol. 37, pp. 1-7.

Lal, B.B. (1981) : Census of India 1981, Series 4, Bihar, Provisional Population Totals, Paper I, and Supplement, Director of Census Evaluation, Bihar.

Lasuen, J.R. (1969) : On growth poles, *Urban Studies*, Vol. 6, pp. 137-161.

Launhardt, W. (1885) : *Mathematische Begriindung der Volkwirtschaftslehre*, Leipzig.

Leontief, W.W. (1951) : "Input-Output Economics", *Scientific American*, Vol. 185, pp. 15-21.

Lever, W.F. (1972) : Industrial movement, spatial association and functional linkages, *Regional Studies*, Vol. 6, pp. 371-84.

Lis, A.G. (1975) : On the question of the composition of economic territorial complexes, *Soviet Geography*, Vol. 16, pp. 20-27.

Logan, M.I. (1966) : Locational behaviour of manufacturing firms in urban areas, *Annals of the Association of American Geographers*, Vol. 56, pp. 451-66.

Logan, M.I. (1970) : The spatial dimensions of economic development : the case of the upper midwest, *Regional Studies*, Vol. 4, pp. 117-25.

Lokanathan, P.S. (1936) : Recent trend in the distribution of cotton mill industries in India, *Journal of Madras, Geographical Association*, Vol. 11, pp. 197-212.

Lokanathan, P.S. (1959) (ed.) : *Techno-Economic Survey of Bihar*, NCAER, New Delhi.

Losch, A. (1940) : *The Economics of Location*, Yale University Press, New Haven.

Luttrell, W.F. (1962) : *Factory Location and Industrial Movement : A Study of Recent Experience in Great Britain*, National Institute of Economic and Social Research, London.

Luttrell, W.F. (1972) : Industrial complexes and regional economic development in Canada, in Kuklinski (ed.) *Growth Poles and Growth Centres in Regional Planning*, Monton, Paris and the Hague. pp. 242-62.

Mahmoud, A. (1977) : *Statistical Methods in Geographical Studies*, Rajesh Publications, New Delhi.

Majid, S.A. (1949) : "*The Industrial* Geography of Bihar", Unpublished Ph.D. Thesis, London University, London.

Majid, S.A. (1949) : Industrial regions of Bihar, *The Indian Nation*, Puja Supplement, Patna, p. ix.

Majid, S.A. (1956) : Copper industry of Bihar, *Geographical Outlook*, Vol. 1, pp.

Majid, S.A. (1959) : Silk production and weaving in Bihar, *The National Geographical Journal of India*, Vol. 5.

Majid, S.A. (1960) : A geographical study of lac and shellec industries of Bihar, *The National Geographer*, Vol. 3, pp. 1-10.

Majid, S.A. (1968) : "Sugar industry in Bihar, *Abstracts of Papers of 21st International Geographical Union Congress*, New Delhi, p. 193.

Mandal, B. (1971) : Manufacturing regions of north Bihar, *The National Geographical Journal of India*, Vol. 17, pp. 52-62.

McNee, R.B. (1960) : Towards a more humanistic economic geography : The geography of enterprise, *Tijdscrift Economische Voor Sociale Geografie*, Vol. 51, pp. 201-06.

Mehta, J.K. (1972) : *Infra-Structure of Economy*, Allahabad.

Mehta, M.M. (1952) : *Location of Indian Industries*, Allahabad.

Mehta, M.M. (1955) : *Structure of Indian Industries : A Statistical Study of Size*, Location and Integration of Industrial Units, Bombay.

Mills, J.S. (1848) : *Principles of Political Economy*, London.

Miller, E.W. (1962) : *A Geography of Manufacturing*, Prentice Hall, London.

Mishra, J.N. (1973) : Making up the gap in power supply, *Commerce*, Vol. 127, no. 3263, Bombay, November 17, pp. 23-24.

Misra, R.P. (1971) : *Growth Poles and Growth Centres in Urban and Regional Planning in India*, University of Mysore Press, Mysore.

Misra, R.P. (1972) : Growth poles and growth centres in the Context of India's urban and regional development problems, in A.R. Kuklinski (Ed.), *Growth Poles and Growth Centres in Regional Planning*, Moutan, Paris and the Hague.

Misra, R.P. *et al.* (1974) : *Regional Development Planning in India : A New Strategy*, Delhi.

Misra, R.P. *et. al.* (1978) : *Regional Planning and National Development*, New Delhi.

Mosley, M.J. (1974) : *Growth Centres in Spatial Planning*, Pergamon Press, New York.

Mountjoy, A.B. (1966) : *Industrialization and Underdeveloped Countries*, Hutchinson University Library, London.

Mukherjee, B. (1956) : Ranchi : A study in urban morphology, *The National geographical journal of India*, Vol. 2, pp. 96-103.

Mukherjee, M.M. (1967) : Manufacturing towns of Bihar, *Transactions of the Indian Council of Geographers*, Vol. 4, pp. 33-40.

Mukherjee, M.N. (1970) : Aspects of recent industrialisation in Chotanagpur, *The National Geographical Journal of India*, Vol. 16, pp. 101-09.

Mukherjee, R.K. (1945) : *Indian Working Class*, Hind Kitab, Bombay.

Mukherjee, R.K. (1965) : *Man and His Habitation*, Popular Prakashan, Bombay.

Myrdal, G. (1967) : *Asian Drama : An Inquiry into the Poverty of Nations*, Vol. 1, Penguin Press.

Myrdal, G.M. (1957) : *Economic Theory and Underdeveloped Regions*, Gerald Duckworth, London.

Narayan, J.P. (1973) : The problem of self-renewal in Bihar, *Commerce*, Vol. 127, no. 3263, November 17, Bombay, pp. 3-5.

Nekrasow, N. (1974) : *Territorial Organisation of Soviet Economy*, Progress Publishers, Moscow.

Neutze, G.M. (1967) : *Economic Policy and the Size of Cities*, Australian National University Press, Canberra.

Norman, G. (1979) : Economics of scale in the cement industry, *The Journal of Industrial Economics*, Vol. 27, pp. 317-22.

Ojha, B.N. (1976) : Power crux of the problem, *The Economic Times*, Sept. 22, Special Vol. 1, p. viii.

Ojha, B.N. (1976) : The success story of electricity in Bihar, *The Bihar Information*, March and April, Vol. 24, pp. 31-32.

Palander, T. (1935) : *Beitrage [Zur Standortstheorie*, Almqvist and Wiksells Boktryckeri, Uppsala.

Pandey, P. (1969) : Industrial landscape of greater Ranchi, *Geographical Outlook*, Vol. 6, pp. 41-47.

Pandey, P. (1970) : *Impact of Industrialization on Urban Growth : A Case Study af Chotanagpur*, Central Book Depot, Allahabad.

Pandey, S.C. (1979) : Mica Processing Industry in Giridih, Unpublished Ph.D. Thesis, Patna University, Patna.

Pathak, C.R. (1968) : The Industrial Growth Dynamics in the Damodar Valley Region, *Abstracts of Papers of the 21st International Geographical Union Congress*, New Delhi, p. 146.

Patni, R.L. (1968) : Criteria for location of Indian plants in India : Changes and problems, *Abstracts of Papers of the 21st International Geographical Union Congress*, New Delhi, p. 76.

Patni, R.L. (1968) : A new method for measuring locational changes in a manufacturing industry, *Economic Geography*, Vol. 44, pp. 210-17.

Perroux, F. (1950) : Economic space, theory and applications,

Quarterly Journal of Economics, Vol. 64, pp. 89-104.

Peter, N. (1972) : *Planning of Industrial Complexes by Means of Geographic Programming*, University Press, Rotterdam.

Pounds, N.J.G. (1951) : Ruhr Area : A problem in definition, *Geography*, Vol. 36.

Prasad, A. (1970-71) : Industries of Chotanagpur : A study in regional pattern of distribution, growth and amplitudes, *Geographical Outlook*, Vol. 2, pp. 71-83.

Prasad, J.M. (1976) : Sick sugar industry of Bihar, *The Indian Nation*, Patna, April 18, p. 4.

Prasad, K.N. (1967) : *Economics of a Backward Region in a Backward Economy : A Case Study of Bihar in Relation to other States of India*, Scientific Book, Calcutta.

Prasad, K.N. (1973) : Economic development of Chotanagpur, *Commerce*, Vol. 127, pp. 54-58.

Prasad, K.N. (1980) : *Problems of Economic Development in the Third World with Special Reference to India*, Sterling Publications, New Delhi.

Pred, A. (1967) : *Behaviour and Location ; Foundations for a Geographic and Dynamic Location Theory*, Part I, Lund Studies in Geography, Series B. 27.

Qaiyum, A. (1981) : Role of steel towns in the regional development in L.R. Singh (Ed.) *New Perspectives in Geography*, Indian University Press, Allahabad, pp 41-46.

Ram, L.N. (1968) : Industrial belts in south-east Chotanagpur, *Transactions of the Indian Council of Geographers*, Vol. 5, pp. 79-90.

Rao, V.L.S.P. (1941) : *Geographical Factor and the Ship Building Industry of India*, Calcutta Geographical Review. Vol. 3.

Rao, V.L.S.P. (1942) : The geographer and the localization of industries, *Journal of Madras Geographical Association*, Vol. 17, pp. 216-21.

Rao, V.L.S.P. (1976) : *Development Strategy for an Agricultural Region*, University of Mysore Press, Mysore.

Rawstron, E.M. (1958) : Three principles of industrial location, *Transactions and Papers, Institute of British Geographers*, No. 25, pp. 132-42.

Ray Choudhury, P.C. (1960) : *Bihar District Geographers*, Champaran, Saran, Shahabad, Singhbhum, Dhanbad,

Ranchi etc., Government Press, Patna.

Renner, G.T. (1947) : Geography of industrial localization, *Economic Geography*, Vol. 23, pp. 167-89.

Ricards, D. (1817) : *The Principles of Political Economy and Taxation*, London.

Richardson, H.W. (1969) : *Regional Economics*, Weidenfeld and Nicolson, London.

Richter, C.E. (1969) : The impact of industrial linkages on geographical association, *Journal of Regional Science*, Vol. 9, pp. 19-28.

Richter, C.E. (1970) : Systematic relationship between industrial linkages and the agglomeration of manufacturing industries, *Review of Regional Studies*, Vol. 1, pp. 37-48.

Riley, R.C. (1973) : *Industrial Geography*, Chhtto and Winders, London.

Robinson, G. and Salih, K.B. (1971) : The spread of development around Kuala Lumpur : A methodology for an exploratory test of some assumptions of the growth pole model, *Regional Studies*, Vol. 5, pp. 303-14.

Royen, W.V. and Bengtson, N.A. (1971) : *Fundamentals of Economic Geography*, Prentice Hall of India Ltd., New Delhi.

Salt, J. (1969) : Progress in industrial geography in R.U. Cooke and J.H. Johnson (Ed.), *Trends in Geography : An Introductory Survey*, Pergamon Press, London.

Sengupta, K.K. (1973) : Bihar, a paradox of plenty and poverty, *Amrit Bazar Patrika*, Calcutta, Wednesday, March 28, p. 10.

Sengupta, N. (1979) : *Destitute and Development : A Study of the Bauri Community in the Bokaro Region*, Concept Publishing Company, New Delhi.

Sharma, T.C. and Coutinho, O. (1977) : *Economic and Commercial Geography of India*, Vikas Publishing House, New Delhi.

Sharma, T.R. (1949) : *Location of Industries in India*, Hind Kitab, Bombay.

Shirokov, G.K. (1973) : *Industrialisation of India*, Progress Publishers, Moscow.

Singh, J. (1964) : *Transport Geography of South Bihar*, National Geographical Society of India, Varanasi.

Singh, J. (1971) : Chotanagpur plateau region, in R.L. Singh (ed.), *India : A Regional Geography*, National Geographical Society of India, Varanasi.

Singh, K.N. (1957) : Morphology of the twin-township of Dehri-Dalmianagar, *The National Geographical Journal of India*, Vol. 3.

Singh, R.L. and Singh, K.N. (1971) : Middle Ganga plain, in R.L. Singh (ed.), *India : A Regional Geography, Varanasi*, National Geographical Society of India, pp. 183-251.

Singh, R.P. and Kumar, A. (1970) : *Monograph of Bihar*, Bharti Bhawan, Patna.

Singh, R.P. (1961) : Bokaro : The future steel town, *National Geographical Journal of India*, Vol. 7.

Singh, Rana Pratap (1968) : "Industrial Geography of Dalmianagar" Unpublished Master Thesis, Patna University, Patna.

Singh, Rana Pratap (1974) : Dalmianagar : A study of the industrial complex, *Indian Geographical Studies, Research Bulletin* No. 2, pp. 36-43.

Singh, Rana Pratap (1976) : Factors Affecting Growth of Industrial Complexes in Bihar, *Indian Geographical Studies*, Research Bulletin No. 7, pp. 66-72.

Singh, Rana Pratap (1980) : The industrial complexes of Bihar, *Geographical Review of India*, Vol. 42, pp. 229-37.

Singh, Rana Pratap (1980) : Growth of small scale industry and its impact on the economy of the Bihar Plain, *Indian Geographical Studies*, Research Bulletin No. 14, pp. 29-35.

Singh, Rana Pratap (1981) : Rural urban migration and its impact on regional development, *Abstracts of Papers, National Symposium on Geography and Regional Development*, November 1-7, Department of Geography, Patna University, Patna, P.E-6.

Singh, U.P. (1975) : "Industrial Landscape of Upper-Damodar Valley", Unpublished, Ph.D. Thesis, Bhagalpur University, Bhagalpur.

Sinha, B.N. (1959) : Heavy industries : Their problems and possibilities in Orissa, *Geographical Review of India*, Vol. 21,

Sinha, B.N. (1972) : *Industrial Geography of India*, World Press Private Ltd., Calcutta.

Sinha, R.P. (1970) : "Industrial Landscape of the Highlands of Chotanagpur" Unpublished Ph.D. Thesis, Bhagalpur University, Bhagalpur.

Sinha, R.P. (1972) : Growth of industries in Bihar, *Geographical Progress, Research Bulletin of India*, pp. 19-67.

Sinha, R.P. (1973) : Industrial landscape of Ranchi, India, *Journal of Geography*, Jabalpur University, Vol. 4, pp. 22-29.

Sinha, R.P. (1974) : Development of industries in Bihar : achievements and prospects, *The Bihar Information*, Jan. pp. 30-67.

Sinha, R.P. (1974) : Growth of industries at Dalmianagar, *The Bihar Information*, Vol. 18, pp. 26-37.

Sinha, V.N.P. (1968) : Industrialization in Ranchi, *Transactions of the Indian Council of Geographers*, Vol. 5, pp. 91-97.

Sinha, V.N.P. (1968) : Ranchi industrial complex in Bihar, *Abstracts of papers of the 21st International Geographical Union Congress*, New Delhi.

Sinha, V.N.P. (1976) : *Chotanagpur Plateau : A Study in Settlement Geography*, Rajesh Publications, New Delhi.

Smith, A. (1976) : *Inquiry into the Nature and Causes of the Wealth of Nations.*

Smith, D.M. (1966) : A theoretical framework for geographical studies of industrial location, *Economic Geography*, Vol. 42, pp. 95-113.

Smith, D.M. (1969) : Industrial location and regional development : some recent trends in north-west England, *Environment and Planning*, Vol. 1, pp. 173-91.

Smith, D.M. (1970) : On throwing weber out with the bathwaters: A note on industrial location and linkage, *Area*, No. 1, pp. 15-18.

Smith, D.M. (1971) : *Industrial Location : An Economic Geographical Analysis*, John Wiley and Sons, New York.

Spate, O.H.K. (1960) : *India and Pakistan : A General and Regional Geography*, Methuen & Co. Ltd., London.

Steed, G.P.F. (1970) : Changing linkages and internal multiplier of an industrial complex, *Canadian Geographer*, Vol. 19, pp. 229-42.

Strong, H. (1937) : Regions of manufacturing intensity in the United States, *Annals of the Association of American Geo-*

graphers, Vol. 27, pp. 23-43.

Taylor, M.J. (1969) : Industrial linkages, seeded growth and the location of firms, *Occasional Paper*, No. 3, University College, London.

Thakur, B. (1975) : Application of sampling method in an industrial area, *Indian Geographical Studies, Research Bulletin No. 5*, pp. 1-11.

Thakur, B. (1979) : Intra-urban location of manufacturing : A test of the hypothesis of spatial changes, *The Deccan Geographer*, Vol. 17, pp. 499-515.

Thakur, J.N. (1975) : Sugar Industry of Bihar, unpublished Ph.D. Thesis, Patna University, Patna.

Thapan, D. (1966) : The iron and steel belt of India, in R.L. Singh, (ed.), *Applied Geography*, National Geographical Society of India, Varanasi, pp. 173-80.

Thomas, P.J. (1948) : *Basic Industries of India*, Orient Longmans Ltd., Bombay.

Thomson, J.H. (1955) : A new method for measuring manufacturing, *Annals of the Association of American Geographers*, Vol. 45, pp. 416-36.

Tinbergen, J. (1961) : The spatial dispersion of production : A Hypothesis, *Schweiz, Zeitschrift fur Volkswrit and Statistic*, Vol. 97, pp. 1-15.

Tiwari, C.B. (1968) : Sugar industry in eastern Uttar Pradesh, *The 21st International Geographical Union Congress*, New Delhi, p. 200.

Tiwari, R.N. (1962) : Glass industry of Uttar Pradesh, *Proceedings of the Summer School in Geography*, Simla.

Tornqvist, G. (1970) : *Contact Systems and Regional Development*, Lund Studies in Geography, Series B, no. 35.

Townroe, P.M. (1970) : Industrial linkage, agglomeration and external economics, *Journal of Town Planning Institute*, Vol. 56, pp. 18-20.

Warneryd, O. (1968) : *Interdependence in Urban System*, Goteborg.

Weber, A. (1909) : *Theory of the Location of Industries*, Translated into English by C.J. Freidrich in 1927, University of Chicago Press, Chicago.

Wood, P. (1969) : Industrial location and linkage, *Area*, No. 2, pp. 32-39.

Wilde, D.P. (1981) : From insulation towards integration : The Australian industrial system in the throes of change, *Pacific Viewpoint*, Vol. 22, pp. 1-24.

Wright, A.J. (1938) : Manufacturing districts of the United States, *Economic Geography*, Vol. 14, pp. 195-200.

INDEX